AMDO LULLABY

An Ethnography of Childhood and Language Shift on the Tibetan Plateau

In Amdo, a region of eastern Tibet incorporated into mainland China, young children are being raised in a time of social change. In the first decades of the twenty-first century, Chinese state development policies are catalysing rural to urban migration, consolidating schooling in urban centres, and leading Tibetan farmers and nomads to give up their traditional livelihoods. As a result, children face increasing pressure to adopt the state's official language of Mandarin.

Amdo Lullaby charts the contrasting language socialization trajectories of rural and urban children from one extended family, who are native speakers of a Tibetan language known locally as "Farmer Talk." By integrating a fine-grained analysis of everyday conversations and oral history interviews, linguistic anthropologist Shannon M. Ward examines the forms of migration and resulting language contact that contribute to Farmer Talk's unique grammatical structures, and that shape Amdo Tibetan children's language choices. This analysis reveals that young children are not passively abandoning their mother tongue for standard Mandarin, but instead are reformatting traditional Amdo Tibetan cultural associations among language, place, and kinship as they build their peer relationships in everyday play.

SHANNON M. WARD is an assistant professor of anthropology at the University of British Columbia, Okanagan.

ANTHROPOLOGICAL HORIZONS

Editor: Michael Lambek, University of Toronto

This series, begun in 1991, focuses on theoretically informed ethnographic works addressing issues of mind and body, knowledge and power, equality and inequality, the individual and the collective. Interdisciplinary in its perspective, the series makes a unique contribution in several other academic disciplines: women's studies, history, philosophy, psychology, political science, and sociology.

For a list of the books published in this series see p. 247.

Amdo Lullaby

An Ethnography of Childhood and Language Shift on the Tibetan Plateau

SHANNON M. WARD

UNIVERSITY OF TORONTO PRESS
Toronto Buffalo London

Toronto Buffalo London
utorontopress.com
Printed in the USA

ISBN 978-1-4875-5866-6 (cloth)
ISBN 978-1-4875-5867-3 (paper)
ISBN 978-1-4875-5869-7 (EPUB)
ISBN 978-1-4875-5868-0 (PDF)

Library and Archives Canada Cataloguing in Publication

Title: Amdo lullaby : an ethnography of childhood and language shift on the Tibetan plateau / Shannon M. Ward.
Names: Ward, Shannon M., author.
Series: Anthropological horizons.
Description: Series statement: Anthropological horizons | Includes bibliographical references and index.
Identifiers: Canadiana (print) 20240417429 | Canadiana (ebook) 20240417550 | ISBN 9781487558673 (paper) | ISBN 9781487558666 (cloth) | ISBN 9781487558680 (PDF) | ISBN 9781487558697 (EPUB)
Subjects: LCSH: Anthropological linguistics – China – Amdo (Region) | LCSH: Children – China – Amdo (Region) – Language. | LCSH: Ethnicity in children – China – Amdo (Region) | LCSH: Amdo dialect – Social aspects – China – Amdo (Region) | LCSH: Amdo (Tibetan people) – Socialization – China – Amdo (Region) | LCSH: Amdo (Tibetan people) – China – Amdo (Region) – Ethnic identity. | LCSH: Amdo (China : Region) – Languages.
Classification: LCC P35.5.T5 W37 2024 | DDC 495/.4 – dc23

Cover design: Val Cooke
Cover images: iStock.com/AlKane (top); Author (bottom)

We wish to acknowledge the land on which the University of Toronto Press operates. This land is the traditional territory of the Wendat, the Anishnaabeg, the Haudenosaunee, the Métis, and the Mississaugas of the Credit First Nation.

This book has been published with the help of grants from the University of British Columbia, through the Scholarly Publication Fund and Aspire Fund, using funds provided by the Vice-President, Research & Innovation.

University of Toronto Press acknowledges the financial support of the Government of Canada, the Canada Council for the Arts, and the Ontario Arts Council, an agency of the Government of Ontario, for its publishing activities.

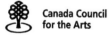

Canada Council for the Arts
Conseil des Arts du Canada

ONTARIO ARTS COUNCIL
CONSEIL DES ARTS DE L'ONTARIO
an Ontario government agency
un organisme du gouvernement de l'Ontario

Funded by the Government of Canada
Financé par le gouvernement du Canada
Canada

Dolma, Lhamo, and Sonam: May you always remain children of the snow mountains.

Contents

Figures and Tables

Figures

Tables

Acknowledgments

All language, spoken, written, and signed, carries traces of its social history. Although *Amdo Lullaby* closely analyses conversations from fifteen months of field research, it was composed through more than fifteen years of talking, thinking, and being with others.

My dear friends from Wellesley College, where it was cool for women to nurture our arcane interests, have supported me in building a career as a linguistic anthropologist of Tibet. Anastasia Karakasidou, Deborah Matzner, and Adam Van Arsdale provided indispensable guidance early in my career. Anthea Cheung, Kathleen Sprague, and Marie Vasek listened to me talk endlessly about language in diaspora, spent many early mornings reading and writing with me in coffee shops, and encouraged me to not give up. Your friendship has helped this project come to fruition.

Opportunities for immersion-based language learning, and the patience of many teachers, allowed me to acquire the language skills necessary to conduct field research with Amdo children. Isabelle Onians facilitated the early stages of my Tibetan language learning and, in 2011, may have been the first person to hear me correctly configure central Tibetan's direct evidential marker with a first-person subject when I recounted to her my experience of dreaming about a white yak. In the summer of 2014, Isabelle also encouraged me to study in Amdo over tea in a Kathmandu courtyard. I am indebted to the Chinese Language Program at New York University and the Tibetan Language Program at Columbia University for supporting me on a winding path of studying multiple Chinese and Tibetan languages and writing systems.

My fieldwork in Amdo was financially supported by a National Science Foundation Doctoral Dissertation Research Improvement Grant (programs in Cultural Anthropology and Linguistics), the New York University Graduate School of Arts and Sciences's MacCracken

Fellowship, and the New York University Department of Anthropology's Annette Weiner Fund. I am grateful for the companionship of Giulia Cabras, Agnes Conrad, Pete Faggen, Judith Petry, and Timothy Thurston during my student life in Xining.

My intellectual community in New York City allowed me to integrate theories and methods from anthropology, linguistics, and Tibetan history to address my broad interest in how languages move along with their speakers. At home in New York, scholars of Tibet helped me parse and process linguistic data from my fieldwork. I thank Palden Gyal for the time we spent listening and relistening to Amdo Tibetan talk, and Tenzin Norbu Nangsal and Sonam Tsering for opening my eyes to the links between Tibetan speech and literature. Your guidance helped me, retrospectively, hear new meanings in my fieldwork conversations. Robbie Barnett's breadth of knowledge of contemporary activism and cultural production in Tibet shaped my interest in locating political ideologies within children's social worlds. Lauran Hartley assisted me in finding textual sources related to education in Amdo/Qinghai. Gray Tuttle introduced me to nuanced ways of interpreting overlapping histories of empire in Amdo. Over lovely dinners on the Upper West Side, David Feingold and Heather Peters encouraged me to think across borders by uniting my research experiences in the Tibetan diaspora and in Amdo.

At New York University, on Waverly Place, my time with fellow linguists and anthropologists Eli Dollarhide, Jacqueline Hazen, Becky Laturnus, Schuyler Marquez, and Jessica López-Espino shaped my thinking about the objectification and materiality of language, and the forms of inequality that circulate through everyday talk. I thank Sonia Das for sharing with me frameworks for examining the colonial histories that co-constitute language ideologies, Fred Myers for helping me place Amdo within global movements for Indigenous sovereignty, and Emily Martin for supporting my inquiries into developmental psychology. Gerald Roche strengthened my conviction in the relevance of Amdo children's language socialization to scholarship on language endangerment. Elinor Ochs's close engagement with my work inspired me to attend to children's experiences of language and to compose *Amdo Lullaby* through thick ethnographic description in an attempt to convey these experiences.

At the University of British Columbia Okanagan, conversations with Christine Schreyer helped me integrate literature on language revitalization and children's psychosocial development. Fiona McDonald's inquiries into the ethnographic documentation of sensory experience inspired my analysis of sound and embodiment. Conversations with

Guofang Li and Yumjyi gave me new insights into education policy in China, which helped me grasp the rapidity of change to schooling practices in China's borderlands. Shanneen Chiu supported the analysis and translation of transcripts included in chapter 5. I was fortunate to have the opportunity to collaboratively examine transcript material from chapters 2 and 3 with UCLA's Center for Language, Interaction, and Culture, and the University of Alberta's Language, Communication, and Culture Colloquium Series. During forested walks, Allison Hargreaves and Susan Frohlick provided invaluable mentorship regarding the process of manuscript composition and submission. With David Geary, Sara Shneiderman, and Mark Turin, I considered how to apply my findings from Amdo to develop new directions in research with the Tibetan diaspora.

Multiple scholars provided valuable feedback on drafts of this manuscript. Two anonymous reviewers through the University of Toronto Press strengthened my analysis of embodied interaction and ensured the accuracy of my representations of Tibetan language and Chinese state policies. Early comments from Anne Brackenbury gave me permission to more freely express my ethnographic voice in narrative form. Alessandro Duranti provided meticulous feedback on the framing and argumentation of sections of the text. I am grateful for a year of Zoom-based writing with Marie-Eve Bouchard, Hannah McElgunn, and Britta Ingebretson. Candy Goodwin and the Co-Operative Action Laboratory at UCLA carried this work through the COVID-19 pandemic, especially by thinking with me about the connections between embodiment and language forms.

Chapters 1 and 4, as well as the closing scene to the monograph, include material from my essay "Playing with Language Boundaries: Heteroglot Standard Language Ideology and Linguistic Belonging among Amdo Children," in Gerald Roche and Gwendolyn Hyslop, eds., *Bordering Tibetan Languages: Making and Marking Languages in Transnational High Asia* (Amsterdam: Amsterdam University Press, 2022), 31–52. Chapter 2 includes material from my article "Spatializing Kinship: The Grammar of Belonging in Amdo, Tibet" in *Pragmatics* 32 (3): 452–87. The original publishers have generously provided permission for the reuse of this material.

Between the years when I conducted fieldwork and composed this monograph, the Chinese state has enforced more coercive governance of its borderlands. At the time of publication, the state's surveillance of Tibetan communities, in general, and repression of Tibetan language activism, in particular, mean that the families and community members whose voices animate *Amdo Lullaby* cannot be identified.

I express my deepest gratitude to them for sharing with me their languages and histories for this book. It is my great hope that my ethnographic representation of our shared experiences does justice to their community.

In her ethnography of Kaluli children's language socialization, Bambi Schieffelin (1990) documented how children named other persons with the possessive form of an object that they regularly exchanged (152). When I became her student, Bambi became "my mind." I dedicate this book to Bambi, along with the children I met during fieldwork, for our many years of thinking together.

Preface

The idea to conduct research on language shift among Tibetan children came to me in 2011, when I spent a summer in the Himalayan hillside town of Dharamsala, India, as an undergraduate student. My years as a young adult in Massachusetts had been shaped by my community's interest in education for global citizenship. As a high schooler and undergraduate, I had been given the opportunity to study at several universities and cultural centres across South Asia, where I learned to speak and read first in Hindi, then Nepali, and then Tibetan. Studying new languages through immersion gave depth and meaning to my long-standing interest in grammar. The Nepali word for tea, *chiya*, would slowly reveal itself as I used its Hindi counterpart, *chai*, to order spiced milk tea on foggy mornings in Kathmandu. I could combine the letters that are pronounced "a" and "ma" in Hindi, Nepali, and Tibetan to write the word *Amma* (mother) on postcards to the women who generously hosted me during my studies.

During the summer of 2011 in Dharamsala, however, I found that studying Tibetan was raising more questions than it answered – questions that reached beyond grammar to draw in the social and cultural practices of language. I had just spent a semester studying abroad in Kathmandu and had participated in daily Tibetan-language classes. I had moved to Dharamsala, the home of the 14th Dalai Lama and seat of the Tibetan government-in-exile, to work as a volunteer English teacher, continue learning Tibetan, and conduct ethnographic research for my undergraduate senior thesis project. I quickly found that my usual language-learning strategies were ineffective in this community of migrants from across the Tibetan plateau. When I asked someone to write down a spoken word or phrase in my notebook, what emerged on the page did not seem to correspond to what they had said. Sometimes, I could understand a person when they were addressing me, but if they turned to a friend or family member, their speech suddenly changed beyond my recognition.

I found that it was easiest to communicate with young children. Tibetan children born in India spoke in a way that generally correlated with the phrases and sentences I was memorizing from my favourite textbook, the *Manual of Standard Tibetan* by Nicolas Tournadre and Sangda Dorje (2003). After studying these grammatical patterns, I could understand most of what children said to one another. When a parent would address a child, however, I often understood only a few words that the adult had spoken. If the child answered back, they used the very same words and structures that filled my textbook. Parents and children accommodated each other's distinct ways of speaking. However, when I asked why their grammars did not seem to match, neither parents nor children could easily explain. It seemed that code-mixing, or the use of distinct grammars in a single conversation, was outside of the speakers' conscious awareness. Over time, I realized that, because the children's parents had migrated to Dharamsala from many different regions of Tibet, they spoke varieties of Tibetan that were not mutually intelligible and that linguists consider to be separate languages. Children were using what is known as *spyi skad* (common speech), a lingua franca derived from Lhasa's dialect, that they had been exposed to from birth in their diasporic community. Their parents from Tibet could understand this language, but many did not speak it.

Other features of children's language also facilitated our communication. Children played predictable games and repeated them over and over. This gave me more than one shot at interpreting new words and phrases. One of my most frequent playmates was Khangmo, a dimpled five-year-old whose mother, Tsomo, attended my English class and owned the restaurant with the most delicious *mog mog* (Tibetan dumplings) in town. Tsomo had come to India ten years earlier, from the eastern Tibetan province known as Amdo. She had grown up south of a great salt lake called Tsho Ngonpo (Tib. *mtsho sngon po*), or Blue Lake, before her parents sent her to India to continue her education in one of the schools for Tibetan migrants administered by the Tibetan Government-in-Exile. One day in late June 2011, I was sipping hot, sweet Indian chai in Tsomo's restaurant while monsoon rains pounded the thickly forested hills beside us. Tsomo and I were discussing how the Tibetan word *sngon po*, in the name for Tibet's great salt lake, can mean blue, green, or turquoise when describing the shifting hues of waters and skies. Khangmo sat in Tsomo's lap, contentedly swinging her legs back and forth in rhythm with the rainfall. When the rain suddenly let up, Khangmo interrupted our talk. She grabbed my hand and led me outside. Several other children also emerged from nearby buildings, and we came together to form a circle.

Often the first to coordinate play, Khangmo instructed those of us in the circle to close our eyes while she ran laps around our perimeter. Without warning, she slapped a shorter boy on the top of the head, shouting in the standard *spyi skad "pœ la ḍo!"* (Let's go to Tibet!). Like a game of duck-duck-goose, the boy dashed out of his spot in the circle and tried to complete one lap before Khangmo could catch him. Khangmo easily overtook him. She settled into the circle, saying contentedly, "ŋa *pœ-la leb-soŋ*" (*I* made it to Tibet). The goal of the children's game was to pretend to return to their parents' homeland.

I thought about how deeply the homeland must be capturing the imaginations of these children, who would likely never visit Tibet itself due to the challenges of moving between India and China's vast territory. I wondered how the presence of many different Tibetan languages affected children's connection to this imagined homeland. While the children shared a newfound home in India, their families' different ways of speaking showed their diverse origins. I wondered how and why these Tibetan languages were changing so quickly once they had been displaced from their homelands. That summer in Dharamsala, I decided that I would pursue a PhD to find out. Two years later, I enrolled in the doctoral program in anthropology at New York University and focused my study on linguistic anthropology.

By the time I began my studies, Tsomo and Khangmo were also living in New York City. They had settled in Queens, a quick subway ride away from me, with the goal of obtaining American citizenship so that they might one day be able to safely return to visit their family. I made the decision to conduct research in Amdo, Tsomo's homeland in eastern Tibet, on the same evening that Khangmo gave me an idea that would eventually become the title of this book. It was September 2015, and I had begun my third year of graduate school. Khangmo, Tsomo, and I had just finished eating dinner at a small Tibetan restaurant in Jackson Heights, Queens. I was grateful for the time to catch up with them before my semester was fully underway. We were wandering down Broadway towards the subway station where we would part. We were mostly speaking in English. Tsomo had gained confidence in her knowledge of English since moving to New York, and Khangmo was now entering fifth grade at her local public school.

As we arrived at the subway stop, Tsomo exclaimed that she was exhausted. Khangmo jokingly announced, "I'll sing you to sleep with a Tibetan lullaby." Khangmo began to hum the tune to popular song, a tribute to Tibet's salt lake, Tsho Ngonpo. Then, she belted out a verse.

"dʑok̚ʰtsatʰaŋ jul la nor lik̚maŋ-ŋa!" (The nomad's grassland is filled with cattle and sheep!), Khangmo shouted to make her voice heard in the noisy station. I noticed that Khangmo's pronunciation of the Tibetan words for "nomad," "grassland," and "sheep" seemed accented. I mentioned this out loud as my train approached.

"Now, because she only speaks Tibetan to *me*, Khangmo got an Amdo accent," Tsomo explained. I stepped through the subway doors as Khangmo shouted, "I sang an *Amdo* lullaby."

It seemed that Khangmo's speech had changed since moving from India to New York. In India, she spoke the standard diasporic Tibetan of her peers, but, in New York, she spoke with features of her mother's native variety of Amdo Tibetan, known as *rong skad* or "Farmer Talk." I was curious as to how and why young Tibetan children like Khangmo adapted their ways of speaking as they moved. I wondered about the potential social and cultural consequences of their language change throughout migration.

As a dual Canadian-American citizen and a doctoral student, I had privileges that Tsomo and Khangmo did not. I could travel to their homeland in Amdo and live in a community of Amdo Tibetan speakers. I could investigate how Tsomo's mother tongue was changing with new generations of child speakers. I decided to undertake my dissertation research in the region south of Tsho Ngonpo, where Tsomo was born and raised. I started Mandarin classes to ensure I could communicate with non-Tibetan speakers in China. In August 2016, I enrolled as a foreign student at a university in Xining, the provincial capital of Qinghai, the mainland Chinese province that encompasses most of Amdo.

This book is based on fifteen months of ethnographic and linguistic research that I conducted between 2016 and 2018 in Amdo/Qinghai, in preparation for my doctoral dissertation. I settled on the title, *Amdo Lullaby*, which borrows from the phrase Khangmo invented on that September evening in 2015, for several reasons. Khangmo's own Amdo lullaby responded to her new social world in New York City. When Khangmo sang, she adopted her mother's Amdo Tibetan language to sustain an important social relationship and mark her Tibetan identity in a new country and community. Khangmo's Amdo lullaby therefore suggests that young children's intuitive, creative uses of language build connection and continuity in the face of social change. The word "lullaby" also invokes discourses of language loss. "Sleeping languages," or those that currently have no fluent speakers, are waiting for revitalization. Languages like Tsomo's native Amdo Tibetan Farmer Talk are on the verge of sleep when children stop speaking them in favour of the dominant languages of standard Tibetan, English, and Mandarin. The connection of lullabies to young children also calls to mind the central role of first language acquisition in sustaining linguistic diversity.

The past decade of learning with Tibetan children like Khangmo has taught me that children do not passively abandon minoritized languages for more dominant ones. Nor do they naturally acquire the mother tongues spoken by their family members. The process of language acquisition crucially depends on cultural practices and social relationships. When children learn to speak, over several arduous years in their early lives, they must learn not only a language, but also how to make themselves understood in particular social and cultural contexts. From the perspective of structural linguistics, the language systems children learn to produce are in flux. The target of any child's language acquisition is dynamic, not static. Ethnography, the key method that anthropologists use to study cultural practices, can reveal particular behaviours, norms, and beliefs that influence how children learn to speak. Ethnographic methods for documenting languages can also shed light on the changing linguistic structures that children produce as they grow up.

This book uses ethnography to critically examine the pathways that multilingual Tibetan children such as Khangmo follow as they learn language. A world away from New York City, the children we will meet inhabit a borderland at the edge of Tibet and China, where multiple languages influence each other's structures, and languages carry the ideological weight of the political histories that unite their speakers. In this setting, children are adapting, and adapting to, shifting definitions of the boundaries of languages. As adults, it is not always easy to listen to children. The careful excavation of young people's words reveals forms of social action and cultural knowledge that we often overlook. The close examination of children's everyday talk shows that meaning is not inherent in the content of what we say, but forged dialogically, in and through our embodied interactions with one another.

Narrative and Transcription Conventions

Amdo Lullaby is a work of ethnographic writing, composed for scholars and students of anthropology and Tibetan studies. Ethnographic writing uses interpretive data from fieldwork – in this case, audio-video recorded naturalistic conversations with families and children, audio-recorded oral history interviews with adults, and fieldnotes created by the author during participant observation – to construct a narrative account of the emergence of culture in a specific sociohistorical moment. To a Tibetan studies audience, this sociohistorical context is highly familiar, recognizable through existing scholarship on Tibetan history, policy, literature, and languages. To my knowledge, *Amdo Lullaby* is the first study that examines Amdo Tibetan children's everyday language use, and the first book-length study about Tibetan children growing up in the People's Republic of China. The voices of young children, as well as the methods used to document and represent these voices, remain novel for the field of Tibetan studies. To linguistic anthropologists, the methods used to record, transcribe, and analyse children's voices are familiar. However, the specific details of Amdo Tibetan children's lives, in a historical borderland between overlapping empires that is now integrated into the Chinese nation-state, are not. Narrative ethnography grounded in this sociohistorical setting provides anthropologists with an additional theoretical perspective on how diverse processes of colonization shape children's language use.

My methodological choices during fieldwork and writing are built from my positionality – my language background, my lived experience in transnational Tibetan communities, my scholarly commitment to the fieldwork methods of linguistic anthropology, and my ethical commitment to privilege, to the very best of my ability, children's voices over adults' interpretations and rationalizations of what they say and mean. Because my positionality has influenced how materials from fieldwork were first constructed as "data" and subsequently integrated into narrative form, audiences from both anthropology and Tibetan studies will benefit from a detailed description of the research methods and social theory that guided my interpretive choices. All potential errors or omissions that have resulted from these interpretive choices remain my own.

Approach to Ethnographic Narrative

Amdo Lullaby represents and analyzes the practices through which Amdo Tibetan children constitute the boundaries between languages and their speakers in a time of cultural change. By communicating an author's experiences of field research in narrative form, ethnographies depict "real cultural events" in order to illuminate the dialogic processes that build cultural, ideological, moral, and linguistic systems (Clifford 1986, 98). Because researchers actively participate in these dialogic processes, any resulting ethnography depicts the contestable perspectives of the author. While anthropologists acknowledge subjectivity in the research process, ethnographic writing remains grounded in the author's engagement with actual events experienced, and real people encountered, in the course of fieldwork.

In this book, you will meet two main households from Amdo, in contemporary Tsholho Tibetan Autonomous Prefecture (Tib. *mtsho lho bod rigs rang skyong khul*; Ch. *Hainan zangzu zizhizhou*), Qinghai Province, China. Each household has three young children, who were the primary participants in my longitudinal field research. Given ongoing state censorship in this region, protecting the confidentiality of all participants is particularly important. Furthermore, ethnographic writing is most effective when its narrative form also communicates the ethnographer's lived experiences of fieldwork, which requires careful attention to the sequencing of events. To address these two major issues in representation, I have used several writing strategies.

First, the participants are given pseudonyms. Rural places that research participants inhabit are also given pseudonyms: Tsachen Village and Lungma County. While these places are referenced with pseudonyms, details of which events – historical and in the ethnographic present – took place in which location have not been altered. That is, all events depicted in Tsachen occurred in one village in Tsholho Tibetan Autonomous Prefecture, and all events depicted in Lungma occurred in the county seat in Tsholho Tibetan Autonomous Prefecture within which Tsachen sits.

Second, I have created some composite characters. Since the family's migration history, ages, genders, and occupations are documented, complete details of their kin relationships could leave participants vulnerable to identification. I have therefore created some secondary characters to allow the reader to conceptualize historical and translocal kinship ties without risking identification. Specifically, I have amended kin relationships in the generation of the children's grandparents and great-grandparents, such as including or excluding some marriage partners or siblings, and changing relationships between some siblings and cousins. These secondary composite characters appear primarily in the kinship chart (fig. 6) and prevent the family from being identified through their complete kinship structure. Also, I have taken additional steps to ensure that the family's recorded oral histories remain accurate while preserving each individual's confidentiality. In the section "Remembering Hualong" in chapter 1, I have attributed quotations from more than one oral history interview to the individual characters depicted in the scene. I have made additional efforts to preserve the anonymity of participants outside of the focal family, whose words were documented in the course of participant observation in public places in Xining and Tsachen. Specifically, I have attributed the public words and behaviours of some individuals to members of the focal family.

Third, to effectively translate my own lived experience of fieldwork into narrative form, I have created some scenes as composite depictions. These scenes were developed based on the location and time of more than one event I participated in during fieldwork and are juxtaposed for narrative purposes. Specifically, autoethnographic transitions into and out of transcript excerpts were built from repeated everyday experiences and did not always occur immediately before or after the presented transcript.

Transcription, Analysis, and the Depiction of Speech

Each method of ethnographic fieldwork and data collection – audio-video recording spontaneous talk, audio-video recording scheduled ethnographic interviews, and traditional participant observation involving note-taking in the absence of recording – produces a particular form of documented linguistic material used for distinct analytic goals.

The foundational material used to build this ethnography is transcriptions of audio-video recorded spontaneous conversations with young children. To create these transcriptions, I worked with research participants using principles from interaction analysis, a method that examines how speakers create shared meaning in their communicative practices through resources including grammatical forms, turn-taking, gesture, and touch (Gumperz and Cook-Gumperz 2008, 18). Interaction analysts create annotated transcriptions that preserve phonetic and grammatical details of spoken language, which often do not align with formal, prescriptive grammars. Rather than aiming to create a fixed grammar, interaction analysts look for patterns within their specific corpus of data and seek to privilege the interpretations of participants, as they are revealed turn by turn in collaborative transcription sessions, over those of the researcher. Beyond depicting the form of spoken languages, interaction analysis thus identifies the elements of communicative practice that participants themselves regard as meaningful. Following the method that Elinor Ochs (1988) and Bambi Schieffelin (1990) developed for interaction analysis in the study of language socialization, I conducted collaborative transcription of spontaneous talk with children's primary caregivers and documented caregivers' comments about talk as an essential part of my ethnographic record. Sometimes, we asked children to participate in transcription by clarifying their intended meaning in a segment of talk. I used participants' reactions to identify meaningful patterns and to choose representative transcript excerpts.

These processes of transcription require interpretive choices and forms of selective attention derived from the researcher's goals (Ochs 1979). To highlight children's voices, as well as the Tibetan mother tongue, while attending to the complexity of multigenerational, multilingual speech, I developed conventions to document the sounds and grammatical forms that speakers repeatedly used. During fieldwork, I created a phonological inventory of the Amdo Tibetan mother tongue, known locally as Farmer Talk (Tib. *rong skad*) (tables 1 and 2), by comparing my recorded material to existing phonological inventories of Amdo Tibetan Farmer Talk from different localities (Hua Kan 2002, Padma Lhundrup 2009). Because the International Phonetic Alphabet (IPA) allows a researcher to depict sound variation in a conventionalized manner for audiences unfamiliar with the documented language, I chose the IPA to represent Amdo Tibetan speech. My transcripts depict each spoken morpheme in the IPA, a gloss that identifies its grammatical category and function, as well as a translation of each line of speech.

When pronunciations differed from my phonological inventory, I generally chose to highlight the phonetic form that the speaker actually employed. This means that transcripts, at times, differ significantly from previously documented grammars of Amdo Tibetan. Existing scholarship justifies preserving grammatical irregularities in transcribed speech, since these seeming mistakes can provide insight into overlooked language patterns. For example, in an analysis of the acquisition and use of ergative marking in Samoan, Elinor Ochs (1985) found that applying judgments of "error" to young children's speech obscured sociolinguistic variation in adult speech *to* children. Using phonetic forms of speech is therefore useful in the study of child language, because children's grammatical irregularities may defy prescriptive grammars while pointing towards unacknowledged, community-wide patterns in speech production and reception. Following the principle that native speakers are the experts of their own languages, I have preserved translations that I created during fieldwork, avoiding back-translation or amendment to remain grounded in the interpretive choices that I made collaboratively with my participants.

In general, I analysed material from ethnographic interviews and participant observation for its content more than its form. To transcribe audio-recorded ethnographic interviews, I worked with a local community member to create a word-by-word transcription and translation. I have depicted translated quotations from this material in English. A select number of translated quotations are taken from my fieldnotes, which I hand recorded during real-time conversations that were not audio-video recorded. While audio-video recording delays but does not prevent selective interpretation, it does allow for fine-tuned analysis of linguistic forms with the expertise of native speakers. Quotations rendered from fieldnotes thus represent a different, real-time interpretive process that may introduce grammatical errors.

A final note that, as in other ethnographic methods, the positionality of the researcher influences the form and content of resulting data. Some of my recorded material provokes questions about how participants may have consciously or unconsciously regimented their speech based on my language background. Urban families who participated in this research study were highly educated, with knowledge of multiple varieties of Tibetan as well as Mandarin and English. Some had spent time living abroad, both in India and in the United States. These participants were also aware that I initially came to the field with much greater competence in central Tibetan and Mandarin than in Amdo Tibetan. Adults may have used Mandarin loan words for place-names and historical events that they would have spoken in Tibetan to a different audience. In several conversations, adult speakers also seemed to code-mix between standard Amdo and central Tibetan. Instances of code-mixes potentially shaped by the researcher's positionality are marked with endnotes in the body of the text.

Romanization and Transcription Conventions

Throughout this book, spoken Amdo Tibetan is depicted in the IPA, accompanied by an English translation in parentheses. I have

Table 1. Amdo Tibetan Farmer Talk consonant inventory

		Bilabial	Labio-dental	Alveolar	Retroflex	Palatal	Velar	Uvular	Glottal
Plosive	*voiceless*	*p p*^{h}		*t t*^{h}			*k k*^{h}		
	voiced	*b*		*d*			*g*		
Nasal		*m*		*n*		*ɲ*	*ŋ*		
Affricate	*voiceless*			*ts ts*^{h}	*ʈʂ ʈʂ*^{h}	*tɕ tɕ*^{h}			
	voiced			*dz*	*ɖʐ*	*dʑ*			
Fricative	*voiceless*		*f*	*s*	*ʂ*	*ɕ*	*x*	*ʁ*	*h*
	voiced		*v*	*z*	*ʐ*	*ʑ*	*ɣ*		*ɦ*
Approximant		*w*		*r*		*j*			
Lateral approximant				*l*					

Table 2. Amdo Tibetan Farmer Talk vowel inventory

	Front	Central	Back
Open	*i*	*ɨ*	*u*
Mid	*e*	*ə*	*o*
Close	*a*		

transcribed spoken Mandarin in the Pinyin Romanized transliteration system and depicted it in bold to differentiate it from Amdo Tibetan. All segments of talk labelled as "excerpts" come from audio-video recordings of spontaneous conversations. The body of the book integrates these excerpts as dialogue, presented in an IPA transcription and an English translation. For readers seeking more information on the details of speakers' morpho-syntax or turn-taking behaviours, the appendix includes morpheme-by-morpheme glossing and a modified conversation analysis notation of each excerpt.

For quotations from oral history interviews and fieldnotes, I have provided an English translation of the original speech and have not included glossing. When the form of a specific word or phrase within these segments is significant, I have included a Wylie (for Tibetan) or Pinyin (for Mandarin) transliteration in parentheses.

For single words and phrases that have equivalents in written Tibetan, I have used the Wylie (1959) Romanized transliteration system. Wylie allows for easier cross-referencing with existing scholarship in Tibetan studies.

For personal names, place names, and kinship terms, I have used Romanization that approximates the English pronunciation. When a place name has a counterpart in written Tibetan, I include this in parentheses the first time the name appears.

The glossary includes place names and kin terms, as well as translations of the words and phrases rendered in Wylie and Pinyin throughout the text. The glossary is alphabetized based on the first appearing letter (including Tibetan superscribed letters).

AMDO LULLABY

Introduction

After more than two decades of publishing in the colonial language of English, Kenyan author Ngũgĩ wa Thiong'o vowed to adopt Gikuyu, his mother tongue or first language, as his primary medium of expression. In *Decolonizing the Mind*, a composition that grapples with language oppression, Ngũgĩ asserted, "The choice of language and the use to which language is put is central to a people's definition of themselves in relation to their natural and social environment, indeed in relation to the entire universe" (Thiong'o 1986, 4). Ngũgĩ's decision to use the language he learned in early childhood for his artistic expression came only after an education and illustrious career in English. His retrospective account illustrates the enduring significance of mother tongues for establishing senses of belonging and provides insight into the struggles of many adults to reclaim the cultural worlds of their childhoods. We know less about the everyday struggles and triumphs of young children who are learning languages within diverse structures of colonization in the twenty-first century. From their earliest social interactions, these children must actively navigate pressures to conform to cultures and worldviews dissociated from their mother tongues.

This book is about how senses of perduring cultural identity are rooted in languages, which are themselves rapidly changing and highly dynamic systems. It appears at a time when the global foundations of colonization are threatening the sustainability of most of the world's languages.[1] First-hand experiences show that intergenerational language loss matters not only as a consequence of political domination and economic exploitation. For example, Polish-Canadian author Eva Hoffman (1990) chronicled the sense of alienation that accompanied her loss of Polish and language shift to English. Linguistic anthropologists Michèle Koven (2007) and Kathryn Woolard (2011) have presented complementary scholarly perspectives on how adults adapt their social identities to fit multilingual repertoires that shift across their lifetimes. Language shift, or the gradual abandonment of a mother tongue for a more dominant language, threatens sustainability more generally because language is a medium for establishing social relationships, cultural practices, and senses of belonging. Ruptures in the transmission of language systems can therefore contribute to social and cultural ruptures.[2]

Given the worldwide acceleration of language shift, the dynamism of language systems is often interpreted as fragility. However, with each instance of talk, speakers make choices that influence the vitality of their languages. A key goal of this book is to highlight the linguistic choices that young children make in situations of social and political change. Most commonly, scholars examine the politics of language in the institutionalized contexts of language policy or education. Even personal accounts of language loss, like that of Ngũgĩ, tend to focus on highly institutionalized settings that have explicitly sought to erase diverse languages. However, in young children's everyday experiences of language, we can see cultural continuity in the face of significant political constraints on expressions of diversity.

This book shows how young children in Tibet participate in community efforts for cultural survival through their emerging language use, even when adults view children's speech as evidence of language loss. In Tibetan communities, language is both the key medium through which young children build sociality and an ideological focal point for articulating a shared Tibetan Buddhist identity. By examining ethnographic scenes from Tibetan children's everyday play and closely analysing their talk, I show how children are forming their identities through language in a time of social change. Focusing on children's everyday family interactions, I ask: How do young children form identities as speakers or non-speakers of their mother tongues? And, how does the dialogic emergence of social relationships in everyday talk influence the vitality of young children's mother tongues?

By following the language-learning trajectories of young children from one extended family, I show that Tibetan children are actively responding to community-wide language shift as they build their social identities. My central argument is that these children are not passively abandoning their mother tongues but, instead, are incorporating new urban places and associated language varieties into traditional Tibetan associations between language, place, and kinship. As they learn language, children are therefore creatively reformatting a central facet of Tibetan cultural worlds.

The Setting

"Tibet" is the name of a vast region, historically united by a Buddhist empire, linguistically united by a common literary language, and culturally united by a shared spirituality and common livelihood practices. Known in Tibetan as *gangs ljongs*, "the land of snows," Tibet stretches from the western Himalayas of northern Pakistan through the Inner Asian deserts of northwestern China. As anthropologist Sara Shneiderman explains, the approximately six million people who identify as Tibetan draw on both a national imaginary, locating themselves through their shared political history, and an ethnic imaginary, locating themselves as peripheral subjects of the states in which they reside (2006, 10). In terms of land area, the majority of greater Tibet is currently located within the People's Republic of China (PRC), but Tibetans also trace their homelands to territories incorporated into India, Nepal, and Bhutan. Tibetan communities remain rooted to the particular local histories of their homelands while also recognizing transnational connections. These communities share a literary language that is sacred to their Buddhist religion. In contrast, spoken Tibetan languages vary greatly by region and locality. In Tibet, language is thus an important resource for constructing individual and collective identities. Tibetans use language to build social relationships in everyday talk, to express belonging to their homeland, and to articulate a common ethnonational identity that hinges on a Buddhist worldview.

These components of Tibetan linguistic identity are rebuilt through the creation of new speakers – that is, as young children learn their mother tongues. However, as inhabitants of a complex borderland, children growing up in Tibet have been faced with rapidly changing political and economic circumstances that have influenced the structures of spoken Tibetan languages by spurring migration and language contact. Most recently, the PRC has implemented structures of colonial rule in the name of economic development, intensifying language endangerment (Roche 2021a). In 1959, the military of the PRC suppressed an uprising in Lhasa, imperial Tibet's capital city. This led to the exile of the 14th Dalai Lama, Tibet's spiritual and political leader, to Dharamsala, India. An estimated 80,000 Tibetans followed their leader into exile. A flourishing Tibetan diaspora, supported by an exile government, was established. Today, an estimated 128,000 Tibetans live in diaspora, spread outside of their homelands.[3] Many are the descendants of those who left Tibet between the 1950s and 1980s. These exiled Tibetans have adopted a common language, *spyi skad* (common speech), based on the Lhasa dialect of central Tibetan.

While diasporic Tibetans have a common language, the vast majority of Tibetan people continue to speak local mother tongues, or *yul skad* (literally, land speech), which are unique to their homelands. Most of these homelands are currently incorporated into mainland China's provinces of Qinghai, Sichuan, Gansu, and the Tibet Autonomous Region. Since the first decade of this century, the migration of Tibetans out of China has mostly ceased, due to stricter border controls as well as expanded economic and educational opportunities within China. Despite these increased opportunities, Tibetans living within China's borders face significant challenges to language vitality and associated forms of cultural survival.

The Chinese Communist Party (CCP) asserts a unified nation-state, whose citizens are classified into fifty-six *minzu*, or "nationalities" – the Han majority and fifty-five *shaoshu minzu* (minoritized nationalities).[4] Despite significant ethnic and linguistic diversity among Tibetan communities, the state categorizes Tibetans (Ch. *zangzu*) as a single minoritized nationality, with a single recognized language embodied in the written standard. Diverse Tibetan *yul skad* are dominated by this view of a standard Tibetan language, as well as by the state's official language of Mandarin. Growing up as a Tibetan in China therefore requires confronting a sense that one's mother tongue is somehow dissociated from one's national identity as well as the physical place of one's homeland, in which it also inherently rooted. It requires managing family and peer relationships in a time when the Tibetan homeland itself appears to merge more seamlessly into the Chinese state. Within Tibetan areas of China, rural-to-urban migration is encouraging the use of Mandarin, thus destabilizing the linguistic resources traditionally used to build everyday relationships in Tibetan families. Young Tibetan children must navigate the tension inherent to their families' competing desires to use Mandarin to participate in a modernizing Chinese nation-state, to assert Tibetan cultural survival through a standard Tibetan language, and to form their intimate family relationships in diverse *yul skad*.

These competing desires create a dynamic tension between linguistic continuity and assimilation, which is particularly apparent in Amdo (Tib. *a mdo*). Amdo, which sits at the historical border between Tibet and China, was one of the three major regions (Tib. *chol kha gsum*) of imperial Tibet, along with U-tsang (Tib. *dbus gtsang*) and Kham (Tib. *khams*). The birthplace of the 14th Dalai Lama, Amdo is located in what is now northwestern China, encompassing most of Qinghai Province, as well as the outskirts of Sichuan and Gansu Provinces. This book is set among Amdo Tibetan children from one extended family, who are living in two very different settings. Some children are located in their

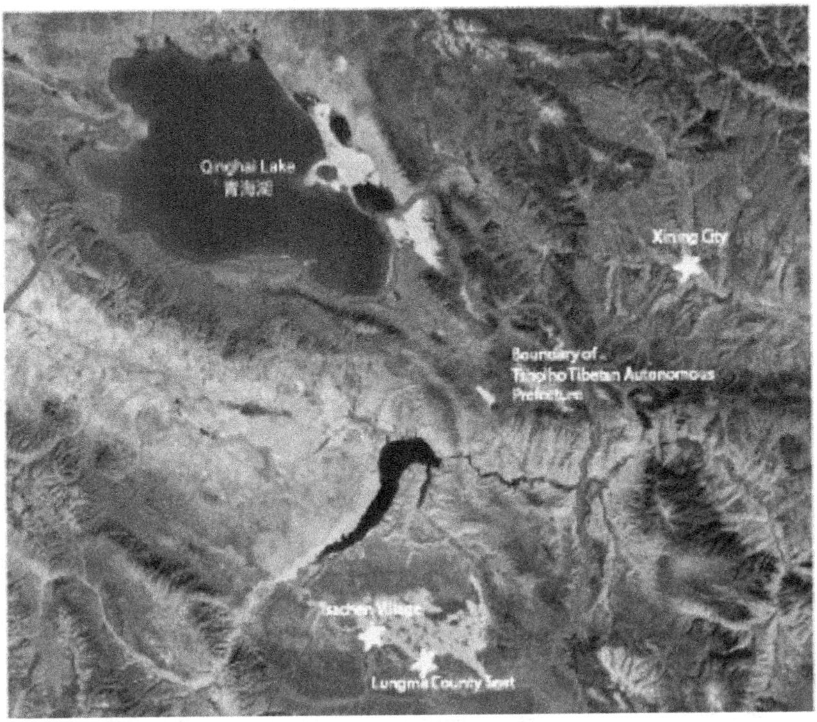

Figure 1. Locations of field research in Amdo

Source: Created with images from Google Earth (with data from Landsat/Copernicus). The visible imagery has unknown date information.

homeland, a rural village called Tsachen, in Tsholho Tibetan Autonomous Prefecture, Lungma County, Qinghai Province.[5] Other children from the same extended family have moved from Lungma County to Xining, Qinghai's provincial capital city.

Because this borderland region has been ruled, at different times, by Tibetan, Mongolian, Manchu, and Chinese empires, as well as Hui Muslim warlords, Amdo's inhabitants have diverse ethnic and linguistic identities. The Chinese state currently recognizes thirty-seven distinct nationalities (Ch. *minzu*) in Qinghai province alone (Goodman 2004b, 382). In Tsholho Tibetan Autonomous Prefecture, Tibetans form the largest nationality (68.3 per cent), followed by the Han Chinese (21.5 per cent) and Hui Muslim nationalities (7.8 per cent).[6] Tsholho also includes members of the Tu, Mongol, and Salar nationalities. Xining is, by Chinese standards, a small city. Home to more than 2.2 million people, Xining's population is approximately 74 per cent Han Chinese, 16 per cent Hui Muslim, and 5.5 per cent Tibetan, with smaller numbers of people from Amdo/Qinghai's thirty-four additional nationalities (Grant 2016, 142).

These demographic details are important to understanding the Tibetan language, which has been shaped by long histories of ethnolinguistic contact. In line with their belief in a unified language, which supports a common national identity, Tibetan people often describe "Tibetan" as one language with three major dialects that correspond to the imperial provinces of Amdo, U-tsang, and Kham. From the perspective of contemporary linguistics, Tibetan is better understood as a language family, because the varieties spoken across these regions and among Tibetans living in diaspora are not mutually intelligible. Based on field research, linguists recognize fifty-four Tibetan languages that are historically related to the classical Tibetan literary language (Ward and Roche 2020, 371). Linguists estimate that ethnic Tibetans living within China speak as many as sixty distinct languages, some of which are not historically related to literary Tibetan (Roche and Suzuki 2018, 1255).

Most Tibetans in Amdo speak a language named "Amdo Tibetan" (Tib. *a mdo skad*) after its native region. According to recent estimates, Amdo Tibetan has 1.8 million native speakers (Eberhard, Simons, and Fennig 2023). Amdo Tibetan can be further divided into spoken dialects, or mutually intelligible language varieties, known locally as *yul skad. Yul skad* are diverse mother tongues learned in early childhood and used in the home. Amdo Tibetan people also differentiate their *yul skad* into two major occupational categories: *rong skad* (Farmer Talk) and *'brog skad* (Nomad Talk). Because farming communities have had more enduring contact with neighbouring groups who speak Turkic, Mongolic, and Sinitic (Chinese) languages, Amdo Tibetan Farmer Talk shows more extensive internal linguistic diversity than Amdo Tibetan Nomad Talk. Most Amdo Tibetan people conceptualize Amdo Farmer Talk as encompassing multiple *yul skad*, and Amdo Nomad Talk as corresponding to a single *yul skad* (fig. 2).[7]

Comparing rural and urban children's daily lives and language use makes apparent how state-led economic development campaigns are contributing to language shift in Amdo. Urban living has dissociated young children from important Buddhist cultural practices, as well as traditional childrearing practices that emphasize peer relationships and free play. Urban children have opportunities for socio-economic mobility through schooling and educational enrichment that are not accessible to their rural peers. Urban parents support their young children's social

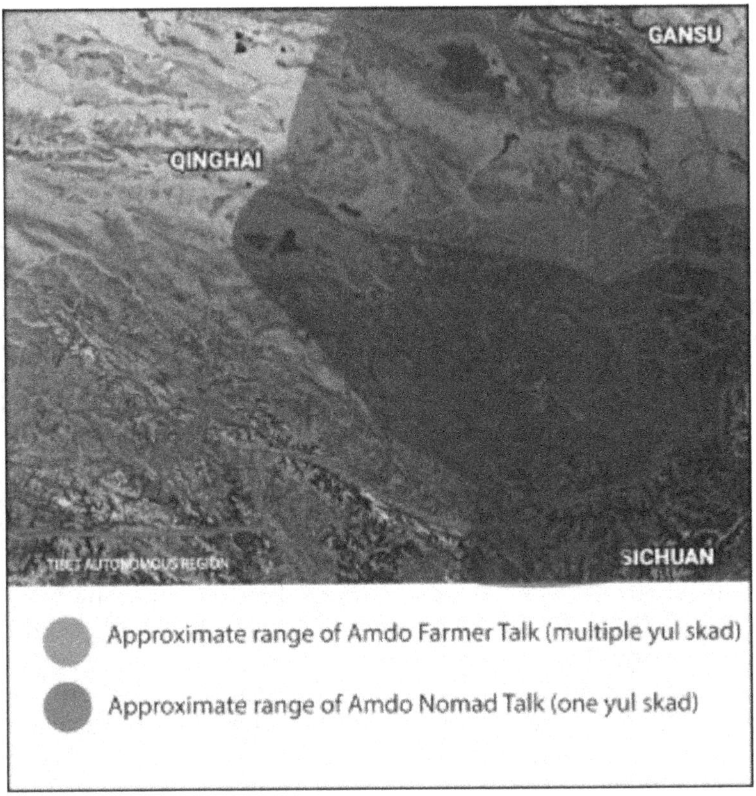

Figure 2. Approximate range of Amdo Tibetan Nomad Talk and Farmer Talk

Source: Created with images from Google Earth (with data from Landsat/Copernicus). The visible imagery has unknown date information.

and linguistic development by organizing reading groups and enrolling children in extracurricular lessons for English, dance, music, and the arts. In fact, many urban Amdo Tibetan parents use verbal routines commonly prescribed by Euro-American psychologists to boost young children's social and cognitive development, including one-on-one play and orchestrated co-reading.[8] Despite this extraordinary parental investment, urban Amdo Tibetan children experience language shift to Mandarin and associated ruptures of their close family relationships. Because they are growing up in a community where expressions of ethnic and linguistic difference are closely surveilled, urban children lack the social context for enacting intuitive language play in their mother tongue.

To examine the effects of urbanization on Amdo Tibetan language vitality, this book focuses on speakers of one variety of Amdo Farmer Talk, specific to Tsachen Village in Tsholho Tibetan Autonomous Prefecture. I compare how children living in their rural homeland and in the provincial capital city speak with different members of their families and in different social settings. By closely examining these young children's language use, I theorize how children's choices about language influence their everyday social relationships and intersect with the broader transformation of Amdo cultural worlds. I found that Amdo Tibetan children mediate the tension between their communities' aspirations for socio-economic mobility and cultural survival by incorporating new language varieties and new urban places into traditional associations between language, place, and kinship. As they do so, young Amdo children are unknowingly reinforcing inequalities between rural and urban persons in contemporary China.

$^{n}t^{h}$on pa: "Arrival"

In late August 2016, I arrived in Qinghai Province from my home in New York City with a plan to study young Amdo Tibetan children's language acquisition and socialization. For the previous six years, I had studied the Tibetan language (Tib. *bod kyi skad yig*) in various forms, first from textbooks co-authored by Western linguists and scholars from central Tibet, next from the vast array of classical and modern texts that I pored through in the dimly lit basement of the Starr East Asian Library at Columbia University, and finally from a group of Amdo scholars and friends living in New York City. I was fascinated, as the object of my study constantly shapeshifted. The Tibetan language seemed to transform between text and talk, between the voices of various interlocutors, and even in the voice of a single speaker who could move seamlessly between varieties of Tibetan when addressing co-present friends or video-chatting with family members a world away in Tibet. My training as a linguistic anthropologist had convinced me that what we call "languages" are dynamic, emergent, and far from clearly bounded. I sought to understand how one target language was being defined, and thus constructed, by its youngest speakers.

On an evening a few weeks after my arrival, I walked down a wide avenue in central Xining. Neon lights from hotels, bars, and restaurants flashed, vibrantly dizzying. I made my way into a café, where cigarette smoke and the steam from fresh espresso commingled around the crowded tables. I glimpsed the face of my new friend, Norbu, an undergraduate student at the local university. Norbu had invited me for tea that evening and promised to introduce me to some of his classmates. I approached the corner table where he was seated. After I sat down, our discussion shifted to the topic of research.

When I explained to Norbu that I had come to Amdo to study Tibetan children's language acquisition, he pointed out a central problem: I was in Xining, and no Tibetan children in Xining speak Tibetan. Most of Xining's population identifies as Han Chinese. Formal bilingual schooling is available only in rural areas of Amdo, where most of the population is classified as Tibetan (Ch. *zangzu*). Because they lack access to formal schooling in Tibetan, Norbu suggested, urban Amdo children speak only Mandarin. I would have to travel somewhere else, like his home village, Tsachen, if I wanted to meet Amdo children who actually speak Tibetan.

"*Xining-na xɕik̚me-la?*" (There's not even one child in Xining?), I asked Norbu in Amdo Tibetan.

"*xɕik̚ la jo-ɕi-re*" (Well, there might be one), Norbu conceded and pulled out his cellphone. Before I could order my tea, Norbu rose from the table, calling to me "^{n}*dʑo-ba*!" (Let's go!) as he rushed out the door and hailed a taxi.

As I caught up to Norbu and slipped into the taxi, he explained that we were going meet his relative and her nephew at a nearby mall. A speedy five minutes later, we were striding up an escalator in an expansive, gleaming shopping complex. Norbu led me to an indoor playground, where his relative, Tsering Kyi, stood smiling in the doorway. As we made our way over to Tsering Kyi, she gestured to a toddler, her nephew, who was standing in front of an elevated play station and filtering lime-green kinetic sand through his tiny, dimpled hands.

Ani (Aunt) Tsering Kyi directed the toddler in Amdo Tibetan, "*Sonam, Ani demo-ze*" (Sonam, say hi to Ani).

As I crouched down, Sonam called out the Amdo Tibetan greeting "*Ani demo*" (Hi, Ani), reaching out his hand for a shake. As he looked towards me, Sonam caught sight of my cellphone and turned his outstretched hand to point. Sonam shouted out, now in Mandarin, "***gei wo***!" (Give it to me!).

All three of us adults burst out in laughter, noting the ironic contrast between Sonam's friendly Amdo Tibetan greeting and his use of the state's official language to issue a command.

Ani Tsering Kyi teasingly called out to Sonam, "*ra-ma-lik̚*," a phrase that literally means "neither goat nor sheep" and is used to characterize code-mixing, or the use of multiple languages in a single utterance. She then posed a rhetorical question to Sonam, "*tɕʰo ŋo-mə-tsʰa-ni?*" (Aren't you ashamed?).

Ani Tsering Kyi framed Sonam's simultaneous use of Amdo Tibetan and Mandarin as unnatural and socially inappropriate. Her comments nonetheless remained light-hearted. Coupled with Norbu's earlier insistence on the difficulty of locating urban Amdo children who speak in Tibetan, Ani Tsering Kyi's reaction to her nephew's language use made me wonder what might lead adults to conclude that urban Amdo children do not speak their mother tongue. Sonam had spoken to me in his Amdo *yul skad*, in addition to Mandarin. I suspected that, like other urban children, he frequently moved between his extended family's rural home in Tsachen and his nuclear family's apartment in Xining. I wondered if there were social pressures that would lead Sonam and children like him to choose to speak Mandarin rather than their Amdo *yul skad*.

Children's Agency in Language Shift

Amdo's diverse *yul skad* have historically served as a basis for social belonging, due to foundational cultural associations between language, place, and kinship. The Amdo adults we will meet in this book recognize that both rural and urban children face social pressures to use Mandarin instead of their native Amdo Tibetan Farmer Talk. The pressure to speak Mandarin dissociates children from their families and homelands. Most adults have responded to concerns about language loss by advocating for children to study written Tibetan. Most adults do not recognize the cultural and linguistic practices that their children *do* maintain despite the dominance of Mandarin.

In the chapters that follow, I examine young children's everyday interactions with their peers and caregivers to show that, paradoxically, Amdo Tibetan children's cultural knowledge is leading many to stop speaking their mother tongues. I approach children's uses of language in everyday play as a manifestation of their intuitive knowledge of cultural practices. While the tradition of generative linguistics tends to view language abilities as innate, anthropological research on language acquisition suggests that the social and cultural practices of everyday talk shape a speaker's emerging grammar. This capacity for language to structure itself through interaction is known as "reflexivity" and interfaces with cultural knowledge, especially in the course of language acquisition (Taylor 2000, 486). Cultural knowledge governs the everyday conversations in which speakers use metalanguage, or talk about talk, to represent language itself. Specific grammatical forms, such as reported speech and deixis, serve as particularly rich sources of metalanguage (Lucy 1993) while also playing an important developmental role in language acquisition. The reflexive capacity of language leads children to construct models of languages, as well as models of *speakers* of languages, during everyday talk.

Within linguistic anthropology, the paradigm known as "language socialization" emphasizes reflexivity in language acquisition, arguing that children simultaneously learn to use language while they learn cultural practices through language (Schieffelin and Ochs 1986, 2). Complementary experimental evidence suggests that a language's grammatical structures shape cognition, implying that children learning different mother tongues may be acquiring different ways of thinking.[9] Language socialization theorists nonetheless argue that actual language use, rather than grammatical structures alone, influence cultural patterns of thought and behaviour. In fact, linguistic anthropologists more generally highlight how ideologies, or cultural belief systems that shape identity, drive change to language structures. From this perspective, language shift happens not simply because children lack input in a given mother tongue. Rather, children stop using their mother tongues when community-wide patterns of language use and language ideologies conspire to encourage them to speak a more dominant language.

Despite children's central role in language shift, most scholarship on issues related to language endangerment has focused on adults' language use. In fact, endangered languages are categorically defined as those no longer being acquired as mother tongues, or first languages, by young children. The exclusion of children from the very definition of endangered languages leaves room for investigating how ongoing, community-wide language shift shapes young children's experiences of language acquisition and socialization (Meek 2019). Previous ethnographic research of children's conversations has consistently found that children's linguistic knowledge exceeds the expectations of adults. For example, studies of young children's role play show that children associate distinct styles of speaking with different social identities (García-Sánchez 2014) and that, when children act out the identities of adult characters, they use language forms they do not produce in other settings (Andersen 2014). As anthropologist Amy Paugh (2005) found in a study of language socialization in the Dominican Republic, adults discouraged children from speaking their mother tongue, Patwa. Outside of adult supervision, however, children used Patwa to playfully enact different adult roles, such as bus drivers and school teachers. This finding suggests that children have not only linguistic knowledge of Patwa but also cultural knowledge of who can or should use it. Although young children growing up in endangered language communities may not openly use their mother tongue, they often possess more linguistic knowledge than they reveal on a daily basis. Further, adults' belief that children cannot speak their mother tongue may actually lead children to identify as non-speakers in the first place.[10] It is necessary to examine young children's language use in historical and cultural context to understand the specific factors that are driving language shift in any community.

A Brief History of Amdo

While Tibet's history has been animated by intersections of decentralized states and imperial centres, Buddhist institutions have remained the foundation of Tibetan cultural worlds.[11] In the seventh century, Tibetan king Songtsen Gampo built a Buddhist empire, centred in Lhasa. Interactions between imperial Tibet and China's Tang dynasty are documented in both Tibetan and Chinese sources (Shakabpa 2010, 110). In 783, a treaty between Tibet and China established the boundaries of Tibet as far east as the current borders of Qinghai and Gansu Provinces (Schaeffer, Kapstein, and Tuttle 2013, 6). Between the ninth and the twelfth centuries, the Tibetan empire experienced a period of fragmentation, followed by a cultural and religious renaissance. From the twelfth century until the fall of the Qing dynasty in 1911, Tibetan Buddhist polities retained significant power across the Tibetan plateau while engaging in patron-client relationships with Mongol (Yuan), Chinese (Ming), and Manchu (Qing) imperial elites (Shakabpa 2010, 199–200). From a perspective that privileges historical continuity in Tibetan sovereignty, Buddhist monastic institutions developed and maintained governance structures that were recognized and supported by external imperial powers (Dawa Norbu 2001, 137–42).

Tibetan-language sources first began to refer to Amdo as a coherent territory in the seventeenth century.[12] In this period, the Gelukpa (Tib. *dge lugs pa*) school of Tibetan Buddhism had gained dominance on the Tibetan plateau, in part, through the patronage and military support of Mongolian rulers. In 1578, the Mongol ruler Altan Khan had met a prominent Gelukpa lama, Sonam Gyatso, in Amdo. Altan Khan bestowed him with a Mongolian title, *Dalai*, or "Ocean," a translation of his Tibetan name that indicated his vast knowledge (Goldstein 1999, 8). Sonam Gyatso's lineage became known as the Dalai Lamas. Over the next decades, the Mongols provided military support to the Gelukpas in Tibetan sectarian conflicts. From 1642 to 1717, the Khoshud Mongols governed Tibet from a base in Tsho Ngonpo (known in Mongolian as Kokonor), while acknowledging the sovereignty of Gelukpa monastic polities. Meanwhile, east of Amdo, the Manchu Qing began to consolidate imperial rule over China. The Qing dynasty rose to power in 1644, maintaining control over China until 1911, while managing diplomatic relationships with Tibetan, Mongol, and Hui Muslim authorities in Amdo. By 1724, the Mongol influence in Amdo had waned due to internal conflicts (Goldstein 1999,16). In response, Qing authorities incorporated Amdo's monastic polities into their territory.

The Qing recognized the sovereignty of Amdo's monastic polities, and, in fact, strengthened their governance powers with legal and military support.[13] In Amdo's monastic polities, nomads and farmers participated in mutually beneficial subsistence strategies. Settled villagers who cared for livestock depended on nomadic camps for herding and, in turn, provisioned camps with goods such as fuel and food. Villagers and nomads intermarried, which often resulted in settled households gradually moving towards more nomadic subsistence practices over time (Ekvall 1968, 21–8). Despite being self-sufficient in their subsistence strategies, Amdo's monastic polities relied heavily on the Qing courts and military to resolve disputes with Mongolian, Hui, and other Tibetan communities.[14] In particular, competitions over pastureland often resulted in considerable tensions. The interdependence of farmers and nomads under monastic polities contributed to a social boundary between these two occupational groups, which is maintained today partly through the linguistic distinction between *'brog skad* (Nomad Talk) and *rong skad* (Farmer Talk).

While patronizing Amdo's monasteries, the Qing sought to classify their subject populations and territories, which provided a foundation for later articulations of assimilationist language and ethnic policy. The Qing relied on cartography, or the mapping of territories, and ethnography, or the supposedly naturalistic description of the inhabitants of these territories, to expand their vast empire (Hostetler 2001). With the technologies of censuses, cartographies, and ethnographies, the Qing demarcated five main political constituencies: Manchu, Han, Mongol, Tibetan, and Hui or Muslim. The Qing also experimented with language reform as a means of consolidating power. Qing-era reformers sought to overcome differences between written Chinese and various spoken Chinese languages (Ch. *fangyan*) and looked to Beijing's dialect of spoken Chinese as a potential standard (Tam 2020, 42, 77). The Qing's efforts to strengthen their governance while simultaneously recognizing the autonomy of existing polities led to complex interactions among their constituencies. In the late nineteenth century, the Qing appointed some Hui Muslim leaders in civil-military posts in response to rebellions on the northwestern frontier (Weiner 2020b, 33). One group of Hui military leaders, the Ma clan, gained control over northeast Amdo, eclipsing the political authority of Tibetan monastic polities in this region.

In 1911, the Qing dynasty collapsed due to internal conflicts combined with the external threats of British, Soviet, and Japanese expansion. A new nation-state, the Republic of China, was created. It was ruled by the Republican Party, or Guomindang (1912–49). The Guomindang was opposed by the Chinese Communist Party. In order to legitimate rule over the Qing's former territories, Guomindang leaders drew on the Qing's pre-existing demarcation of five major ethnic constituencies.[15] In Amdo, they maintained an allyship with the ruling Ma clan. Although the Guomindang adapted the Qing's confederate model, they professed a newfound emphasis on *minzu tuanjie* (national unity). At the new capital in Nanjing, President Sun Yat-sen declared, "The foundation of the state lies in the people's ability to unite the Han, Manchu, Mongol, Hui and Tibetan territories into a single country (Ch. *yi guo*) and to unite the Han, Manchu, Mongol, Hui, and Tibetan races into a single people (Ch. *yi ren*)" (as cited in Leibold 2007, 38). State discourse in the Republican era therefore advocated for unifying *shaoshu minzu* through *hanhua* (literally, the act of "becoming Chinese"), in order to preserve the nation's territorial integrity (Leibold 2007, 5).[16] Drawing, in part, on Qing practices of ethnography and language reform, Republican scholars used different survey methods to document the languages spoken by Han and non-Han nationalities (Ch. *minzu*) (Tam 2020, 135–6). The designation of any language as a dialect of Chinese (Ch. *fangyan*) was taken as scientific proof of membership in the Han nationality, and the demarcation of non-Chinese languages justified the boundaries of minoritized nationalities (ibid.). In the Republican era, the modes of ethnic classification inherited from the Qing thus carried new ideological consequences. *Minzu tuanjie* became a moral and political imperative, and the explicit demarcation of minoritized nationalities justified coerced assimilation.

By the mid-twentieth century, internal conflict between the Republicans and Communists had come to a head, while, in Amdo, the Ma clan continued their military reign. The Communist People's Liberation Army intervened in ongoing conflicts between the Ma clan and Amdo's Tibetan monastic polities. In 1949, revolutionary Mao Zedong led the Chinese Communist Party to victory and founded the People's Republic of China. The Republican Guomindang retreated to Taiwan. The Ma clan, allied with the Guomindang, followed them into exile.

During the transition from Republican to Communist rule, efforts to ensure control over the entire breadth of the former Qing territory intensified. In contrast to the explicit assimilationist discourses of the

Guomindang, the CCP borrowed from Soviet nationality policy to cultivate a narrative of the historical unity of its fifty-six *minzu*. As historian Benno Weiner asserted, "when the CCP first arrived in Amdo, it was both fully confident that Amdo's diverse inhabitants were part of a self-evident multi-national state and equally sure that these same people were often unaware and even hostile to this otherwise objective fact" (2020a, 44). In response to the belief that Amdo inherently belonged to the Chinese nation, the CCP employed a bureaucratic apparatus, the United Front (Ch. *tongyi zhanxian*), to manage relationships with Amdo's existing political elites while encouraging epistemological adherence to the CCP's vision of a multi-national state. With the United Front, the CCP balanced opposing desires to maintain the political stability of existing governance structures, subservient to the Communist state, and to liberate its subjects from backwards, "feudal" theocracies (Weiner 2020b, 22).

From 1949 to 1958, Amdo's monastic polities generally accepted the CCP's presence, although some engaged in anti-state activities (Weiner 2020b, 162–3). By 1958, the CCP had hastened their goals for collectivization, and Tibetan efforts to avoid the collapse of their monastic governance structures erupted in a series of rebellions (ibid., 164–8). These rebellions provided justification for the CCP to topple monastic polities. In response to anti-state activism, the CCP initiated a program of Democratic Reforms (Ch. *minzhu gaige*) that aggressively redistributed pastoral land rights and replaced religious and lay leaders with state officials. The 1958 Democratic Reforms initiated a cataclysmic shift by destroying Buddhist governance structures. Prior to 1958, Qinghai province alone was home to 722 Tibetan Buddhist monasteries with over 60,000 monks and nuns. By the time the program officially ended in 1962, only eleven monasteries remained intact (Kolas and Thowsen 2005, 45–6).

The Communist Party framed this integration of Amdo, and of greater Tibet, into the Chinese nation-state as a "peaceful liberation" (Ch. *heping jiefang*) from a barbaric system of feudal rule. Tibetans' own narratives present this historical moment as one of radical disjuncture between an "old society" (Tib. *spyi tshogs rnying pa*), which existed prior to the rise of the PRC, and a "new society" (Tib. *spyi tshogs gsar pa*) under Communist rule.[17] These terms are, in fact, neologisms calqued directly from the Mandarin terms *jiu shehui* (old society) and *xin shehui* (new society). Amdo Tibetans today use the Mandarin and Tibetan terms interchangeably, which highlights the foreignness of these concepts in a Buddhist society that interprets history through successive lifecycles rather than linear stages of economic development. The CCP's aggressive campaigns for collectivization, political integration, and epistemological assimilation necessitated the destruction of Buddhist institutions. These initiatives not only reorganized subsistence practices but dismissed Buddhist philosophy, the very foundation of Tibetan cultural worlds, as a primitive form of false consciousness. As a result, state goals for national development could not be articulated through local Tibetan cultural logics or local Tibetan languages.

During the ensuing Cultural Revolution (1966–76), the state continued to radically redistribute wealth and dismantle the political power structures of pre-Communist Amdo society. Official translators from the People's Liberation Army combined the written Tibetan words for "new" (Tib. *gsar pa*) and "change" (Tib. *brje ba*) to make *gsar brje* (revolution). This neologism was added to the Tibetan word for "culture" (Tib. *rig gnas*) to create the phrase *rig gnas gsar brje* (Cultural Revolution). During the Cultural Revolution, the widespread practice of "socialist education" (Ch. *shehui zhuyi jiaoyu*) forced Tibetans to narrate the terrors of monastic rule in public "struggle sessions" (Tib. *'thab 'dzing*). This public practice of historical revisionism aimed to break Tibetans' faith in their religious leaders and monastic institutions. Instead, following the Cultural Revolution, Tibetan people rebuilt their lives around Buddhist monasteries, spiritual leaders, and philosophical and literary traditions. As Tibetan poet Tsering Woeser aptly notes, the Tibetan neologism *rig gnas gsar brje* can be rendered back into Chinese with the homophonic phrase *renlei shajie*, meaning the "killing and destruction of humanity" (2020, xv).

In the late twentieth century, the damages of the Democratic Reforms and the Cultural Revolution contributed to environmental disruptions that devastated Amdo Tibetan practices of mutually beneficial farming and pastoralism. As part of their efforts to redistribute land holdings during the 1958 Democratic Reforms, the Communist Party established state-owned collective farms in existing agricultural settlements. As a result of redistribution, Amdo farmers' private land use was drastically restricted. Many had no choice but to labour in the state-owned collective farms alongside exiled political prisoners from central and eastern China, in a practice that was framed as social welfare (Rohlf 2016, 70). Meanwhile, pastoralists were forced to give up their herds of yak, cows, and sheep. Many of these animals were shipped to industrial centres and slaughtered, their meat exported for profit (Demick 2020, 46). Using Amdo's plateau grasslands for collectivized agricultural cultivation rather than local grazing and pastoralism created widespread famine. Despite these dire consequences, the CCP continued to promote collectivization, compounding environmental disaster while glorifying rural villagers as the ideal political subjects (Makley 2005, 47).

Mao Zedong's death in 1976 contributed to the end of the Cultural Revolution. Mao's chosen successor, Hua Guofeng, would lead for only two years before a prominent revolutionary and party member, Deng Xiaoping, became paramount leader in 1978. Tibet experienced another radical transformation during Deng's leadership. He initiated a series of economic reforms (Ch. *gaige kaifang*) that decollectivized agriculture, liberalized some sectors of China's economy, and supported cultural revival among minoritized nationalities. Tibetans avidly restored their monasteries, expanded secular bilingual education, and engaged in artistic production. In fact, Deng's plans for economic modernization *required* the participation of intellectuals, educators, artists, and entrepreneurs (Weiner 2020a, 50). Amdo, in particular, became a locus of Tibetan cultural production. Intellectual and artistic circles flourished in eminent monasteries such as Rongwo (Tib. *rong bo'i dgon chen*) and Labrang (Tib. *bla brang bkra shis 'khyil*), as well as in Xining's universities. The relatively early introduction of secular education, especially in Tsholho Tibetan Autonomous Prefecture (Thurston 2018a, 150–1), facilitated the participation of Amdo people in cultural revival. Widespread bilingualism in Mandarin also expanded the reach of Amdo Tibetans' religious, intellectual, and cultural activities (Maconi 2008, 178). Against the backdrop of this Tibetan cultural renaissance, Deng's market reforms brought new economic prosperity to eastern China. By one estimate, the total percentage of China's population living in poverty dropped from 75–100 per cent to 6.7–13.2 per cent between 1978 and 1996 (Yao 2000, 447).

By the first decade of the twenty-first century, the Chinese state sought to extend this prosperity to its far western territories. The Open Up the West Campaign (Ch. *xibu da kaifa*), which began in 1999 and is planned until 2050, brought significant socio-economic change to the Tibetan plateau by furthering the state's vision of civilization through urbanization (Ptáčková 2020, 22). Justified through state-sanctioned discourses that equate economic development with the advancement of China's minoritized nationalities, the Open Up the West Campaign represents a series of fragmented, underfunded policies administered by local bureaucrats (Goodman 2004a, 319). Despite inconsistencies between state discourses and local execution, the Open Up the West Campaign has transformed land use and subsistence strategies in Amdo. With the twin goals of restoring forests and grasslands, as well as modernizing Tibetans' livelihoods, a range of prefecture-level mandates across Amdo have once again curtailed farmers' land use, and sought to settle nomadic herders (Ptáčková 2020, 17–20). Additional investments in transportation infrastructure have increased rural

Tibetan communities' access to schools and hospitals, while connecting Amdo to eastern China and contributing to an influx of Han Chinese migrant workers and settlers. Combined with nomadic resettlement, migration has remodelled the seats of rural Tibetan autonomous prefectures into bustling urban centres. Alongside urbanization, state discourse surrounding Tibet's incorporation into the Chinese nation-state has shifted from a narrative of political liberation to one of socio-economic mobility. According to this narrative, economic development is a state-provided gift that supports Tibetan cultural survival (Yeh 2013, 3). The Open Up the West Campaign has defined civilization through modernization, transforming the image of the ideal political subject from the rural peasant farmer into the modern urban citizen.

Amdo families' adaptations to the campaign's ongoing, fragmented development policies complicate this political narrative of cultural survival through economic development. For example, the demarcation of protected ecological zones, alongside the allocation of pastureland and farm plots to individual families, has intensified internal disputes over grazing and farming territories (Yeh 2003). At the same time, with the rise of a market economy and constraints on land use, traditional Amdo practices of farming and pastoralism are no longer economically viable as a family's sole occupation. In response, Amdo adults are seeking employment in county and prefecture seats or the provincial capital. Although the stated goal of the Open Up the West Campaign was to promote equality between eastern and western China, the imperative for market employment has compounded Tibetans' economic exclusion. Economist Andrew Fischer (2013) showed that Tibetans' lack of opportunities for equal employment and urban mobility are distinct from the disadvantages faced by rural Han Chinese people. In fact, development campaigns such as Open Up the West structurally reproduce the marginalization of minoritized nationalities by introducing new forms of economic stratification alongside urbanization. As Ptáčková asserted, with the Open Up the West Campaign, "hundreds of thousands have risen out of poverty [while] similar numbers have become impoverished through the rising costs of living and the loss of their livelihoods" (2020, 16).

While a market economy has brought cities to previously rural places, education policies have motivated migration out of villages and into cities. Chinese laws requiring nine years of primary education date to 1986, but these have been enforced in many parts of Amdo only in the past twenty years (Wright 2019, 28). In 2011, Qinghai Province announced the successful implementation of universal primary school education (Ying 2023, 857). Alongside the enforcement of compulsory education, the state introduced village-based pre-schools, while promoting a School Consolidation Policy (Ch. *hebing zhengce*) that centralized rural primary and secondary schools into boarding schools in county and prefecture seats. The School Consolidation Policy has served young children from nomadic and remote communities, while also removing them from their rural homelands. Many Amdo families have openly embraced opportunities for formal, secular education in boarding schools (Ying 2023, 868). With the belief that school achievement will facilitate upward socio-economic mobility, rural parents are investing in their children's secular education, although only a decade earlier, most had preferred for their children to attend monastic schools or support household labour (Gyal 2019, 17–18). Many parents have rented rooms in county and prefecture seats as a way to mitigate the psychological, social, and cultural risks posed by boarding schools (Yeh and Makley 2019, 6). For example, Wang's (2013) study of a secondary boarding school in Xinghai County, Tsholho Tibetan Autonomous Prefecture, found that approximately one in six students had a relative staying in the nearby county seat to help care for them (as cited in Ying 2023, 858). While parents who lack the economic resources to integrate into urban economies are forced to board their children without family support, the wealthiest families are increasingly moving to Xining, where their children attend Chinese public day schools.

Rural-to-urban migration carries substantial consequences for language vitality, because urban living, even in county- and prefecture-level seats, can dissociate children from their relationships with peers and family members who speak their mother tongue. The Chinese state also grounds language rights in territories, complicating language vitality outside of the rural homeland. The PRC's 1954 Constitution provided minoritized nationalities with the right to use their written languages in the governance of autonomous counties and prefectures, as well as in schools in autonomous counties and prefectures. Of the fifty-five minoritized nationalities, twenty-one, including Tibetans, have implemented formal bilingual education in rural autonomous areas (Zhang and Tsung 2019, 292). Bilingual education generally follows two models: either the minoritized language is used as the medium of instruction, and Mandarin is taught as a subject, or Mandarin is used as the medium of instruction, and the minoritized language is taught as a subject. Prior to the turn of the century, in Tibetan autonomous prefectures in Qinghai, most schools operated in Tibetan, with Chinese taught as a subject (Ma and Renzeng 2015, 107). In Xining, all children must attend Mandarin-medium schools. There are no options for formal Tibetan-language study. Families who choose to move to Xining therefore give up all legislated protections for Tibetan-language education.

Furthermore, the ever-changing landscape of education policy means that even legislated language rights provide little support for children to continue to use their mother tongues. Although the Chinese Constitution allows for the use of minoritized languages in autonomous counties and prefectures, state and provincial education policies have shifted since the 1990s from accommodating the recognized languages of minoritized nationalities to promoting standard Mandarin (Zhou 2017, 470–1). In 2010, Qinghai's provincial government announced a ten-year plan to increase Tibetan students' proficiency in Mandarin, with the goal of changing the medium of instruction in all Tibetan schools to Mandarin, with Tibetan offered as a single subject (Zhang and Tsung 2019, 293–4). The plan was met with widespread protests across Amdo.[18] Some prefectures, including Tsholho Tibetan Autonomous Prefecture, retained their model of Tibetan-medium education, with Mandarin offered as a subject. However, the extent of Tibetan-medium education across the province, as well as its popularity, has continued to decrease since 2010. Graduates of Tibetan-medium high schools continue to have the option to write their university entrance exams in Tibetan (Ch. *minkaomin*) and to attend Tibetan-medium university programs. However, graduates of Tibetan-medium degree programs often lack opportunities to use their skills in market employment, where demand for Mandarin language skills reigns supreme. Policies for school consolidation, as well as the segregation of Tibetan-medium education in rural areas, have thus increased Amdo families' reliance on formal education for socio-economic mobility. Meanwhile, education policies have intersected with the rise of market labour to simultaneously spur rural-to-urban migration and entrench inequalities between rural and urban families.

In contemporary Amdo, economic development has complicated Tibetan struggles for meaningful cultural survival, political autonomy, and language vitality. In the past generation alone, Amdo families have come to depend on the market economy for employment, schooling, medical care, and transportation. These are entitlements that the Chinese state carefully controls by allocating social benefits and language rights through one's place of habitation.[19] Amdo families must therefore choose whether to abandon their homeland, traditional livelihoods, and access to formal Tibetan education in the hopes that city life will provide their children with a more stable future. The current generation of Amdo Tibetan children is navigating this tension between opportunities for cultural and linguistic continuity and an increasing reliance on standard Mandarin for socio-economic mobility.

Chapter Outlines

The chapters that follow trace the contrasting language socialization pathways of rural and urban Amdo Tibetan children. I use the stories of Sonam in Xining, and Norbu's nieces Dolma and Lhamo in Tsachen, to exemplify broader patterns in my complete corpus of ethnographic and linguistic data. The chapters are sequenced to demonstrate two emerging forms of change: first, developmental patterns in language and social behaviour from infancy through early childhood, and, second, trends in migration that are increasingly drawing Amdo Tibetan families away from their rural homelands to the provincial capital. While rural and urban children used distinct language forms at different ages, all were grappling with the potential for language loss that accompanied their families' aspirations for education, urban living, and socio-economic mobility.

Chapter 1 narrates the history of Dolma, Lhamo, and Sonam's extended family, in order to examine the foundational association between land, language, and kinship that shapes Amdo Tibetan cultural worlds. Drawing from the theories of Mikhail Bakhtin (1981), I situate contemporary processes of linguistic differentiation – between the Tibetan and Chinese languages, and between different varieties of spoken Amdo Tibetan – in the context of personal narratives about the region's political history. By analysing ethnographic scenes of children's play as well as excerpts of family histories collected from ethnographic interviews, chapter 1 shows how political history is influencing the current language choices of young Amdo Tibetan children. Despite pressures for assimilation to more dominant languages, rural children continue to recognize the social meanings of Amdo's distinct *yul skad*. Specifically, in their everyday play, Tsachen's children mark place-based belonging by characterizing the voices of Tibetan people from different regions. Despite the cultural continuity that children enact by recognizing Tibetan linguistic diversity, adults' reactions to children's play demonstrate pervasive language ideologies that are leading to the reinterpretation of language variation in light of anxieties over language shift to Mandarin.

Chapter 2 examines contrasting patterns in rural and urban children's production of the key grammatical structures that are used to achieve joint attention. Drawing from theories of the development of peer culture through verbal interaction (Corsaro 1992), I demonstrate that children in rural Tsachen use salient grammatical features of the *yul skad* to reproduce associations between their village homeland and their kin relationships, in a cultural practice that I call "spatializing kinship." In urban Xining, infants and young children engage mostly in dyadic play with a single caregiver in their family home and lack access to multi-party play with related peers. Despite this constraint, urban adults spatialize kinship by focusing shared attention on children's non-present peers, imaginatively locating them in extended family relationships. Before age three, urban Amdo Tibetan children also use the features of the *yul skad*'s grammar that are involved in spatializing kinship. After beginning preschool, however, they shift to prefer Mandarin's grammatical structures. As they spatialize kinship, rural children build peer relationships that allow for cultural and linguistic continuity. Urban children, in contrast, are socialized out of their knowledge of the *yul skad* as they grow up.

While chapter 2 demonstrates the loss of cultural and linguistic practices among urban children, chapter 3 examines commonalities in rural and urban children's expressions of emotion. It analyses routinized displays of compassion, love, and interdependence in everyday family interactions in Tsachen and Xining to show how adults and children model for each other appropriate expressions of emotion and, in so doing, use the *yul skad* to identify as Tibetan Buddhist people. By integrating literature on affective stance – or the social alignment of displays of emotion in interaction – with Buddhist theories of emotion and cultural interpretations of attachment theory, I show how routinized displays of compassion help children build foundational family relationships while also reproducing an opposition between Tibetan and Chinese ethnic identities. Through this analysis, I suggest that connections between language socialization and affect contribute to Amdo Tibetan children's senses of belonging and difference.

In contrast to earlier chapters, which attended to the cultural meanings of linguistic diversity, chapter 4 analyses standard language ideology, or the shared belief in a single, correct language. The chapter traces historical details of education policy in Qinghai Province, which associate ethnolinguistic communities with fixed territories and literary languages. I suggest that these education policies have contributed to a standard language ideology with three components – the belief in a literary standard, the valorization of Amdo Nomad Talk over Amdo Farmer Talk, and negative attitudes towards code-mixing – that encourage children to identify as monolingual, rather than multilingual, speakers. This community-wide standard language ideology is enacted in everyday talk through performances of linguistic allegiance and shaming routines that target children's uses of code-mixing. Through these instantiations of standard language ideology, adults overlook children's existing forms of linguistic knowledge and position urban children, in particular, as the agents of language shift. Amdo's standard language ideology has therefore deepened the divide between rural and urban cultural worlds, contributing to urban children's identification as speakers of Mandarin.

Although chapter 4 examined a prescriptive standard language ideology, chapter 5 documents how urban children build multilingual identities that recall their families' histories of cultural and linguistic hybridity. In "I Read," a family-organized reading group in Xining, multi-ethnic preschoolers learn to read together in English and Mandarin. A small group of mothers created "I Read" to foster acceptance of multilingualism within the socio-political limits placed on Tibetan-language advocacy. In light of competing pressures to address the loss of the *yul skad* in the city, and to help their children integrate into multi-ethnic peer groups, Amdo parents created collaborative, structured reading activities that were grounded in a language ideology that positioned English in opposition to Mandarin. Despite the framing of reading activities through this language ideology, the sequential unfolding of collaborative reading offered children opportunities to creatively blur language boundaries.

Together, the chapters show how Amdo Tibetan children are actively shaping their cultural identities through language, in the context of rapid social change accompanying urbanization. While the increasing dominance of Mandarin in Amdo Tibetan communities has contributed to language loss, children continue to adopt the Tibetan cultural values associated with Buddhist morality and place-based language variation. Children identify as rural or urban persons and, by extension, as speakers or non-speakers of their *yul skad*. Therefore, even when they abandon the *yul skad*, Amdo Tibetan children maintain cultural emphases on place-based identity and Tibetan Buddhist morality that have traditionally been realized through Tibetan linguistic differentiation.

Chapter 1

Local Histories and Language Variation in Amdo

ཡུལ་ས་རེ་རེ་གཙང་ཆུ་ཡོད། སྡེ་བ་རེ་རེ་སྐད་ཡོད།
Every valley has its river; every village has its language.

Tibetan proverb

^{n}*dzo-wa*: "Travelling"

During my fieldwork, when I was not in Xining, I lived in Tsachen, a small village in Lungma county. Nestled at the base of a winding highway, whose final mountain pass rises above a plateau desert and is dotted with billowing *rlung rta*, prayer flags stamped with the auspicious image of a "wind horse" (fig. 3), the village of Tsachen evens out onto a plateau ridge above a monastery.

In Tsachen, I stayed in a household with two young girls, Lhamo and Dolma, ages three and five at the start of research in August 2016. Their baby sister, Yangkyi, was born in March 2018. Nearly half of Tsachen's fifty families are related. This extended family traces their heritage to Hualong County (Tib. *dpa' lung rdzong*; Ch. *Hualong huizu zizhixian*), approximately 250 kilometres northeast of Tsachen. In Tsachen, the local *yul skad*, or spoken mother tongue, demonstrates the family's migration history because it shares grammatical features with the *yul skad* of Hualong.[1] Lhamo and Dolma have never travelled farther away from their home than Lungma's county seat. Nonetheless, in their everyday play, they revealed an intuitive knowledge of Tibet's linguistic diversity, including the distinctiveness of Tsachen's *yul skad*.

One day in early October 2016, Lhamo and Dolma were playing at the local temple (Tib. *ma ni khang*) with their cousins, Dawa, age five, Tenzin, age two, and Yangmo, age one. The temple grounds include a spacious courtyard used for circumambulation, as well as a cement exercise plot

Figure 3. The author at the final mountain pass between Xining and Tsachen

with several pieces of steel fitness equipment. These exercise plots, which are common throughout China, are provided by municipalities to encourage health and wellness. To an outsider, the exercise equipment – covered with bright green but chipping paint – may seem out of place beside the white clay altars, smoking with juniper incense, that dot the temple's periphery. For Tsachen's children, the exercise plot provides a convenient platform for imaginative play as it is used by few adults (fig. 4). Adults prefer the Buddhist practices of circumambulation (Tib. *skor ba*) and prostration (Tib. *phyag 'tshal*), performed to increase spiritual merit, as their main form of exercise.[2]

Having burst through the gate that frames the temple grounds, Lhamo, Dolma, and Dawa ran towards the exercise plot. Toddlers Tenzin and Yangmo trailed behind them. The three older children scrambled atop a stationary bicycle, slipping their feet one over another on the metallic pedals. Tenzin and Yangmo, too small to mount the bicycle unassisted, watched from the sidelines. The older children began to "travel" (*^{n}dʑo-wa* in the *yul skad*), by naming places to which the group would navigate. As each of the young travellers offered up a destination, they shifted the pronunciation of their chosen place name to imitate the speech of its local inhabitants. Dawa, often the first to

Figure 4. Tsachen's children play near the *ma ni khang*

initiate a line of play, yelled "Lhasa!" with an exaggerated pitch contour, indicating the phonemic tone of central Tibetan that is absent in his native Amdo Farmer Talk.[3] "Golok!" (Tib. *mgo log bod rigs rang skyong khul*; Ch. *Guoluo zangzu zizhizhou*), Dolma responded, accelerating the pedals as she reached deep into her throat to pronounce the fricative consonants that are said to manifest the strength of nomads from this region of southern Amdo. Dawa took another turn, bringing the children home to "Tsachen." As is typical in their *yul skad*, Dawa merged the two consonants *tsʰa* and *tɕʰa*, which contrast in other varieties of Amdo Tibetan.

In their travelling game, Dawa and Dolma portrayed characters from across Tibet by using linguistic features to mark each place's unique *yul skad*. A verbal action that may appear insignificant, such as shifting a single sound feature, may actually point out children's awareness of social distinctions. Drawing from philosopher of language Mikhail Bakhtin (1981), linguistic anthropologists assert that social distinctions are created through the shared interpretation of groups of linguistic features. The resulting "voices" serve as typified social identities, marked by recognizable ways of speaking (Agha 2005, 43). Focusing on the enactment of voices in the course of everyday talk, Erving Goffman (1981) suggested that participants use voicing strategies to manage their shifting relationships. Voices emerge in talk because the bounded, unitary nature of any given language is illusory and subject to change during interaction. From this perspective, languages are interlocking systems that become recognizable through ordered sets of distinctions between sounds, structures, and words. When a community associates patterned linguistic features with a common social identity, these distinctions in ways of speaking give rise to social differentiation (Bakhtin 1981, 270–2). Dolma and Dawa, for example, characterized Amdo nomads and farmers from different places with contrasting sets of linguistic features, such as the presence of tone or fricative consonants.

Bakhtin further argued that every instance of language use recalls the historical development of a given social category. As he wrote, "language is not a neutral medium that passes freely and easily into the private property of a speaker's intentions; it is populated – overpopulated – with the intentions of others" (1981, 294). Bakhtin thus emphasized that, in each utterance, a speaker grapples, often unconsciously, with the social history of a particular language form. These insights into the cultural organization of linguistic diversity can clarify how Tsachen's children are using language to form their identities in a time of social change. Dolma and Dawa demonstrated their shared interpretation of place-based social distinctions when they contrasted Tsachen's *yul skad* with the voices of Tibetans from Lhasa and Golok. They were also reproducing knowledge of which ways of speaking are accepted and valued in these places. This knowledge is rooted in political history, but is also changing in the current historical moment of rapid urbanization.

Seated last on the bicycle, younger sister Lhamo claimed her space in the travelling game by calling out, "Xining!" Like other places across greater Tibet, Qinghai's provincial capital is known by both a Tibetan name, Ziling, and a Mandarin name, Xining. Even the name of the children's own village, Tsachen, meaning "grassland" in Tibetan, has a Mandarin counterpart, Sha Shan, meaning "sand mountain." This Mandarin name is perhaps an intentional pun that references the village's desert-like landscape while imitating the sounds of its original Tibetan name. As a centre of the Tibetan intellectual renaissance following the Cultural Revolution, and home to the pre-eminent Kumbum Tibetan monastery (Tib. *sku 'bum byams pa gling*), Xining arguably sits within the boundaries of Tibet, despite its political incorporation into mainland China. Given that the children had named all other places in Tibetan, why did Lhamo voice the city's name in Mandarin?

When considering code choice alone, Lhamo's association of the provincial capital with the Mandarin language shifted the rules of the travelling game. Dolma and Dawa, however, seemed not to notice. Without delay, they incorporated Lhamo's turn into the game. They slotted the Mandarin place name into an Amdo phrase, calling, "*Xining na* ^{n}*dʐo*!" (Let's go to Xining!), while accelerating the bicycle's pedals. Dolma and Dawa's lack of attention to the sudden use of a Mandarin place name suggests that Lhamo did not significantly alter the premise of the game. Lhamo was still characterizing places through the voices typical of their Tibetan inhabitants. She was enacting a Tibetan person from Xining. This imaginary Tibetan urbanite was speaking in Mandarin.

The associations between specific places and distinctive ways of speaking are constructed through a history of everyday choices about how to use and interpret language. In this chapter, I demonstrate how Dawa, Dolma, and Lhamo's performances of linguistic diversity emerge from local histories of migration and associated forms of language contact, or the meeting of historically unrelated language communities. I integrate excerpts from their family's oral histories, which I collected through ethnographic interviewing, with a discussion of the language ideologies, or cultural beliefs about languages and their speakers, that shape how contemporary Amdo Tibetans interpret linguistic diversity. The story of how the children's extended family first settled in Tsachen demonstrates that Lhamo, Dolma, and Dawa are reproducing meaningful social distinctions by switching between different Amdo Tibetan *yul skad*. The story of some family members' recent migration to Xining clarifies why the children recognized the mother tongue of urban Tibetans as Mandarin. In the context of this history, it seems that, when they play, Lhamo, Dolma, and Dawa are making claims about whose voices are recognizable and legitimate in which places. They are defining what it means to be a Tibetan speaker in contemporary China.

The Farmer and the Nomad: Reformatting a Salient Linguistic Distinction

Amdo Tibetan communities embrace multiple, internal linguistic distinctions that reproduce spiritual connections to the land, demonstrate common religious affiliations, and perpetuate kinship bonds. Amdo Tibetans recognize these sociolinguistic distinctions through place-based *yul skad*. In Amdo, diverse *yul skad* are encapsulated within a larger, categorical boundary between farmers and nomads, and the associated language varieties of Farmer Talk (Tib. *rong skad*) and Nomad Talk (Tib. *'brog skad*). Because Nomad Talk shares structural features across multiple places, it is generally considered to be a single *yul skad*. Farmer Talk, in contrast, exhibits more extensive internal variation, encompassing multiple recognized *yul skad*. Variation within the Amdo Tibetan language is therefore formatted according to two major social distinctions: the occupational difference between farmers and nomads, and the unique forms of place-based belonging symbolized in each of Farmer Talk's *yul skad*. During their travelling game, Dawa and Dolma reproduced these social distinctions when they contrasted the voices from aristocratic Lhasa and nomadic Golok with those of their own farming village.

In Amdo today, the occupational identities of farmers and nomads intersect with a social and political division between rural and urban persons. The social significance of rural and urban identities in China is due, in part, to the state's system of household registration (Ch. *hukou*), which, since the 1950s, has restricted access to social services based on one's birth place. With higher-quality educational and medical services located in urban areas, many rural people seek to change their registered place of habitation to a city. Since 2014, reforms to the *hukou* system have transferred powers over registration to municipal governments, opening up opportunities for rural migrants to more easily access services in smaller cities like Xining.[4] The opportunity for urban living nonetheless comes at a significant cost. In order to obtain an urban *hukou*, migrants must give up their rural land rights.[5] The desire to access socio-economic mobility is leading many rural Amdo Tibetans to choose to move to urban centres, even at the cost of their territorial, cultural, and linguistic rights.

Broader policy changes associated with the Open Up the West Campaign (Ch. *xibu da kaifa*) have catalyzed desires for urban living. The campaign channels revenue from the provincial government to county bureaucracies through subsidies for local development projects (Ch. *xiangmu*) (Gyal 2019, 22–3). These development projects have urbanized previously rural places, bringing dense housing, highways, and amenities such as electricity and running water to county seats. Efforts to settle nomadic communities have also intersected with the project economy. Monetary incentives as well as restrictions on herd size and grazing area have motivated many nomadic families to move into semi-urban housing blocks (Cencetti 2014, 159–60). Farmers are also adapting to rapidly evolving constraints on the size and type of their agricultural plots. These land-use policies are framed in terms of ecological preservation and poverty alleviation, a narrative that met with little overt resistance from Amdo Tibetan families in Tsachen, who viewed payments through the project economy as a reasonable incentive to modify their farming practices. More specifically, Tsachen's families discussed the cosmopolitan advantages of access to market labour, on which they increasingly depend to support their rural households.[6]

State and provincial development policies are undergirded by a shift in political discourse that equates civilization with urbanization. From the 1950s to the 1980s, media, propaganda, and social policies portrayed the ideal citizen as a peasant farmer. Since the 2010s, the Chinese state has instead heavily invested in promoting a "Chinese dream" (Ch. *zhongguo meng*) grounded in the city. Public service announcements, educational materials, and state-run media present urban citizens as cultured and sophisticated. For example, the Grade 1 Tibetan-language textbooks used in Lungma County idealize urban living. One page portrays a mother and child, dressed in traditional Tibetan clothing and standing in front of a television broadcasting tower in Xining. The text accompanying the image reads "Tsering asked his mother, 'What is this tower?' His mother said, 'This is the television broadcasting tower. It can show us the beauties of the material world. Truly wonderful!'" (translated by the author) (fig. 5).

Despite their desires to participate in urban economies, Tsachen's families share spiritual connections to their homelands, which they reinscribe through daily circumambulation, ritual offerings to sacred features of the landscape, and seasonal visits to local and regional pilgrimage sites. Rooted in these rural homelands, Amdo's diverse *yul skad* perpetuate place-based belonging. However, explicit discourse about languages positions Nomad Talk as an ideal, imagined standard. In both Tsachen and Xining, adults valorized two characteristics of Nomad Talk. First, they described Nomad Talk as a "pure" language (Tib. *pha skad gtsang ma*), untouched by language contact with non-Tibetan communities (Prins 2002, 41–2; Thurston 2018b, 205). Adults specifically cited the pronunciation of consonant clusters, reduced in many spoken varieties of Farmer Talk, as evidence of Nomad Talk's unchanging nature. Second, adults accentuated perceived similarities between literary Tibetan and Nomad Talk. Adults identified spellings that represent consonant clusters, as well as verbs that have been grammaticalized as evidential particles in other spoken varieties, as features that are shared between literary Tibetan and Nomad Talk.

Due to the significance of literary Tibetan in Buddhism, these associations solidify the nomad's role as an emblem of purity, as well as an embodiment of a shared cultural heritage. Popular historiographies hold that, during imperial Tibet's prosperity in the seventh century,

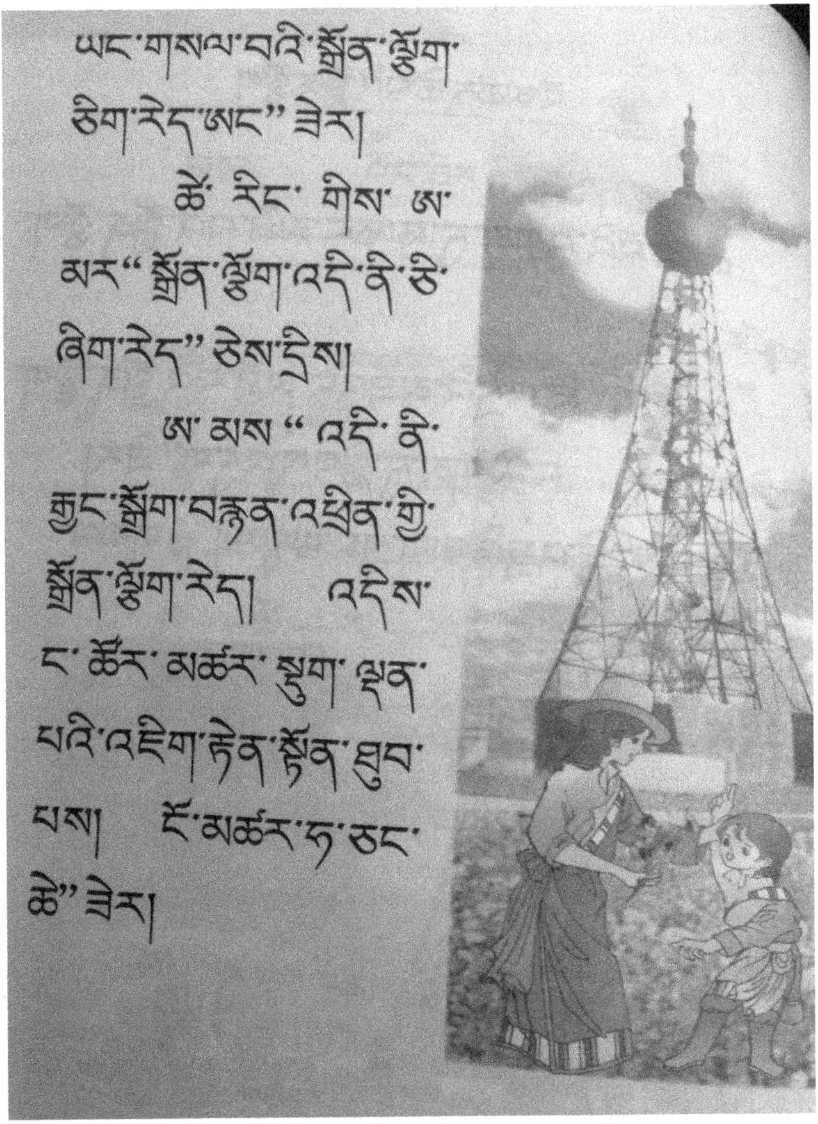

Figure 5. Page from Grade 1 Tibetan textbook

King Songtsen Gampo sent a renowned scribe, Thonmi Sambhota, to study Buddhist scriptures in India. Thonmi Sambhota returned to Lhasa with a Tibetan script that he had modelled on Sanskrit. The Tibetan script allowed for the translation of Sanskrit texts and gave rise to a rich tradition of Tibetan grammatology. Tibetan grammatology uses Buddhist doctrine to analyse the classical Tibetan language and serves as the foundation for the study of literature and linguistics in Tibetan monasteries and universities. By grounding a shared linguistic heritage in Tibetan Buddhism, the idealization of Nomad Talk challenges state discourse that promotes assimilation through urbanization, instead locating civilization in the figure of the nomad.

While this standard language ideology reclaims the value of rural Tibetan livelihoods, it also intersects with state efforts to locate Tibetan heritage within the Chinese nation. The central and provincial governments fund artistic programming in the form of theatre, music, and dance performances, interpreting Tibetan culture through the lens of China's national history. Drawing from typified representations of Tibetan heritage, performance imagery such as white tents, yak, and headdresses depict Tibetans as nomads. The state also contributes to Tibetan-language standardization by operating Tibetan radio and television programs. Xining is home to two Amdo Tibetan media broadcasting stations (Tib. *mtsho sngon bod skad rgyang sgrog khang* and *a mdo brnyan 'phrin khang*), where programming is performed in a distinctive speech register that accentuates similarities between classical literary Tibetan and Nomad Talk.[7] A linguistic survey of state-operated Amdo Tibetan media reported the consistent use of the phonology of Nomad Talk with grammatical borrowings from literary Tibetan (Green 2012, 8). The literary speech register used in state-sponsored media therefore supports a standard language ideology that represents pan-Amdo heritage through the nomad. This standard language ideology reinscribes the occupational distinction between farmers and nomads, at the very moment that many Amdo Tibetan families are choosing urban livelihoods.

How do children navigate the fact that language ideologies contradict the economic and occupational choices of their families? While the standard language ideology explicitly articulated in discourse values Amdo Nomad Talk, children rely on additional cultural knowledge to interpret linguistic features and to build their models of Amdo Tibetan grammar during everyday interaction. In fact, the categorical sociolinguistic distinction between Amdo Farmer Talk and Amdo Nomad talk erases embedded forms of linguistic diversity between diverse *yul skad*, as well as the broader forms of language contact and multilingualism that have historically shaped cultural worlds on the Tibetan plateau. Amdo Tibetan children demonstrate knowledge of these layered forms of linguistic diversity in everyday talk. Adults' reactions to children's speech, however, may challenge the cultural knowledge that children are reproducing through their language use.

^{h}*ta-ki* ^{n}*dʑo*: "Travelling by Horse"

Tsachen's children imaginatively travel using multiple modes of transportation. In addition to pedalling on the stationary bicycle in the temple complex, Lhamo and Dolma frequently enlisted their adult relatives to serve as vehicles. Back in October 2016, even as the sun began to set, dipping below the *ma ni khang*'s gold awning, Lhamo and Dolma had not tired of their travelling game. Hurrying home to beat the bitter chill that descended into the valley as the sky darkened, the children exited the temple's gate. Lhamo and Dolma, Dawa and Tenzin, and Yangmo dispersed towards their respective households. I joined Lhamo and Dolma. As we meandered home, the girls scaled the mud walls that stand between household compounds and deftly scrambled up solar-powered lamp posts gifted by the county government. At night, these lamps make Tsachen's dust appear white and glowing as moonlit snow, the children's footprints blown over by the plateau wind.

When we reached home, Ama was preparing a rich soup of pulled noodles (Tib. *'then thug*) in a mutton bone broth. The noodles simmered atop an iron stove fuelled with dried cow dung patties and sparse pieces of timber, the warmth spreading through the entire house. Fashioned in the traditional Amdo layout, the stove's iron belly stretched to open out under a brick platform (Tib. *khang*). By unrolling a mattress and several yak-wool throws each evening, Ama would transform the platform into the most comfortable of beds. After dinner, the embers would provide enough warmth for us all to sleep comfortably, cocooned in thickly fluffed synthetic blankets. These blankets, which are ubiquitous in markets stretching from Xining to Kathmandu, are a cheaper alternative to traditional yak-wool throws.

As Ama flicked knobs of stretched wheat dough into the aromatic, bubbling broth, Akha Norbu sat atop the *khang*. Lhamo and Dolma ran over to him, climbing atop his knees and shouting, "^{n}*dʑo-ba!*" (Let's travel!).

Akha Norbu, clearly familiar with this request, complied. He asked the girls, "*gaŋ-ŋa* ^{n}*dʑo-ba?*" (Where should we travel?). Without waiting for an answer, Akha Norbu began to gallop his legs, one girl mounted on each.

"^{h}ta-ki mgoloɣ-na ^{n}dʑo-ba" (Let's go to Golok by horse), he shouted, reaching deep into his throat to exaggerate the fricative consonants that mark Amdo nomads' husky voices. Akha Norbu was more explicit than the young children when explaining whose voice he was enacting. He added, *"ŋa mgoloɣ dʐok̚-pa jin"* (I'm a nomad from Golok). This made the girls giggle, somewhat maniacally, as they hung onto Akha Norbu's arms to avoid tumbling to the ground below the *khang*.

Before the girls could suggest a new destination, I interjected. I had noticed something about how Akha Norbu had spoken the name of his imagined destination. He had introduced a new language form that I, only two months into my stay in Amdo, did not fully understand. He had each added the particle *-ba* to the end of his utterance, as the girls had when initiating the travelling game. Since arriving in Amdo, I had encountered many word- and sentence-final particles in Amdo Tibetan Farmer Talk that, like *-ba*, seemed to have no equivalent in other varieties of Tibetan. In fact, when I transcribed a segment of talk for the very first time in August 2016, I was shocked that the verbs presented a morphological pattern of multiple, linked particles quite distinct from the Tibetan grammar I had studied in India, Nepal, and New York City. When I asked about the particles in transcription sessions, my Amdo Tibetan assistants would state that these features had "no meaning." If the particles articulated no obvious semantic meaning, they must have been serving a grammatical function.

Trying to grasp an opportunity to learn more about the grammatical function of this particle, I asked, *"tɕimo zək̚-kə 'ba' ze-nə-re?"* (Why does one say "ba"?).

Akha Norbu chuckled, responding, *"ŋa-ts^{h}o Amdo roŋ^{h}ke re. ŋa-ts^{h}o k^{h}abta ts^{h}am-ts^{h}am mə-sel-kə"* (It's our Amdo Farmer Talk. Our speech is sometimes not clear). It seemed that pointing out this particle had made Akha Norbu self-conscious about his speech.

"mə-sel-kə ze-na wo^{r}jik̚ mə-^{n}dʐa-kə-re?" ("Not clear" means it's not like written Tibetan, right?), I inquired further.

"o re" (Yes), Akha Norbu confirmed. He elaborated, *"ŋa-ts^{h}o roŋ^{h}ke daŋ wo^{r}jik̚ mə-^{n}dʐa. Amdo dʐok̚^{h}ke wo^{r}jik̚ ^{n}dʐa-kə"* (Our Farmer Talk is different from written Tibetan. Amdo Nomad Talk is like written Tibetan). With this statement, Akha Norbu articulated the standard language ideology that associates Amdo Nomad Talk with the literary language and the value of purity.

"^{n}di-ne, dʐok̚^{h}ke '^{h}ta-ki Golok̚-na ^{n}dʑo-ba' mə-ze-nə-re-wa?" (So, then in Amdo Nomad Talk you wouldn't say *'^{h}ta-ki Golok̚-na ^{n}dʑo-ba,'* right?), I joked, pointing out the disjuncture between the utterance's structure and Akha Norbu's invocation of a Golok nomad's voice. According to

his own description, an Amdo nomad would not use an unclear *-ba* to end an utterance.

"o re, re" (Oh, yes, yes), Akha Norbu responded, chuckling.

Drawing Akha Norbu back into the travelling game, Dolma shouted out *"Xining-na ^{n}dʑo-ba"* (Let's go to Xining!). I realized that my interruption had broken the game's rhythm when, rather than galloping away to Xining, Akha Norbu reformulated Dolma's suggestion: *"Sileŋ-na ^{n}dʑo ze-nə-re"* (One says "let's go to Ziling"). Akha Norbu had substituted the Tibetan place name of the provincial capital city, Ziling, for its Mandarin name, Xining. Notably absent in his reformulation was the particle *-ba*. With these subtle changes, Akha Norbu corrected Dolma's utterance and offered a standard response that lacked a key feature of Tsachen's yul skad.

"Sileŋ-na ^{n}dʑo!" Lhamo and Dolma called out over and over. They incorporated Akha Norbu's correction, while their uncle neighed and galloped his legs. If Lhamo and Dolma maintained Akha Norbu's correction in future iterations of the game, how would they mark the difference between farmers and nomads? How could they return to Tsachen if the game no longer allowed them to speak in their own *yul skad*?

Amdo language ideologies assert that Amdo Farmer Talk is unlike literary Tibetan due to farmers' sustained contact with non-Tibetan speakers. While Farmer Talk's divergence from Old Tibetan is supported by scholars, the negative characterization of Farmer Talk as "unclear" is not. In general, nomadic communities have maintained dense but insular social bonds, often limiting their external relationships to settled Tibetan communities. As a result, Nomad Talk remains relatively homogeneous, retaining phonological and grammatical features of Old Tibetan that contemporary speakers locate in the classical literary language.[8] In contrast, farming communities have maintained extensive relationships with other villages and nomadic communities through trade, religious education, and marriage, facilitating linguistic convergence.[9] Local varieties of both Amdo Tibetan and Chinese (Ch. *Qinghai hua*) serve as lingua francas, and settled Han and Tibetan communities practise bilingualism in these languages (Janhunen 2012, 180; Tribur 2017b, 182). Historically, Amdo communities exchanged wool, hides, and horses for Chinese goods.[10] Multi-ethnic communities practising Tibetan Buddhism, including speakers of Oirat and Khalkha Mongolian, and Tu speakers of Mongghul, Mangghuer, Wutun, and Manegacha, used literary Tibetan in oratory, and may have used Amdo Tibetan in monastic education (Dechun and Roche 2017, 10–12). While documentation of cross-linguistic marriages in multiethnic communities remains sparse, existing studies suggest that families practised constrained multilingualism, with women tending to adopt the language of their husband's family (ibid., 8).[11] Today, Amdo merchants sell yogurt, butter, and barley in urban markets, and Han Chinese migrants work as manual labourers in Tibetan autonomous prefectures. These patterns of multilingualism suggest that linguistic convergence has not simply emerged from contact between distinct monolingual populations, but "through the ways that languages were interwoven in the praxis of individuals" across Amdo's history (ibid., 5). However, contemporary anxieties over the loss of Tibetan language and culture encourage the erasure of this linguistic hybridity in favour of promoting a standard language. Because their mother tongues do not conform to the recognized standard, child speakers of Farmer Talk's *yul skad* grapple with contradictory language attitudes; while Tsachen's *yul skad* marks place-based belonging, it is also overtly described as impure and inauthentic. Attitudes towards the *speakers* of Farmer Talk's diverse *yul skad* provide further insight into the difficulties they face in forging a valued linguistic identity.

Although Akha Norbu seemed to be encouraging Dolma not to speak in their mother tongue, he had, in the past, explained his own frustrations with how Tibetans and non-Tibetans alike look down on Amdo farmers. Akha Norbu explained that nomads and Tibetans from other regions say that Amdo farmers have assimilated to the culture and language of the Han Chinese settlers who increasingly occupy Amdo's agricultural lands. "The inhabitants of Lhasa's Yarlung valley, where our Tibetan Buddhist culture originates, were farmers and not nomads," Akha Norbu had mused one day. "Only later did Tibetan nomads convert to Buddhism," he asserted. In fact, the current 14th Dalai Lama was born into an Amdo farming family in northeastern Qinghai. As a toddler, he was identified as the incarnate deity and brought to Tibet's capital. "Also," Akha Norbu had continued, "there are farmers in every country in the world. No one assumes that an American farmer is similar to a Chinese farmer, so why should people say that Amdo farmers are like Chinese farmers?" Akha Norbu resisted normative narratives that identify nomads' voices as authentic markers of Tibetan identity and that devalue Amdo farmers' languages and livelihoods. Tsachen's local history further complicates these normative narratives. Like other villagers, Lhamo and Dolma's family had not always been farmers, and they had not always lived in Tsachen.

A Local Family History

Amdo Tibetan kinship groups unite communities on multiple scales. The *khyim tshang* (household) refers to the persons who live together in a residence. As is common across greater Tibet, households can be either patrilocal, residing with paternal relatives, or matrilocal, residing with maternal relatives. In Tsachen, Lhamo and Dolma's household is matrilocal. It is made up of the girls; their mother, Ama; their father, Apha; their maternal grandmother, Ayi Khangmo; and their maternal grandfather, Aphu Tsering. Their maternal aunt, Ani Pemba, and uncle, Akha Norbu, also frequently visit for extended stays. While Ani Pemba lives with her husband in another village in Lungma County, Akha Norbu had moved to Xining to study Tibetan history at university. Lhamo and Dolma's relatives Sonam and Yeshi live in a patrilocal household in Xining. Sonam and Yeshi are the grandchildren of Ayi Khangmo's first cousin, Aphu Lhundhup (fig. 6).[12]

Sonam and Yeshi sometimes visit the rural homeland during their summer holidays. They are first cousins, their fathers the two children of Aphu Lhundhup. Sonam and Yeshi live together in a joint household in Xining with both sets of parents and their paternal grandparents.

The shared history of these two households demonstrates how Lhamo and Dolma's intuitive marking of different voices is intertwined with Amdo's political history. Both households are united into a larger kinship unit, known as the *tsho ba*. In Amdo, the *tsho ba* was historically organized under the tutelage of a single *bla ma*, a Buddhist teacher affiliated with a local monastery. The *tsho ba* shared grazing land and intermarried, a practice known as *mi brje* (literally, "person exchange").[13] In return for spiritual and political leadership from their *bla ma*, the *tsho ba* would sponsor construction and upkeep of the monastery grounds, pay taxes in cash, grain, or animal products, and provide labour to care for the monastery's fields and animals. Frequently, families would plan for their second-born sons to become monks. Monastic life provided a holistic education in literary Tibetan as well as religious philosophy. Having a son join a monastery also helped manage the inheritance of multiple children, as most families followed a model of patrilineal descent, in which the first-born son was entitled to the family's wealth. Moreover, Amdo Tibetans emphasize that, when monks and nuns devote their lives to religious study, they experience some respite from the material world (Tib. *'jig rten*) and the suffering associated with it. Despite their removal from the concerns of householders, monks and nuns serve as a conduit through which lay people can access spiritual refuge.

In the first decades of the twentieth century, the extended family's *tsho ba* and central monastery was located about 250 kilometres northeast of Lungma County, in contemporary Hualong, today administered as an autonomous county of the Muslim Hui *minzu* (Ch. *Hualong huizu zizhixian*). Akha Norbu's great-grandparents (Dolma, Lhamo, and Yangkyi's great-great-grandparents) lived in one of Hualong's highland villages,

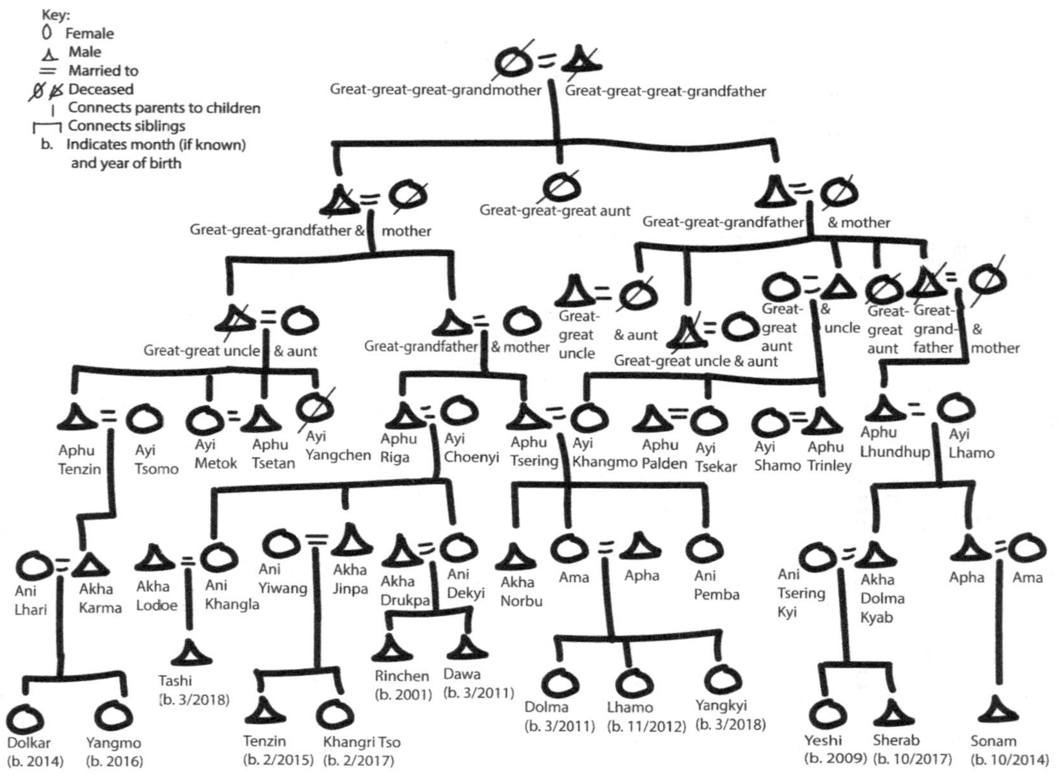

Figure 6. Kinship chart

where they practised a combination of settled farming and pastoralism. The family maintained a settled residence as well as fields of grain and vegetables, owned a herd of several hundred yak, sheep, goats, and cows, and participated in seasonal, migratory grazing. While the *tsho ba* lived in a village inhabited only by ethnic Tibetans, nearby villages were occupied by another minoritized community, known as the Salar. The Salar are recognized by the Chinese state as a distinct *minzu* (Ch. *salazu*). The Salar people live as settled farmers and practise Islam. They speak a Turkic language whose sentence-final particles, including *-ba*, are shared with the *yul skad* of Hualong's Tibetan villages. Amdo Tibetans describe this marker of structural linguistic convergence with Amdo Farmer Talk as "unclear," as demonstrated in Akha Norbu's reaction to the girls' use of the particle *-ba* in their travelling game.

Despite these overtly negative characterizations of Amdo Farmer Talk, the structure of Tsachen's *yul skad* marks belonging to the *tsho ba* and recalls the family's migration history. Dolma, Lhamo, and Yangkyi's great-great-grandparents were the last generation of the *tsho ba* to grow up in Hualong. Although most members of this generation had passed away before Lhamo and Dolma were born, Akha Norbu and his siblings vividly remember stories of the Hualong homeland and of the events that brought their family to Lungma County. Once the *tsho ba* departed Hualong, their *yul skad* moved along with them. The speakers of this *yul skad* built new associations between its linguistic features and the places in which their everyday lives unfolded. When adults correct children's uses of the *yul skad*'s unique grammatical features, as Akha Norbu did when "travelling" with Lhamo and Dolma, they are reinterpreting the traditional cultural meanings of language variation in Amdo. Adults are negatively evaluating children's uses of the *yul skad* and encouraging them to speak in voices that they consider to be more authentically Tibetan.

Remembering Hualong

Akha Norbu had grown up listening to stories about Hualong from his great-grandfather. Sometimes, after dinner and before the family went to bed, Akha Norbu would recount to me the tales that came from this place, whose Tibetan name (Tib. *dpa' lung*) means "land of heroes."

Back in October 2016, after we finished eating our dinner of rich *'then thug*, Dolma and Lhamo settled onto the *khang* to prepare for bed. I slipped out of the household's compound and walked along the ridge that marks the village's boundary. Soft moonlight fell on the far mountainside, illuminating the circumambulation path surrounding the monastery in the valley below. I lifted my gaze when I heard footsteps approach behind me. Akha Norbu, Aphu Tsering, and Ayi Khangmo had joined me. As we conversed that evening, Akha Norbu spoke about his great-grandfather.

"At the time that my great-grandfather lived in Hualong, life was very happy," Akha Norbu explained. "In Hualong, the fields were very big, and we had so many animals. If only we had stayed in Hualong. It was a happy place. Our life was convenient and simple." In Hualong, the *tsho ba* had access to fertile fields and cared for a modest herd of about a hundred yak, sheep, goats, and cows. The family's year-round residence in Hualong marked them as *rong ma 'brog* (literally, "neither farmer nor nomad") as opposed to full nomads, or *'brog pa*, who keep settled residences only during the winter months. Akha Norbu's great-grandfather would take the animals out to graze for several weeks at a time, returning to the village once his food and other supplies had expired. Akha Norbu recalled hearing tales of one spotted goat, great-grandfather's favourite, who always carried his bags on its camel-like back. The *tsho ba* members visited their local monastery to perform daily circumambulation, to participate in prayer festivals, and to seek Tibetan medical treatment.

These memories portrayed a peaceful past that would soon be ruptured by political conflict accompanying the fall of the Qing dynasty. From the late nineteenth century until the founding of the People's Republic of China in 1949, Tibetan monastic polities in northeastern Amdo remained under the control of the Ma clan, a group of Hui militarists whose former sphere of influence is today located in Gansu, Ningxia, and Qinghai Provinces. In the last decades of the Qing dynasty, officials in Xining established a series of military-controlled agricultural settlements surrounding Qinghai's great salt lake, Tsho Ngonpo. The Ma family taxed the settlements and sent the revenues to Xining to be distributed among local elites (Haas 2013, 112). After the Qing dynasty fell to the Nationalists' Republic of China, the central government sought to manage conflicts between competing militarists in this region. Qinghai was granted provincial status under the Republic of China in 1929. Ma Qi (1869–1931), who had been a military commander during the late Qing dynasty, became the first provincial chairman. He would serve for five years, before being succeeded after his death by his brother, Ma Lin (served 1931–6), and then his nephew, Ma Bufang (served 1936–49). The Ma clan aggressively sought to limit the central government's influence in Tibetan and Mongolian territories. Rather than allowing for centralized governance of their territory, the Ma family independently managed relationships with existing Tibetan and Mongolian polities in Qinghai.

The ties of the Ma clan to Amdo's monastic polities shaped the *tsho ba*'s history. In Hualong, the *tsho ba* paid taxes in grain and wool to their local monastery. The head *bla ma*, in turn, shared these with the Ma clan's provincial government. Through such economic relationships with Tibetan and Mongolian constituencies, the Ma clan built a monopoly over the skin and fur trade, supported the Mongolian salt trade, and instituted taxation on the Tibetan wool trade. Horse farms and planned grazing ranges in Qinghai's grasslands were also used to support the Ma clan's growing provincial army (Haas 2013, 132–5). The relationships between Amdo Tibetan herders and farmers, monastic polities, and the Ma clan allowed for a period of relative stability in Hualong until the early 1930s. The same was not true for other places in Amdo. In the first decades of the twentieth century, the Ma clan suppressed a Tibetan rebellion over taxation in what is now Xunhua Salar Autonomous County (Ch. *Xunhua salazu zizhixian*), and occupied Amdo's famous Labrang monastery several times to quell fighting between Tibetan and Hui bands. By the late 1930s, larger-scale conflicts were brewing. The Chinese civil war between the Communists and Nationalists reached into Amdo. Ma Bufang's military had allied with the Guomindang (Chinese Nationalist Army) against the Communists' Red Army (Ch. *Hongjun*), later named the People's Liberation Army (Ch. *Renmin jiefangjun*). The *tsho ba*'s autonomy was shattered.

As I walked along the village ridge with Akha Norbu, Aphu Tsering, and Ayi Khangmo, the mid-autumn moon rose higher. The monastery's gilded rooftop glinted against the darkening desert sky. Akha Norbu continued to narrate his great-grandfather's story.

The Guomindang entered Hualong, he explained, and "the *bla ma* of our Tibetan people gave the village to Ma Bufang." Ma Bufang demanded that all the village's young men join his army to resist the Communists. Having heard of Ma Bufang's violent incursions in Xunhua and Labrang, those who were able fled southwest. "My great-grandfather and his family left Hualong empty-handed," Akha Norbu explained. He elaborated, "It was like having to seek refuge in another country because of warfare. They had no house. They had no animals. They couldn't return to their own homeland. After my family escaped, Ma Bufang let the Hui people settle in the deserted land."

Akha Norbu continued to narrate the hardships his great-grandfather endured: great-grandfather had crossed the Yellow River with his brother, mother, and sister. They eventually arrived in Lungma County, where there was open farmland. His mother and sister settled in Tsachen, at that time a small hamlet in the shadow of the highland desert plain. The mother and sister of Akha Norbu's great-grandfather built a simple home of mud and brick and participated in the village's communal farming of wheat, barley, and potatoes. As the civil war raged on, Ma Bufang's army continued southwards along with the Guomindang. For about five years, it was not safe for young men to stay in Tsachen because they could be forcibly conscribed during the army's periodic visits to the village. Instead, great-grandfather and his brother wandered throughout Lungma County. They survived by providing short-term assistance to other families in exchange for food and shelter. They herded animals for nomads and helped villagers with construction projects. Sometimes, at night, they would sneak into Tsachen to visit their mother and sister. In 1949, the victory of the Communists and the founding of the People's Republic of China forced the Guomindang and its military supporters, including the Ma clan, to flee into exile. Only as the People's Liberation Army took control of Qinghai were Akha Norbu's great-grandfather and his brother able to settle.

When Lungma County was incorporated into the People's Republic of China, great-grandfather moved in with his mother and sister in Tsachen, expanding their residence into a joint household that shared a courtyard wall. In Tsachen, great-grandfather married and had two sons, including Aphu Tsering's father. Lhamo and Dolma's household inhabits the original residence of Akhu Norbu's great-grandfather. Tenzin and Khangri Tso, the grandchildren of Aphu Tsering's brother, inhabit the neighbouring residence. Great-grandfather's brother settled in the seat of Lungma County. Great-grandfather's brother also married, and fathered five children, including Ayi Khangmo's father and Aphu Lhundhup's father.

Akha Norbu's narrative demonstrates that the *tsho ba* maintained patterns of kinship, religious affiliation, and spiritual connection, despite coerced migration. Members of the *tsho ba* patronize the local monastery of Lungma County, located in the valley directly below Tsachen. They also partake in pilgrimage to the monastery in Hualong and recognize Hualong's monastic leader as the spiritual head of their *tsho ba*. They provide offerings to land deities (Tib. *yul lha*), located in their current homelands. *Yul lha* are incarnated in land formations such as hills and streams, and preside over the people who inhabit these places. On auspicious dates in the spring and fall, it is believed that the *yul lha* bless these features of the land. Tsachen's villagers take offerings, including branches from trees and cups of water from streams, to adorn their homes and receive the deities' protection. The *tsho ba*'s spiritual connections therefore originated in Hualong but are emplaced in their current places of habitation. Continuity in marriage patterns has also upheld the *tsho ba*'s spiritual unity, allowing children to patronize the family's lineage deity (Tib. *srung ma*).[14] The *tsho ba*'s kinship ties have also allowed for the transmission of the *yul skad* across generations, connecting Lhamo and Dolma in Tsachen to their relatives, Sonam and Yeshi, in Xining. Lhamo and Dolma's maternal grandmother, Ayi Khangmo, and Sonam and Yeshi's paternal grandfather, Aphu Lhundhup, are first cousins.

The *tsho ba*'s forced migration happened to land them in one of only two counties in Qinghai that has provided Tibetan-language education continuously, from before the rise of the People's Republic of China (PRC) to the present. While monastic education traditionally functioned as the pathway into Tibetan literacy, some monastic leaders in Amdo provided financial and logistical support as early as the 1920s to establish secular schools for Tibetan and Mongolian students. These efforts intersected with education planning from the provincial and central governments.[15] By 1931, Qinghai's provincial education department mandated that every monastery operate an associated secular primary school, and, by 1940, the central government required monastic schools to provide training in spoken and written Chinese (Haas 2013, 215–16). In Lungma County, a primary school serving Tibetan and Mongolian students opened in 1926 (ibid., 215), and it maintained Tibetan-language courses during and after the Cultural Revolution (Zenz 2014, 95–6).[16] A constellation of historical factors, including the efforts of former monks who had been forbidden to practise religion during the Cultural Revolution, supported Tibetan education in Lungma. Instead of moving beyond Lungma County, these monks used their knowledge of literary Tibetan to work as teachers in these years, during which Ayi Khangmo and Aphu Lhundhup were children.

As Akha Norbu finished narrating the story of the *tsho ba*'s settlement in Lungma, the sky darkened. We began to walk back to the household compound along with Ayi Khangmo and Aphu Tsering. I shivered, as the air cooled quickly with the deepening night. As we walked, I wondered how Ayi Khangmo had come to Tsachen, and how Aphu Lhundhup had ended up in Xining city. I asked Ayi Khangmo to share her memories of growing up in Lungma's county seat. She obliged, as our feet stirred up dust on the village's pathways.

Ayi Khangmo is the youngest of three siblings. When she was a child, her older brother and older sister would meet their first cousin, Aphu Lhundhup, every day to walk to school. Because she was the youngest daughter, Ayi Khangmo did not attend school. She would watch from the courtyard, sweeping away stray sticks and rocks, as the other children began the two kilometre walk to their schoolhouse. As Ayi Khangmo explained, before the province began to enforce compulsory primary schooling in the early 2000s, it was common for the youngest child to take responsibility for household labour instead of attending school. This practice was not an attempt to deprive children of opportunities or to mark inequalities between children based on their birth order. It was accepted that birth order affected one's family duties and life trajectory. In fact, by engaging in household work, the youngest child could enjoy some advantages, including very close bonds to their parents.

While Ayi Khangmo supported her parents with household work, her first cousin Aphu Lhundhup excelled in school. After several years of study, Ayi Khangmo's older brother and older sister finished Grade 6 and came home to work as farmers. Cousin Aphu Lhundhup continued to study. Lungma County did not yet have a middle school, which would be established at the end of the Cultural Revolution.[17] At age thirteen, Aphu Lhundhup had finished primary school and was eligible to continue his studies in a regional teacher training program. At age sixteen, he graduated and became a Tibetan-language teacher in Lungma's middle school.

As Aphu Lhundhup began his teaching career, Ayi Khangmo entered her teenage years. She continued to support her household by harvesting crops. Both of her older siblings married and moved into their spouses' households. When Ayi Khangmo was only seventeen, her life course intertwined with her great uncle's lineage. Her great-uncle, Aphu Tsering's grandfather, asked for her hand in marriage to Aphu Tsering. As Ayi Khangmo explained, "since our families had *phan tshun che ba* (Tib. a strong relationship), my parents couldn't refuse. Because I was the youngest child, my parents wanted to keep me with them in their village. But, because our families had *'dang che* (Tib. a very close relationship) and were engaged in mutual exchange, they had to give me up." Although Ayi Khangmo was hesitant to leave her home, her great-uncle's reputation eased her anxieties. She trusted his judgment because he had grown up alongside her own grandfather, as part of the same household and *tsho ba*.

At eighteen, then, Ayi Khangmo entered into an arranged marriage with Aphu Tsering. Her parents gifted her a wardrobe of fine clothing, including a lambskin robe, a woollen robe, a printed robe, a cloth dress, a hair piece, and a sash. They had no animals to offer. Ayi Khangmo moved from Lungma's county seat to her new home in Tsachen. Ayi Khangmo later gave birth to three children: Lhamo and Dolma's Ama, their Ani Pemba, and their Akha Norbu. Ayi Khangmo explained that, when her children were growing up, their daily lives were strained, because Ayi Khangmo was busy working in the fields and had little time to truly care for her children. Now that her own children are grown, she enjoys spending time with her grandchildren.

Ayi Khangmo's children and grandchildren would have very different futures than those of her cousin Aphu Lhundhup. Aphu Lhundhup married several years after Ayi Khangmo. While Ayi Khangmo was raising her children in Tsachen, Aphu Lhundhup found passion in his work as a Tibetan teacher in Lungma's county seat. He realized that the worlds of both Tibetan and Chinese literature were closed to his new wife, Ayi Lhamo. Ayi Lhamo had also grown up in Lungma County but had never attended school. Unlike Ayi Khangmo, whose family had chosen for her to stay at home, Ayi Lhamo did not have the option to enrol in school due to her family's class status. As Ayi Khangmo explained, "When she was growing up, her family's *jiejichengfen* (Ch. class status) was considered high. The children of high-status households were not allowed to go to school. That time was called *jiu shehui* (Ch. old society) in Chinese. During the times of the *spyi tshogs rnying pa* (Tib. old society), their circumstances were beyond horrible because their family was wealthy according to the *gongchandang de zhengce* (Ch. Communist Party's policies)."

As Ayi Khangmo spoke, she first used the Mandarin term *jiu shehui* to describe the "old society." In her next utterance, she switched to the Tibetan equivalent, *spyi tshogs rnying pa*. Both terms conventionally denote the period before the founding of the People's Republic of China in 1949, indicating the supposed backwardness and barbarism of pre-Communist governance. During the 1958 Democratic Reforms in Amdo, Tibetans were subjected to coercive practices of "speaking bitterness" (Ch. *suku*; Tib. *sdug bsngal bshad pa*), through which officials forced individuals to publicly recount the horrors of life in the "old society," prior to Amdo's "peaceful liberation" (Ch. *heping jiefang*). Ayi Khangmo had, however, used these terms to describe the years after the Democratic Reforms of 1958 and during the Cultural Revolution. She drew on these terms to describe political upheaval and to characterize the challenges that Ayi Lhamo had faced as a Tibetan child of high class status.[18] Ayi Khangmo therefore inverted the meaning of the "old society," applying it to a time during and not before Communist rule. As she spoke, I imagined Ayi Lhamo as a young child, possibly living in poverty with educated parents and being forbidden from learning how to read and write.

Ayi Lhamo's circumstances improved after she married. The Cultural Revolution had ended. Aphu Lhundhup's teaching position provided them with a stable income. By the late 1980s, Aphu Lhundhup's school expanded. Having acquired Tibetan-language textbooks in mathematics and science, the school provided more opportunities for teaching and learning in Tibetan.

Several years after their marriage, Ayi Lhamo gave birth to two sons. Both attended their father's school and left Lungma County as young adults to study at major universities in Xining and Beijing. The sons eventually settled in Xining in the early 2000s, finding work as Chinese-Tibetan translators with the provincial radio network. Aphu Lhundhup and Ayi Lhamo came to live with them, in a patrilocal joint household, after granddaughter Yeshi was born in 2009.

As Ayi Khangmo narrated Ayi Lhamo and Aphu Lhundhup's move to Xining, I thought about how very different rural and urban children's lives appeared. In Tsachen, Lhamo and Dolma spent their days in free play with related peers or in the local village preschool. After beginning Grade 1, they would attend a boarding school in Lungma county seat, where they would complete a curriculum in written Tibetan, with Mandarin offered as an additional subject. In Xining city, Sonam and Yeshi had access to nearby public schools that they could attend as day students. These schools would give them a range of opportunities for higher education and employment but would provide instruction only in Mandarin. Sonam and Yeshi spent most of their days studying in school, participating in scheduled activities, or watching television in the family apartment.

As we approached the household's gate, I mentioned the issue of inequitable access to Tibetan-language education across Amdo. Ayi Khangmo confided that Aphu Lhundhup had a different opinion about how to best educate his grandchildren. As Ayi Khangmo explained,

> Sonam and Yeshi's parents think that they need to learn both Chinese and Tibetan, so that they will have the knowledge and ability to go anywhere in society, and do whatever they want ... [But] Aphu Lhundhup felt that when they were around three years old, we should have brought them to the homeland in Lungma to study literary Tibetan. Otherwise, his children will know how to speak Tibetan. Their children will know how to speak some Tibetan. But his great-grandchildren will never speak Tibetan. Although they will be Tibetan, they will not know the Tibetan language, just like non-Tibetan people. They will be just like Chinese people.

As Ayi Khangmo described a seemingly inevitable process of assimilation in the city, Aphu Tsering called for us to come to bed. I followed Ayi Khangmo into the house, and the warmth from the *khang* began to radiate around me. I thought about how different threads in this family history were shaping the language practices of Lhamo, Dolma, Sonam, and Yeshi.

Despite forced migration, homelessness, and extended political turmoil, the *tsho ba* maintained its place-based identity through spiritual practices, marriage patterns, and the continued use of the *yul skad*. Even though the Cultural Revolution had blocked Ayi Lhamo's access to education, Aphu Lhundhup was able to work throughout his career to promote Tibetan-language study. Due, in part, to Aphu Lhundhup's successful career, his own children had experienced upward socio-economic mobility by advancing in China's education system and securing professional jobs in Xining. In order to maintain the family's current socio-economic status, however, his grandchildren would have to study Mandarin. Ayi Khangmo and Aphu Lhundhup felt that, with Mandarin education in Xining, their grandchildren and great-grandchildren would not be able to maintain knowledge of spoken and written Tibetan. Despite this prediction of complete linguistic assimilation to Mandarin, earlier generations *had* maintained the *yul skad* even during migration and the reorganization of their livelihood strategies. Given this history of cultural and linguistic continuity, why did the current historical moment, characterized by educational opportunity and socio-economic mobility, seem to all but ensure a radical disjuncture in the transmission of language and culture?

che-ki-^{n}dzo: "Travelling by Car"

The question of why urban living was synonymous with linguistic assimilation circled in my mind as I arrived back at the household compound with Akha Norbu, Ayi Khangmo, and Aphu Tsering. When Ayi Khangmo had discussed Sonam and Yeshi's circumstances in Xining, she seemed to assume that schooling in written Tibetan would allow for the continuity of spoken Tibetan languages. However, Amdo's diverse spoken languages do not align with the written standard used in formal education. Ayi Khangmo's statement left open the questions of which Tibetan language the community wished their children to learn, and of whose voices would be recognized as authentically Tibetan in the context of anxieties over language shift.

Before retiring to my sleeping place on the *khang*, I stopped by the stove to fill a mug of boiling water for drinking. Lhamo and Dolma sat atop the *khang*, no longer lying down and definitely not sleeping.

"*^{h}ta-ki ^{n}dzo-ba!*" (Let's travel by horse), Lhamo begged in a high-pitched voice as she bounced up and down in a fluffy red blanket.

Akha Norbu tried to convince the girls to lie down, to no avail. Instead, Dolma joined in to Lhamo's calls.

"*^{h}ta-ki ^{n}dʑo-ba, ^{h}ta-ki ^{n}dʑo-ba!*" (Let's travel by horse, let's travel by horse!), Dolma called, popping out from under her covers. I noticed the girls' use of the *yul skad*'s particle *-ba*.

"*'ba ba' ma-ze. tɕ^{h}o ^{r}dʑa re-wa?*" (Don't say "*ba ba.*" Are you Chinese?), I heard Akha Norbu respond to Dolma, as I grasped the handle of the kettle on the stove. Dolma and Lhamo both giggled in response, while I nearly dropped the kettle with surprise. I wondered why saying the particle *-ba*, a feature unique to Tsachen's *yul skad*, would make Dolma and Lhamo seem Chinese.

"*'ba' ^{r}dʑa^{h}ke e-re?*" (Is "ba" a Chinese word?), I asked.

"*ha ma-go*" (I don't know), Akha Norbu, now laughing, responded. He went on to explain, "*^{r}dʑa^{h}ke-ne joŋ-nə-re-la. ^{r}dʑami '**zou ba , zou ba** ' ze-nə-re*" (Maybe it came from Chinese. Chinese people always say "*zou ba, zou ba*" [Ch. Let's go]). Akha Norbu was now as energized as the girls.

"*^{h}ta-ki ma-^{n}dʑo! **che**-ki-^{n}dʑo!*" (Don't go by horse! Let's go by car!), Akha Norbu shouted. In line with his directive to Dolma, Akha Norbu did not use the particle *-ba*. But, he did use a Mandarin loan word, *che* (car).

Akha Norbu turned his legs into the wheels of a racing car, and I hopped onto the *khang* to try to fall asleep. As I drifted off, I pondered the disconnect between Akha Norbu's use of a Mandarin loan word and his characterization of Dolma's speech as "Chinese."

In light of the extended family's complex migration history, Bakhtinian theories of language and social differentiation can explain the contradictory language choices at play in the travelling game. Bakhtin's (1981) concept of voice suggested that a single speaker always invokes multiple social and stylistic distinctions, even within the same utterance. He referred to this multiplicity, inherent in language use, as "heteroglossia" (428). Goffman (1981) further emphasized that a single speaking subject enacts multiple voices. A speaker can represent their self, animate the words of other participants, or characterize a "figure" across multiple turns at talk.[19] In this chapter's opening scene, for example, Dolma imaginatively travelled to nomadic Golok by using her own voice to enact the character of a nomad. Her playmates, Lhamo and Dawa, recognized two voices through two distinct play frames. In the social setting of play, where the children foregrounded their personal identities and relationships, they could perceive Dolma's voice as her own. In the imaginative setting of the play activity, the children took on the identities of other people from other places, and Dolma spoke as a nomad.

When Akha Norbu joined in the game, he listened to Dolma's voice through a third frame, reinterpreting the meanings of place-based variation encoded in the *yul skad*. While Dolma had suggested travelling, in her own voice and using her own *yul skad*, Akha Norbu interpreted her voice as "Chinese." Despite the fact that Akha Norbu had himself used a Mandarin loan word, he labelled Dolma's speech, but not his own, as "Chinese." When I questioned Akha Norbu about his label, he rationalized the history of the particle *-ba*, stating that it "came from Chinese." This explanation differed from his earlier assertion that the particle is an "unclear" characteristic of Farmer Talk. In Mandarin, *-ba* is, in fact, a sentence-final particle that indicates a suggestion or request. After more intensive linguistic analysis and a review of literature in language typology, I realized that Akha Norbu's theory of the particle's Mandarin origin was common among Amdo adults but not supported by scholars.[20] The particle *-ba* entered into Tsachen's *yul skad* after protracted contact with the Salar language in Hualong (Simon 2016, 168–72). In contrast, the Mandarin particle *-ba* is a homophone; although it sounds the same as the Amdo Farmer Talk particle, its origin, meaning, and structure are unrelated to Farmer Talk. The use of the particle is therefore unique to Tsachen's *yul skad* and marks the family's migration history because it originated in the Hualong homeland.

Like *-ba*, words or particles that can function in multiple languages simultaneously are known as "bivalent features." Bivalency is an important component of heteroglossia because it underlines how shared, socially learned interpretation is necessary for the recognition of particular voices as well as the recognition of language boundaries. As linguistic anthropologist Kathryn Woolard (1998) demonstrated in her study of bivalency, both speakers and hearers must decide which language(s) a bivalent feature belongs to, thus defining the language being spoken at any given moment. Because of their interpretive flexibility, bivalent features can simultaneously transgress the expected structural boundaries between languages and the social boundaries between groups of speakers. This transgression leaves room for the transformation of voices and their associated social identities. In the travelling game, for example, Akha Norbu first identified *-ba* as an integral part of Amdo Farmer Talk. He nonetheless discouraged Dolma from using the particle, by labelling it as "unclear." Later in the evening, Akha Norbu identified *-ba* as a Mandarin loan word. After many months of transcribing everyday talk, I realized that adults negatively evaluated features of Tsachen's *yul skad*, but only when they were spoken by certain people. I repeatedly encountered the assertion that the particle *-ba* was categorically Mandarin and not Tibetan, but *only* when the particle was spoken by children. It seemed that adults had adopted two language ideologies that were reframing the traditional, place-based meanings of the *yul skad.* First, they valued the speech of nomads as pure and authentic, and ascribed the inverse values of impurity and inauthenticity to features of their *yul skad.* Second, they focused on children's language use as evidence of a shift to Mandarin.

Although adults targeted children as the agents of language shift, children's play maintained the cultural values embedded within place-based language variation. In the travelling game, the children reproduced pre-existing cultural associations between social identities and contrasting ways of speaking by characterizing the voices of Tibetan people from different places. When Lhamo used the Mandarin name for Xining, she may have been applying this cultural framework to an urban place, associated with a new language variety. In other words, Lhamo was adapting a commonly accepted narrative, that urban children speak only in Mandarin, to a traditional form of place-based belonging. She may have been claiming Xining as part of her own Tibetan cultural world. From this perspective, Tsachen's children played with language in a way that contradicted adults' emphasis on language loss and that helped to maintain cultural continuity amidst language shift.

Conclusion: Language Shift between Amdo Histories and Futures

This chapter has explored how Amdo Tibetan cultural worlds are founded on place-based linguistic identities and how children and adults are reinterpreting these identities in the face of rapid urban development. The extended family's oral histories demonstrate the rootedness of their *yul skad* in the rural homelands of Hualong and Tsachen, allowing us to trace specific features of the *yul skad* that manifest heteroglossia in everyday talk. In the context of widespread anxiety over language shift to Mandarin, adults assert a standard language ideology that frames Nomad Talk as a pure marker of Tibetans' Buddhist heritage because of its similarities to the sacred literary language. In contrast, adults describe features of Tsachen's *yul skad* as "unclear" and impure. These features mark histories of language contact with non-Tibetan communities but also invoke intimate forms of place-based belonging shared among families, households, and *tsho ba.* In everyday talk, adults are reinterpreting these features through narratives about progressive assimilation to Mandarin, and finding examples of language shift in children's speech, in particular.

Although adults place responsibility for language shift on children, children's everyday play reveals important forms of cultural continuity.

In rural Tsachen, Dolma, Lhamo, and cousin Dawa reproduced place-based linguistic differentiation when they invoked the voices of Tibetan people from different places. Drawing on their cultural knowledge of the association of language with place, these rural children used Mandarin to mark Tibetan belonging in Xining. In other words, the children retained a key cultural logic by interpreting language variation as a marker of belonging rather than dislocation. While the children maintained cultural associations between place and language variation, urbanization nonetheless represents a historical moment of rupture. Policies for education, nomadic settlement, and the regulation of agriculture have contributed to the consolidation of amenities in urban areas, leaving families with little choice but to abandon their rural homelands. Given the significance of rural homelands to Amdo Tibetan cultural identity, urban living presents challenges to cultural survival that are not limited to language shift. How do children respond to the idealization of urban China, especially when adults' expectations encourage language shift? Chapter 2 investigates this question by looking at details of the grammatical structures that rural and urban children use to build their foundational social relationships.

Chapter 2

The Grammar of Belonging: Spatial Deixis in Situated Family Interaction

ཕ་མ་བུ་རྒྱུད་གཅིག་ལ་བསོད་ནམས་མི་འདྲ་ཁག་ཁག།
Children of the same family each have a different destiny.

Tibetan proverb

In describing the social worlds of children, sociologist William Corsaro asserted that "children creatively appropriate information from the adult world to produce their own unique peer cultures. Such appropriation is creative in that it extends or elaborates peer culture … and simultaneously contributes to the reproduction of the adult culture" (1992, 168). Corsaro emphasized that children build peer cultures through a process of "interpretive reproduction" of adult behaviours. In this chapter, I examine the Amdo Tibetan mother tongue, as well as the cultural practices in which it is used, as a resource for children's interpretive reproduction. I show how, in multi-party play, rural children build grammatical knowledge as they form foundational social relationships. I use the term "spatializing kinship" to refer to the particular verbal practices that rural Amdo Tibetan children use to link their family relationships to places in the village homeland, extending existing functions of the *yul skad* to support the vitality of their mother tongue.

In contrast, in Xining, Dolma and Lhamo's relative, Sonam, mostly engaged in dyadic interactions with an adult caregiver in his family apartment. In dyadic interactions, urban caregivers often talked about extended family members, which helped young children like Sonam orient to non-present peers. Although Sonam's caregivers created continuity by centring kinship in his social world, they could not give him access to multi-party play with peers who shared his mother tongue. Sonam's physical dissociation from his related peers and his homeland affected his trajectory of language learning. While Sonam mostly used the *yul skad* in his first two years of life, he had adopted Mandarin as his dominant language by age three. Sonam never produced the full system of spatial deixis that Dolma and Lhamo used to build peer relationships in the village homeland.

The stark contrast in these children's grammatical repertoires shows that rural-to-urban migration is transforming the social relationships of young urban children *through* their language use. The loss of the Amdo Tibetan *yul skad* is caught up with the loss of kin-based peer relationships and the associated loss of peer culture. Policies promoting socio-economic development overlook these losses by emphasizing the benefits of urbanization for child development. Beginning in the late 1990s, modernization goals articulated by China's central government aimed to increase human capital by boosting young children's *suzhi* (quality) through formal education (Kuan 2015, 37–40). *Suzhi* discourse valorized urban family life and led educators to explicitly seek to assimilate rural children to urban cultural norms.[1] Alongside efforts for modernization through education, state attempts to centre civilization in cities have led many Tibetan parents to associate urban living with their children's future opportunities (Washul 2018, 505–6). Given the role of the mother tongue in establishing children's foundational relationships, examining the contrasting language repertoires of rural and urban children can reveal the consequences of migration for children's social and emotional well-being. The story of how language shapes social attachments begins in infancy.

The Social Basis of Grammatical Knowledge

Within the first months of life, infants form social bonds through cultural routines that unfold in their mother tongues. Although some early communicative behaviours, such as turn-taking, are shared across cultures, research from anthropology and developmental psychology suggests that the most significant universal feature of early language experiences is a profound sensitivity to the interpersonal world (Nelson 2009; Ochs and Schieffelin 1995; Stern 1985). In everyday interaction, participants use patterns in the content and grammatical form of their talk to align their emotional expression, attention focus, intentions, and actions. These patterned uses of linguistic resources respond to the social and spatial settings of interaction. For example, cultural preferences in the physical positioning of pre-mobile infants encourage different forms of participation. Face-to-face arrangements in mother-infant dyads, which position infants as primary addressees, are common to middle-class Euro-American families. In contrast, the triadic arrangements common to Kaluli (Papua New Guinea) and Mayan families allow infants to coordinate attention with more than one conversational partner and facilitate infants' active co-participation from the margins of conversation (León 2014, 82–90; Ochs and Schieffelin 1984, 288–90). While this existing research documents cross-cultural differences, we know less about the contrasting interactive routines *within* families and peer groups that can facilitate language change.[2]

One morning in Tsachen in June 2018, I woke up late. I turned over on the *khang* and grabbed my phone to check the time. It was about 8:30. Ama had arranged fresh bread (Tib. *go re*) and salted milk tea, the regional specialty known as *am dza* (Tib. *am ja*), atop the stove. She had already departed for her morning tasks. Perhaps she was tending to the family's *ba mo* (female cow) and two calves in their small stable or bringing them to the fenced-in grazing plot in the valley. As I mused about Ama's activities, I thought about the years before I arrived and before Dolma, Lhamo, and Yangkyi were born. The family had owned hundreds of sheep and a dozen cows. The animals used to graze freely in the hills that stretch upwards from Tsachen and level out onto a harsh desert plain. Free grazing gave the family more time to tend to crops. In those years, the crop yields were rich enough to support the entire village. The girls' extended family had not lived as full nomads, who herd hundreds of *g.yag* (male yak) and *'bri* (female yak), for more than three generations. Nonetheless, the recent, extensive settlement of nomads across Amdo indirectly influenced their livelihood strategies. Government restrictions on land use, the desire to consume a wider range of goods, and insurance that could be cashed in when animals passed away contributed to a new reliance on the market economy.

I rose up from my resting place and went outside to the courtyard to wash and prepare for the day ahead. Lhamo and Dolma were nowhere in sight. Likely, they had already embarked on a play adventure, digging in a nearby sandpit or stomping around the temple grounds. I returned to the living room and seated myself on the edge of the *khang*. I pulled off a length of *go re* and picked up the mug of steaming *am dza* that Ama had left for me. As I sipped the briny milk tea, I heard a small sound, "*mio:: mio:: mio::*" I turned, surprised to realize that I had not been alone in the living room after all. I saw four-month-old baby Yangkyi nestled under a blanket on the *khang*. Dolma was lying next to her and giggling.

"*mio::-ze:*" (Say "*mio*"), Dolma prompted, quoting baby Yangkyi's sound.

"*mio:: mio::*," Yangkyi intoned, slightly whining.

"mio::," sounded Dolma, taking another turn.

"mio:: mio:: mio::," Yangkyi responded.

"ani Yangkyi 'mio' ze-go-kə" (Ani, Yangkyi is saying *"mio"*), Dolma excitedly called out to me. Dolma and Yangkyi were enacting sound play, a social activity where participants create patterns of vocalization. With imitation, Dolma transformed Yangkyi's vocalizations into a game structured by turn-taking. Yangkyi joined in Dolma's game. Yangkyi showed an awareness of Dolma's contributions when she waited until Dolma was finished to make her next sound. Dolma bonded with Yangkyi by drawing on her cooing to perpetuate the game. Dolma also described Yangkyi's vocalizations as speech. In so doing, Dolma framed Yangkyi as her conversational partner through her own language choices. Specifically, Dolma used a verb of speaking, *ze* (to say), to quote Yangkyi's contribution to me.

Sound play mediates infants' participation in their social worlds. As both Dolma and I could feel when we listened to Yangkyi on that morning in 2018, sound play is not mere evidence of physiological arousal. Although sound play generally does not encode semantic content, it serves other communicative functions. When they play with sounds, participants organize their vocalizations through turn-taking, which is a universal feature of verbal interaction.[3] Developmental psychologists have asserted that, like Dolma, caregivers scaffold infants' participation in turn-taking by providing contingent responses to their vocalizations (Casillas 2014, 55). When they initiate sound play, caregivers are eliciting ongoing participation from infants, but infants do not simply react to their caregivers' turns. Even within their first year of life, infants show agency in their turn-taking behaviour. For example, infants differentiate between caregivers and more frequently elaborate on turns from more familiar caregivers (Tomasello, Conti-Ramsden, and Ewert 1990). Through verbal activities like sound play, infants coordinate vocalization with touch, gaze, and movement to synchronize their emotional states with those around them (Takada 2014, 57–60). These verbal activities form a basis for communicative behaviour. Infants participate in more elaborate forms of communicative behaviour as they gain knowledge of language structures over developmental time.

As infants acquire grammatical knowledge, the mother tongue shapes their systematic perceptions of the social and material world. Experimental evidence suggests that, within the first six to nine months of life, infants show selective attention to the phonemes, or meaningful sound units, of their mother tongues.[4] While infants seem to share universal preferences for certain sound features in their early vocal production, infants' vocalizations show sound patterns characteristic of the phoneme inventory, intonation, and syllable structure of their mother tongues by the time they are nine to ten months of age (Werker and Tees 1999, 524). Between nine and fifteen months of age, infants expand their communicative behaviours beyond coordinating turn-taking and shared emotional states. At this developmental stage, infants express referential meaning and direct shared attention. Specifically, infants coordinate gaze and gesture, especially pointing, to guide others towards interactional goals (Tomasello 2003a, 302–4). As their grammatical knowledge progresses, infants coordinate the embodied communicative behaviours of gaze and pointing with analogous language structures.[5] Deixis, a set of grammatical systems whose referential meaning shifts based on the context of an interaction, is an important resource for facilitating goal-directed communicative behaviour. Young children's production of grammatical deixis therefore represents a social and linguistic milestone because it allows them to manage joint attention in embodied interaction.

While all languages include systems of deixis, the specific contrastive meanings that they encode are not universal. Deixis is made up of words or particles called "deictics" or "deictic markers." Deictic markers are specific to a particular language's obligatory grammatical categories.[6] To interpret the referent of a deictic marker, participants must recognize a common origin point, such as an individual speaker's location or a framework of shared knowledge (Hanks 1992, 51). Shared knowledge can include immediate perceptions, such as the relative location of a co-present speaker and addressee, or broader experiential dimensions of an interactive setting, such as a temporal orientation to the past or future or shared expectations of a speaker's truthfulness (Hanks 2009, 11–12).[7] During any interaction, this origin point is continually shifting. A speaker may move in space, tell narratives about the past or future, or use reported speech to enact different voices. Therefore, participants must continually reorient to a shared origin point by attuning to each other's movements, knowledge states, and affective displays. Infants display these skills through gaze and gesture by nine to fifteen months of age.

Because deictic markers depend on the evolving social and spatial setting of an interaction, their functions are best examined through the analysis of situated talk. In conversation, participants coordinate deictic markers with the material environment in temporally unfolding sequences. Participants use prior turns at talk, as well as dynamic change in the environment, to co-operatively build social action in real time (C. Goodwin 2018, 11). Attending to the turn-by-turn unfolding of social action shows that grammatical systems like deixis serve as a medium for formulating shared cognition in situated verbal interactions.[8] The examination of sequences of embodied interaction in rural Tsachen and urban Xining can therefore reveal how children's language practices contribute to the ongoing (re)formulation of their social bonds.

Spatial Deixis in Amdo: A Brief Linguistic Description

Speakers of Amdo Tibetan Farmer Talk use their language's system of deixis in culturally particular ways. Cultural norms shape children's language production and comprehension by linking grammatical forms to particular aged identities and social relationships (Ochs 1985, 786). In rural Tsachen, routine uses of spatial deixis strengthen young children's social attachments and senses of place. Specifically, children use their *yul skad*'s deictic markers to move throughout the village's hills and valleys, creating autobiographical memories with their peers that are grounded in particular places. While children's play activities locate social belonging in the homeland, particular structural features of the Amdo deictic system also facilitate the formation of associations between kinship and place. Amdo spatial deictics refer to topographical distance, or relative altitude, in addition to relative distance away from an origin point. This means that the referent of an Amdo deictic marker depends on a speaker's vertical or horizontal movement in the course of talk. This feature of the Amdo *yul skad* allows deictic markers to capture the intricacies of multi-party movement in expanded spaces.

Amdo spatial deixis includes two paradigms: locative adverbs and demonstratives.[9] Both paradigms mark a three-way distinction (table 3). The locative adverbs *jar* ("above"), *mar* ("below"), and *har* ("away") indicate an object's topographical location in relation to the origin point. The locative adverbs can refer to locations in the immediate space of an interaction or to displaced locations or events. In rural areas, speakers often use locative adverbs to describe elevation and other features of the landscape.[10] In urban areas, speakers generally use locative adverbs to discuss features of the built environment, such as the positioning of an item on a shelf or a person within a multi-storey apartment building. The three demonstratives *^{n}di* ("here," near the speaker), *^{n}de* ("there," far from the speaker but near the addressee), and *gen* ("over there," far from both speaker and addressee) denote distances away from the origin point, also marking the relative distance between interactive participants.

While rural and urban children's language repertoires vary drastically, especially across developmental time, children in both Tsachen

Table 3. Two paradigms of Amdo Tibetan spatial deixis

Paradigm 1: Amdo locative adverbs			
Form	*jar*	*mar*	*har*
Meaning	Above	Below	Away
Paradigm 2: Amdo demonstratives			
Form	*ⁿdi*	*ⁿde*	*gen*
Meaning	Here (near to speaker, far from addressee)	There (far from speaker, near to addressee)	Over there (far from speaker and addressee)

Table 4: Mandarin spatial deixis

Mandarin deictics		
Form	*zhe*	*na*
Meaning	Near	Far

and Xining have bilingual communicative competence in Mandarin and Amdo Tibetan and produce deictic markers from both languages. The Mandarin spatial deictic system is less elaborate than that of Amdo Tibetan. Mandarin marks a two-way distinction between near and far, with the deictic markers *zhe* (near the origin point) and *na* (far from the origin point) (table 4). Mandarin deictic markers can be modified with additional particles to provide further specificity about the grammatical category of the referent. For example, Mandarin speakers can discuss a location by combining a deictic marker with an adverb (as in *na li* [there]).

The structure of a particular grammatical system does not determine its actual or potential interactive functions; children could use either the Mandarin or Amdo systems of deixis to achieve the same interactive functions. However, recurring language experiences routinize the social functions of particular grammatical systems. In Tsachen, participants spatialize kinship, using deictic markers to create culturally specific associations between their foundational social relationships and places in the village homeland. In Xining, adult caregivers spatialize kinship in dyadic interactions with young children by using deictic markers to imaginatively refer to non-present family members. In both settings, spatial deixis allows participants to sequentially establish joint attention during place-making practices.

Spatializing Kinship: The Formation of Peer Relationships in Tsachen

In Tsachen, Dolma and Lhamo use their *yul skad*'s elaborated system of spatial deixis to form attachments to persons and places, perpetuating the nexus of land, language, and kinship that serves as a focal point of Amdo people's cultural identity. Children in Tsachen spatialize kinship when they use deixis to map their peer relationships in immediate interactive settings and when they link their friendships to the village's enduring geography. In their first months of life, before infants agentively spatialize kinship, adults and older siblings help them to do so.

Back in June 2018, it was now late afternoon in Tsachen. At the household compound, Dolma, Lhamo, Ama, and I shared a lunch of hot milk, dense *go re*, and fried vegetables served by Ayi Khangmo. As we ate, the television blared synthesized Amdo folk songs while dancers circled on the screen.

When lunch was finished, Lhamo and Dolma rushed outside to the household courtyard. We adults followed, bringing freshly salted sunflower seeds along as a snack. Lhamo and Dolma were performing magic tricks with a mop. Ama sat atop the stoop, with Yangkyi on her lap. Several minutes later, Ama's first cousin, Ani Khangla, crossed through the courtyard's gate with three-year-old Tenzin, a relative and neighbour, at her side. Ani Khangla pushed a baby stroller over the household's uneven brick landing. Tenzin held one edge of the stroller as he toddled through the household's entrance. Inside the stroller, Ani Khangla's infant son, Tashi, lay fast asleep. Tashi was born within several weeks of Yangkyi, soon after the lunar calendar wheel turned to the current year of the Earth Dog.

Ani Khangla lifted Tashi out of the stroller and sat him on her lap as she settled next to Ama. Baby Tashi stirred from the activity. Lhamo and Dolma stopped their game, cooing greetings at Tashi. The two girls moved into a semi-circle in front of Ama and Ani Khangla, while Tenzin stood behind them. Dolma and Lhamo began to take on care-taking roles by coordinating Tashi and Yangkyi's mutual orientation.

Excerpt 2.1: "Look at Achi"[11]

"da kʰə-ɲə kʰə-ɲə-a ʰta-ki-joŋ ani" (Ani, make them look at each other), Dolma directed Ani Khangla. As she spoke, she flexed her right hand to point towards baby Tashi and swayed her forearm back and forth to indicate that Ani Khangla should move Tashi to face Yangkyi.

"ja ja" (Okay, okay), Ani Khangla responded. She shifted her body, along with Tashi, to face Ama and baby Yangkyi.

"wumo awu-a ^{h}*ti"* (Girl, look at Awu [older brother]), Dolma instructed Yangkyi. As Dolma spoke, she crouched down, bringing her face closer to the infants'.

Meanwhile, Lhamo circled behind Dolma to join Tenzin in a brief game. She tried, unsuccessfully, to shift Dolma's attention away from the infants and towards her new game with Tenzin. After several unsuccessful attempts at capturing Dolma's attention, Lhamo gave up. She returned to the activity centre Dolma had established. Lhamo stood next to Dolma, and Tenzin followed close behind.

"atɕ^{h}*i* ***gen!"*** (Achi, over there!), Dolma called gently to Tashi. Dolma used the distal demonstrative, *gen*, to indicate Yangkyi's location. In response, Tashi inclined his head towards Yangkyi.

"tɕ^{h}*o-ɲə* ^{h}*ts*^{h}*e-a-de-a"* (You two keep playing), Dolma encouraged. Dolma had noticed the shift in Tashi's gaze. She was defining Tashi's gaze towards Yangkyi as intentional play.

Tashi kept his head turned towards Yangkyi. Lhamo crouched next to Dolma. Both girls were now kneeling on the ground.

*"**gen*** ^{h}*ti-da-kə"* ([baby Tashi] is looking over there), Lhamo added. Lhamo was expanding on Dolma's previous statement. She used the distal demonstrative, *gen*, to describe Tashi's gaze towards Yangkyi. Lhamo then began to describe the relationship between Yangkyi and Tashi.

"a::-ze k^{h}*ər-ki k*^{h}*ə-a k*^{h}*ər-ki awu ra ze.* ^{n}***di****-a k*^{h}*ər-ki atɕ*^{h}*i* ^{n}***di****-a k*^{h}*ər-ki – "* (Hey, she'll say he's her Awu. This one, his Achi, this one, he –). Lhamo stumbled over her words, as she lost the attention of the other participants. Dolma, Ama, and Ani Khangla had started to laugh because the infants were cooing and jerking their limbs.

"aləi ^{n}*də.gə-ne"* (Wow! Like this, then), Lhamo interrupted. Her interjection captured the others' attention, and she took the floor to speak.

"k^{h}*ə-a lo xtɕik̚t*^{h}*on-na-ta atɕ*^{h}*i zer-nə-re"* (When she's a year old, she'll be called "Achi"), Lhamo observed. She pointed to baby Yangkyi as she spoke, and then shifted her arm to point to Tashi. *"*^{n}***di****-a lo xtɕik̚t*^{h}*on-na awu zer-nə-re"* (When this one's a year old, he'll be called "Awu"), Lhamo concluded.

In this pair of utterances, Lhamo defined each infant's kinship role. She used a pronoun to refer to Yangkyi, and the proximal demonstrative, ^{n}*di*, to refer to Tashi. With this deictic marker, she expressed Tashi's proximity to Yangkyi in the circle of participants. At the same time, she was articulating Tashi and Yangkyi's enduring kin relationship. With this choice of words, Lhamo commented on the infants' immediate co-presence and projected their relationship into the future.

"*kʰə-a awu ze-nə-ma-re. kʰə nuwo re ɲima kʰaxi*" (He won't be called "Awu." He's younger by several days), Ani Khangla explained, latching onto Lhamo's utterance. Ani Khangla was correcting Lhamo. Lhamo had used the kin terms "Awu" and "Achi." When used in a caregiving register, these are the generic terms for young children. Although Lhamo's statement was consistent with how a caregiver would refer to the infants, it did not accurately describe how the infants would name each other when they began to speak. When used by peers, these terms denote relative age, so Yangkyi would call Tashi by his first name or a nickname because she is slightly older.

Yangkyi made a small cooing noise, and Tashi turned his head in response. This prompted Dolma to call out, "*a::* ***gen*** *ʰti*" (Hey, look over there!). She was focusing the other participants' attention on Tashi's gaze towards Yangkyi. The other participants looked towards Tashi as Dolma reached out to touch his arm.

"*awu atɕʰi-a ʰti-a-toŋ*" (Awu, look at Achi), Dolma instructed Tashi. Dolma was noticing that Tashi had shifted his gaze towards Yangkyi in response to her vocalization.

"*atɕʰi-a ʰti-a-toŋ-ja*" (Look at Achi), Ani Khangla added, repeating Dolma's directive. The older participants were collaborating to encourage the infants' mutual orientation.

"*atɕʰi* ***gen****! awu Tashi*" (Achi, over there! Awu Tashi), Dolma said. Dolma gently pulled on Tashi's arm, orienting him towards Yangkyi as she spoke. At the end of her utterance, Dolma exhaled and began to giggle.

Tashi followed Dolma's exhale with a breath of his own, making a small sigh. This caused the other participants to laugh. They focused their gaze on Tashi, while he and Yangkyi looked at each other.

"*hi::* ***gen***" (hi:: over there), Ani Khangla added. Ani Khangla was imitating the sound of Tashi's sigh. She used the distal demonstrative, *gen*, to direct Tashi's gaze towards Yangkyi. Lhamo, Ani Khangla, and Ama followed infant Tashi's gaze, turning to look from his face to Yangkyi's.

Dolma and Lhamo remained kneeling for several more minutes. They alternated between moving the infants' arms and legs and commenting on the infants' subtle movements. As the afternoon sun arched downward, the children began to weave in and out of the courtyard gate, no longer content to stay seated. The adults moved into the living room with the infants and lay them side-by-side on the *khang*. Ama boiled water for tea, anticipating a quick descent of the evening chill, while I sat next to the now-sleeping infants. As I watched them, I thought about their early participation in multi-party interaction.

In Tsachen, caregivers – parents, adult relatives, older siblings, and older cousins – used multiple embodied resources to help infants participate in conversation. These resources included body positioning, gaze, and sound play, all of which are coordinated with deictic markers. Caregivers tend to nest infants in their laps, orienting them outwards in multi-party interaction. In contrast to patterns of dyadic caregiver-child interaction common in Euro-American households (Ochs and Schieffelin 1984, 285), nesting provides infants with perceptual access to multiple participants. Nesting also establishes the expectation that participants will simultaneously coordinate attention with more than one person. When Dolma and Ani Khangla commented on Tashi and Yangkyi's gaze towards one another, they were validating this communicative behaviour. Dolma even characterized Tashi's gaze towards Yangkyi as "playing." Caregivers also ratified infants' vocalizations as intentional contributions to the ongoing conversation. As Bambi Schieffelin (1983) found in a study of Kaluli sound play, understandings of metaphor, sentiment, and relationality defined the cultural values that adults heard in children's vocalizations and how they subsequently responded. When she imitated Tashi (*hi::*), Ani Khangla acknowledged his vocalization as meaningful and perpetuated his sound play. Through their responses to the infants' gaze and vocalization, caregivers encouraged Yangkyi and Tashi to act as conversational partners.

The *yul skad*'s system of spatial deixis played a crucial role in facilitating the infants' co-engagement. Caregivers used spatial deixis to scaffold the infants' perceptual attunement to one another. For example, Lhamo, Dolma, and Ani Khangla sequenced spatial deictics to focus shared attention on the infants' gaze and vocalizations and to coordinate the imperative verb *ʰti* (look) with movements of the infants' bodies. With spatial deictics, caregivers also linked Yangkyi and Tashi's immediate proximity on their mothers' laps to their future relationship. These seemingly mundane uses of spatial deixis in embodied interaction established Yangkyi and Tashi's roles as related peers and playmates.

Embodied Play in Tsachen: Strengthening the *yul skad* through Peer Relationships

In rural Tsachen, young children's multi-party play reproduced existing interactive practices that used spatial deixis to coordinate mutual orientation with related peers. At the same time, Dolma and Lhamo created new, enduring associations between their social relationships and particular places in the village. In the course of their play, Dolma and Lhamo moved through their household, the outdoor space of the village, and their relatives' households. Because their activities relied on coordinated movement, they used spatial deixis to establish a shared trajectory of play and form autobiographical memories with one another. Therefore, Dolma and Lhamo's everyday play built dense kinship ties through particular uses of the *yul skad* that were rooted in the landscape, itself. By grounding their friendships in the material environment, Dolma and Lhamo reinforced the dynamic capacity of their *yul skad* to respond to the contexts of their everyday play. The cultural practice of spatializing kinship endured across generations because children sedimented their social bonds through the *yul skad*.

Back in Tsachen in June 2018, Dolma and I were eating breakfast together on a chilly, dry morning while Yangkyi snored softly on the *khang*. Ama returned from outside while we were eating. She sat and joined us for a cup of tea. Then, she wrapped Yangkyi tightly on her back and departed to tend to the wheatfield next to the home of young relatives Yangmo and Dolkar. Shortly after, Dolma and I also went outside. After wandering Tsachen's dusty roads for about ten minutes, we found Lhamo running in circles around the *ma ni khang*. Yangmo and Dolkar were hanging off the handlebars of a stationary bike in the adjacent exercise plot. As Dolma and I creaked open the gate of the temple compound, Dolma began to chase Lhamo. I did my best to catch up to them. After a few rounds of the temple perimeter – a form of play that mimicked *skor ba* – the girls paused. They kneeled down in a patch of grass next to the temple gate. Dolma was doubled over, putting her head low to the ground to catch her breath. Suddenly, she let out a shrieking giggle. She bolted upright, holding a dandelion with a white seed head.

"hor.dzu!" (literally, "blower"), Dolma yelled. She blew on the dandelion stem, sending its delicate seeds floating into the dusty wind. Dolma and Lhamo scrambled to uproot the dandelions that remained in front of them. When there were no stems left to pick, the two girls darted outside the gate. They used spatial deixis to negotiate the trajectory of their shared movement.

Excerpt 2.2: "The One Where We Had Chased the Cats"[12]

"ani ***gen****-na jo-pa"* (There must be some [dandelions] over there, Ani), Lhamo called to me. She pointed past a bend in the village

road, using the distal demonstrative, *gen*, to identify an object of shared attention.

"***gen**-ni **jar** koŋwa ⁿdʑo-ra jo-pa. **ⁿdi**-ni **jar** koŋ **gen**-na jo-pa*" (Let's go over there, to the house up there, there must be [some]. From here, the house way over up there, there must be [some]), Lhamo elaborated. She was pointing to a household whose roof was visible just beyond the bend in the road. Lhamo was suggesting that we converge on the shared goal of moving towards this house. Lhamo used the locative, *jar*, to describe the intended destination. With the contrasting demonstratives *gen* and *ⁿdi*, Lhamo suggested a potential path of shared movement towards this destination.

"***gen**-na jo-nə-ma-re*" (There aren't any over there), Dolma retorted. Dolma had recycled the demonstrative, *gen*, from Lhamo's previous turn to refuse Lhamo's suggested destination. In response, Lhamo moved in beside Dolma so that they were standing shoulder-to-shoulder in the road. Lhamo lifted her left arm, closest to Dolma, to point towards the distant household's roof.

"*jo-ki-a! **gen** ker-ker-wo **gen** min-ne*" (There are! Over there, what about those white ones? Aren't those [dandelions] over there?), Lhamo asked, repeating the distal demonstrative, *gen*. She was providing further specificity about her intended referent, in an attempt to align Dolma's knowledge with her own.

"*kə ma-re!*" (That's not [them]!), Dolma contradicted. Dolma was competing with Lhamo to direct the group's shared movement.

"*ŋa ⁿdʑo ʰta*" (I'll go look), Lhamo said, sprinting towards the household. Lhamo did not accept Dolma's authority to shape the group's shared action. Because her attempt to direct Dolma towards the distant household had not been successful, Lhamo departed. As Lhamo passed the bend in the road, Dolma took my hand and wandered in the opposite direction. Over the next twenty-five seconds, Dolma wondered about where to locate the dandelions. Suddenly, we heard Lhamo call out.

"*wase! hor.dʑu maŋ.ŋa jo-ki-a*" (Wow! There's so many dandelions!), Lhamo shouted. Dolma turned, grabbing my hand. We once again converged on a shared object of attention.

"*ⁿdʑo!*" (Let's go!), Dolma said, already running towards Lhamo. When we arrived, Dolma turned to me and complained, "*ani kʰər-ki ɕob-taŋ-jo-ki*" (Ani, she's already picked all of them).

Rather than aligning with Lhamo's activity of picking dandelions near the household, Dolma suggested a different pathway of collective movement. "***gen**-ni ta maŋ-nə-re-ja*" (Hey, there's a lot over there), she said, turning again as she held my hand. As in the previous turns,

Dolma relied on the distal demonstrative, *gen*, to suggest a new destination.

*"**har**-ra ak^{h}ə-tɕ^{h}o ^{n}dʑo-sa jo-la"* (Up there, there must be a place for us to go), Dolma wondered aloud about a possible path. She dropped my hand and lifted her left palm. With her right forefinger, she mapped out our group's prospective movement on her hand.

"lam zək̚-ke tʂaŋmo zək̚ ^{n}di.mo ak^{h}ə-tɕ^{h}o milu da-ki-jo-no" (There's a straight road, like this, the one where we had chased the cats), Dolma said, circling her finger on her palm. *"^{h}kor-^{h}kor ^{n}di.ni.ta da maŋ.ŋa jo-no"* (Round and round, then there's [a road] with many [dandelions]), Dolma asserted.*"^{n}dʑo ta!"* (Let's go, then!), Dolma concluded. Lhamo turned towards Dolma, indicating her alignment with Dolma's suggested goal. Dolma, Lhamo, and I had finally agreed upon a shared trajectory. Together, the girls darted ahead of me, and I followed them down the winding road.

When they negotiated where to pick dandelions, Dolma and Lhamo used the *yul skad*'s full repertoire of spatial deictics to coordinate collective movement. Both girls displayed authoritative knowledge about the best location for their unfolding play by synchronizing demonstratives and locatives. In so doing, each offered her immediate perceptions as potential focal points for subsequent shared actions. Dolma and Lhamo repeated the spatial deictic markers from previous turns but sequenced them to create competing directives. Each girl transformed the meaning of the other's previous utterance to claim authority over the trajectory of collective movement. Dolma and Lhamo also drew on prior shared activities, projecting their relationship back in time. With spatial deixis, they brought shared memories into the present, telling autobiographical narratives that were rooted in the village landscape and that influenced the unfolding of subsequent, situated actions.

These two excerpts demonstrate that, across developmental time, Tsachen's children experienced continuity in cultural practices that use the grammar of the *yul skad* to build peer relationships. More specifically, they enacted what Corsaro termed the "interpretive reproduction" of culture (1992, 168). Caregivers and older children used spatial deixis to encourage mutual orientation between infants. Young children continued to display mutual orientation to the peer group by using this same grammatical resource to coordinate shared movement throughout the village. Due to this continuity between caregiving practices and peer-group play, Dolma and Lhamo reproduced linguistic resources from the *yul skad* across generations. In their real-time interactions, they also adapted the functions of spatial deixis across conversational turns to manage multi-party play in expanded space. While Corsaro's theory of interpretive reproduction provides a framework for understanding the pragmatic adaptation of linguistic resources in real-time interaction, linguist Lev Michael described how grammatical systems acquire new, enduring functions over longer time periods. Michael (2015) noted that communicative practices can drive change to a language system by increasing the frequency of certain linguistic features. Frequency of use highlights a linguistic feature, predisposing speakers to use it in new ways and novel contexts (100–4). Routine verbal interactions therefore facilitate grammaticalization, or the creation of additional grammatical functions for a particular linguistic feature.

Such forms of functional change within language systems contribute to their vitality. In Tsachen, Dolma and Lhamo sustained their *yul skad* not only by using spatial deixis to coordinate movement in multi-party play. They also created new referents for deictic markers by encoding associations between their peer relationships and the landscape. In the complete corpus of conversations, the children referred to the locations of their peers' households with two phrases: *jar-ka* (upper area) and *mar-ka* (lower area). These phrases modify a spatial deictic (a locative adverb) with a nominalizer (*-ka*) to denote stable locations in the village landscape. In Dolma and Lhamo's formulation, *jar-ka* included the households of Dawa, and Yangmo and Dolkar by the elevated wheatfield, and *mar-ka* included the households of Tashi as well as Tenzin and Khangri Tso towards the valley (fig. 7). By naming their peers' households with deictics, they expanded existing functions of the *yul skad*, demonstrating the process that Michael (2015) termed "culture-driven grammaticalization."

In Tsachen, participants thus used deixis to spatialize kinship on multiple scales. Children formulated directives in face-to-face interaction in intimate space as well as during multi-party play in expanded spaces. Dolma and Lhamo also used the locative adverbs to create metonyms that linked physical places in the village to their peer relationships. Tsachen's children shared two key language experiences that allowed for the stability of the *yul skad* across generations. First, everyday communicative routines of multi-party interaction made spatial deixis particularly salient. Second, conversations using spatial deixis were grounded in the children's immediate material and social environments. In Xining, Sonam's changing uses of spatial deixis across developmental time demonstrate the current fixity of these language experiences in the rural homeland.

Figure 7. The Children's deictic demarcation of Tsachen Village

Spatializing Kinship in the City: Dyadic Interactions in Xining

While Tsachen's dense kinship ties facilitated young children's attachment to their related peers, the cultural significance of the peer group endured within families who had migrated out of the village homeland. This is due, in part, to the grammatical resources that urban Amdo Tibetan families used to talk about non-present people and places. With spatial deixis, participants located each other in the course of face-to-face interaction while also projecting their relationships across time and space. In dyadic play involving one caregiver and one child, urban Amdo Tibetan adults used spatial deixis to imaginatively bring children's non-present peers into their conversations.

Sonam and Yeshi are paternal first cousins, and relatives of Dolma, Lhamo, and Yangkyi (fig. 6). Sonam and Yeshi live in a joint household in Xining, composed of their mothers and fathers, and their paternal grandparents. Unlike Dolma and Lhamo, who spent their days playing with groups of related peers, Sonam and Yeshi frequently participated in dyadic interactions with caregivers or engaged in solitary activities. While Yeshi attended school for eight hours each day on Sundays through Fridays, Sonam tended to play in his apartment with Ama, Ani Tsering Kyi, Ayi Lhamo, or Aphu Lhundhup. After school and on her weekly Saturday holiday, Yeshi often completed homework or attended extracurricular art classes. When Yeshi was not otherwise engaged, she watched television and drew with Sonam. Although Sonam and Yeshi had the opportunity to engage in free play with their related peers only when they visited Tsachen on holiday, their adult caregivers spatialized kinship by including multiple relatives in everyday conversations.

One Saturday morning in early March 2016, I knocked lightly on the door to Sonam and Yeshi's apartment. Sonam's family had invited me over that morning to video-record Sonam's play and then share lunch. I was slightly out of breath, after climbing the six flights of concrete stairs leading to the family's top floor unit. I admired the red brocade curtain that hung from the copper door frame. I reached out to touch an image of the eternal knot, *dpal be'u*, which symbolizes *las*, the endless cycle of birth and rebirth recounted in Tibetan Buddhist teachings. As I ran my finger along the image, woven with multicoloured thread into the middle of the curtain, Ayi Lhamo opened the door. Sonam, aged two years, five months, was standing just behind her legs.

"*Ani demo ze*" (Say hi to Ani), Ayi directed Sonam. Sonam peeked through the gap between Ayi's legs.

"*Ani demo!*" Sonam called out, placing his hands together at his heart in the Tibetan gesture of respect.

"*Demo, demo!*" I responded, as Ayi ushered me inside.

Ayi and I sat down on the large leather sofa in the apartment's living room. Ani Tsering Kyi entered from the kitchen, carrying a kettle of just-boiled water. She placed the kettle on the glass coffee table in front of us and went to retrieve a canister of green tea leaves from a nearby shelf. Ani Tsering Kyi again approached the table. She sprinkled several tea leaves, along with dried *hongzao* – Chinese red dates used to boost immunity in cold weather – into three glass mugs for us adults. As Ani Tsering Kyi filled each mug with steaming water, she explained that seven-year-old Yeshi was in her bedroom, working on a drawing for an art class she would attend that afternoon. As Ayi Lhamo and I began to sip our tea, Sonam bounded around the coffee table and plopped himself on the floor next to Ani Tsering Kyi. Ani Tsering Kyi kneeled down, settling in next to him. She reached for a car catalogue, gleaming with silver photographs, that lay on the coffee table.

Excerpt 2.3: "Let's Go, Yeshi!"[13]

"*ŋi-kə awu*[14] *ra ŋi-ɣɲi-kə che-a ^{h}ta rema*" (Awu and I, let's both look at the cars, quickly), Ani Tsering Kyi suggested. Ani accommodated the current social situation to Sonam by drawing him into dyadic play as we adults continued to chat.

"*awu che ^{h}ta*" (Awu [will] look at cars), Sonam responded, moving to sit in Ani's lap. As is common among Amdo toddlers, Sonam referred to himself in the third person, with the generic kin term that caregivers use to address young male children. With format tying – the repetition of syntax from a prior turn at talk that functions to continue or transform a line of social action (C. Goodwin 2006, 449; M. Goodwin 1991, 177–8) – Sonam entered Ani's game.

"*awu-kə che. awu che gaŋ re? ani ɕol-a-toŋ*" (Awu's car. Which is Awu's car? Tell Ani), Ani prompted, using format tying to expand the previous activity of shared looking into picture identification.

"***^{n}di***" (This one), Sonam asserted, pointing to the image of a black SUV. With the proximal demonstrative, *^{n}di*, Sonam linked the image in front of him to an imagined scenario of owning the car. Sonam and Ani used this deictic marker as a foundation for format tying, as they continued to build shared understanding in their evolving game.

"*ani **^{n}di** si-kə che re*" (Then, whose car is this?), Ani prompted. Ani recycled the deictic marker from Sonam's previous turn, pointing to a red sedan.

"*ani-kə*" (Ani's), Sonam added.

"*ani-kə che re*" (It's Ani's car), Ani responded. She expanded Sonam's response into a grammatically complete sentence. Sonam then initiated a new turn.

"***^{n}di** awu-kə che*" (This, Awu's car), Sonam asserted, pointing to the red sedan and contradicting his previous statement. With this turn, Sonam used format tying to reuse and transform the meanings of his and Ani's past turns. He created a dispreferred second, or unexpected response, to Ani's just prior utterance.[15]

Then, Sonam escalated his claims of ownership with repetition: "^{n}***di*** *awu-kə* ***che***. ^{n}***di*** *awu-kə re-ja!*" (This, Awu's car. Hey! This one's Awu's). Sonam moved his finger, pointing repeatedly to both the black SUV and the red sedan.

In her next turn, Ani used format tying to once again transform the meaning of Sonam's statement. "*awu daŋ atɕ*^{h}*i-kə* ***che***" (Awu and Achi's car), Ani responded. She had recycled and reformulated Sonam's previous turn into a preferred response that included older sister Yeshi. Ani was indicating that Sonam's insistence on claiming ownership of all the cars did not align with her intended goal for the game.

Next, Ani asked a prompting question that emphasized Sonam's family relationships. "^{n}***di*** *ap*^{h}*a-kə* ***che*** *re-la?*" (Isn't this one Apha's car?), Ani suggested, pointing to the black SUV. With this rhetorical question, Ani displayed another potential response that Sonam could recycle into a preferred second. Ani was attempting to bring Sonam into alignment with her goal of attributing ownership of the cars to different family members. In Ani's intended activity trajectory, Sonam would express belonging to his family by discussing the imagined car owners.

"*ma-re! awu-kə re!*" (No! It's Awu's!), Sonam yelled. Instead of repeating the content of Ani's suggested response, Sonam drew on the verb from Ani's prior turn to provide another dispreferred second. By this point in the conversation, Sonam was expressing continued disalignment with Ani's goal. Ani was guiding Sonam to orient towards his relatives, which is an important cultural norm in Amdo Tibetan family conversations. Sonam was violating this norm by refusing to include other family members in his imagined scenario.

In response to Sonam's disalignment, Ani shifted the content of her prompting questions. "*o:: awu-kə re awu-kə re*" (Oh, it's Awu's, it's Awu's), Ani seemed to concede, as she repeated his statement of ownership. With her next utterance, however, Ani indicated that she was not accepting Sonam's suggested line of play. Ani began to ask Sonam to name parts of the car. She was attempting to shape the activity trajectory by engaging Sonam in an entirely new line of play.

"^{n}***di*** *tɕ*^{h}*i re?*" (What's this?), Ani asked, pointing to the SUV's large front tire.

"^{n}***di*** *awu-kə* ***che*** *re*" (This is Awu's car), Sonam stubbornly asserted, using the proximal demonstrative, ^{n}*di*, from Ani's prior turn to repeat the content of his previous assertion.

"^{n}***di che****-kə* ^{h}*korlo zək̚ re-ja ze-go*" (You should say, "This is the car's wheel"), Ani said. She was correcting Sonam's statement with a directive. Ani was no longer subtly suggesting preferred responses. She was instructing Sonam in how to respond now that the line of play had shifted.

"ʰkorlo!" (Wheel!), Sonam called out. He had finally offered a preferred second, or expected response, to Ani's directive, joining in her desired trajectory of social action.

Over the next minute and twenty seconds, Ani and Sonam expanded on this line of play. Ani asked Sonam to name particular parts of the car, and Sonam responded with preferred seconds that accurately described the objects. With the proximal demonstrative, *^{n}di*, serving as the basis for format tying, Sonam and Ani negotiated shared social actions in their imaginative discussion of the car images. Ani also shaped the evolution of their co-constructed knowledge by using demonstratives in prompting questions and directives.[16]

Ani turned a page in the catalogue, unexpectedly revealing images of car interiors. Ani used this change in the material environment to initiate a new line of play. Building on the basis of shared knowledge that she and Sonam had established about the cars' owners, Ani began to tell a story. She continued to use spatial deixis to fancifully transport other family members into her plot.

"a::" (Ah!), Ani exclaimed, verbally marking the new line of play. *"awu lʰodʐa-na ^{n}dʑo-kə tɕʰi* ***<u>che</u>*** *ʰkor-re"* (Awu, to get to school, you drive the car!), Ani suggested.

"atɕʰi Yeshi ***^{n}de*** *tsʰok̚-kə-dʑɨ-taŋ"* (Have Achi Yeshi sit there), Ani said. She used the medial demonstrative, *^{n}de*, and pointed to the image of the car's passenger's seat to specify her meaning.

"awu ***^{n}de*** *tsʰok̚-taŋ"* (Awu, sit there), Ani added, now pointing to the driver's seat. Ani had placed Sonam and Yeshi next to one another in her unfolding story. Her use of the medial demonstrative, *^{n}de*, carried Yeshi into the physical space of the world of the story.

"awu ***<u>che</u>*** *ʰkor-re, 'atɕʰi lʰodʐa-na ^{n}dʑo! rema xok̚! ʱwe kʰər-ra xok̚' ze-na"* (While Awu's driving the car, he says "Achi, let's go to school! Come quickly! Come and bring your schoolbag!"), Ani added. She voiced Sonam's imagined words to Yeshi by shifting her intonation.

"mm hmm," Sonam replied, smiling and nodding his head to indicate his engagement in the unfolding plot.

"awu ***<u>che</u>*** *ʰkor!"* (Awu, drive the car!), Ani directed.

In the next utterance, she again shifted her intonation to voice an imagined statement from Sonam. *"atɕʰi naŋ-ŋa ^{n}dʑo-ja! lʰodʐa go-na soŋ!"* ("Achi, go inside! Go into the school!"), Ani said, animating Sonam's imagined words to Yeshi.

"bi:: bi::" (Beep beep!), Ani called, pretending that Sonam had honked the horn. Ani pressed her finger on the image of the steering wheel in the car catalogue.

"'tʰon-taŋ-a' zer-toŋ-a. jin-na?" (Say "We arrived!" Right?), Ani added. With this confirmation-seeking question, Ani bridged the imagined world of the story with the immediate social world of storytelling. She was prompting Sonam to actively participate in developing the plot.

"eh eh," Sonam grunted, providing a backchannel cue (Goffman 1976, 264) that indicated his continued interest. Over ten more turns, Ani advanced the story's plot. She portrayed Sonam returning home to retrieve his other family members. Together, the family then drove to pick up Yeshi at school.

"***gen** da tsʰə da.kə tsʰə ze-ta?*" (What about all those, over there?), Ani asked, anchoring her narrative in the catalogue's pictures as she pointed to the back seats in the car. Ani continued her turn by answering the question she had just posed. *"awu-kə ʰkor-taŋ"* (Awu, drive), Ani said, pointing to the driver's seat. *"apʰa* ^{n}***de** tsʰok̚-kə-dʑɨ-taŋ"* (Make Apha sit there), Ani said, pointing to one of the back seats.

"ama ^{n}***di** tsʰok̚-kə-dʑɨ-taŋ"* (Make Ama sit here), Ani added, pointing to the adjacent back seat. Ani used contrasting demonstratives to locate Sonam with his parents in the car. She was continuing to integrate the catalogue's visual form into her story, while also including non-present family members.

Next, Ani advanced the plot by quoting what Sonam would say when the family arrived at Yeshi's school. *"'ama tsʰaŋ* ^{n}*dʑo'-ze. awu-kə che ʰkor, 'zər zər zər zər zər!'"* ("Let's go to Ama's house!" Awu's driving the car, "zoom zoom zoom zoom zoom!"), Ani added.

Sonam then took a turn. *"Yeshi* ^{n}*dʑo"* (Yeshi! Let's go!), Sonam yelled, calling to Yeshi from within the story world.

Hearing Sonam's explosive enthusiasm, Yeshi emerged from her bedroom to ask where Sonam was going. She had thought Sonam was calling her to leave the apartment. I laughed along with Ani Tsering Kyi and Ayi Lhamo, as we explained the plot of Ani Tsering Kyi's story. Yeshi shrugged and retreated to her bedroom. She did not return to the living room until lunch was served.

In everyday conversations, the intertwined worlds of stories and storytelling iteratively build each other (Ochs and Capps 2001, 36–40). Participants use social cues, previous turns at talk, and objects in their material environment to collaboratively shape an evolving plot. Because narratives can relocate events in space and time, urban caregivers like Ani Tsering Kyi used storytelling to bring non-present relatives into dyadic conversations with toddlers. Spatial deixis is a potent resource for linking an internal story world to the social world of storytelling. By imaginatively placing family members in the car catalogue's pictures, Ani Tsering Kyi used spatial deixis to both displace referents in space and time and locate them in the immediate interactive setting.

Urban Amdo Tibetan toddlers participated in the cultural practice of spatializing kinship through their caregivers' prompts. However, despite the focus on kin relationships in their family conversations, as they grew up, urban children tended to build friendships with non-related peers. They also stopped using spatial deixis to imaginatively create multi-party play during dyadic family interactions. In their imaginary car ride to school, Yeshi's response to Sonam's unexpected call provided insight into why school-aged children largely move their peer relationships outside of the home. Although Sonam called Yeshi into his evolving story, Yeshi did not elaborate on Sonam's call or on Ani Tsering Kyi's explanation of Sonam's intentions. Rather than joining in their game, Yeshi returned to her bedroom and worked on her art project until the next scheduled activity – a family meal.

By age three, urban Amdo Tibetan children have entered preschool, where they participate in a hierarchical and achievement-oriented school system. In urban centres like Xining, children are expected to read basic Chinese characters and perform common mathematical operations like addition and subtraction before entering Grade 1. Urban preschools teach these skills while socializing children into academic routines. They offer structured group lessons in reading, math, and exercise, and assign classroom duties like wiping down tables between activities or sweeping the floor after snack time. The tempo of children's days thus involves moving between structured activities at home and school and completing independent study activities. The spatial settings through which urban children move – from bedroom to car to schoolroom and back – do not allow for extensive unsupervised play. In rural Tsachen, children's peer culture depended on the freedom to move. With their relatives, children moved throughout the space of the village and created diverse assemblages of play activities. Although urban Amdo Tibetan toddlers use the *yul skad* to form their foundational family relationships, time and space collaborate to displace them from their related peers as they grow up.

Urban Childhoods and the Displacement of the *yul skad*

As Sonam aged, his days were no longer filled with intimate, dyadic interactions with a single caregiver. He increasingly participated in activities with peers outside of his home. In October 2017, Sonam turned

Table 5. Number of spatial deictics in one-hour samples of Sonam's talk

Age	Amdo Locative: Upper	Amdo Locative: Lower	Amdo Locative: Away	Amdo Demonst.: Proximal	Amdo Demonst.: Medial	Amdo Demonst.: Distal	Man-darin: Proximal	Man-darin: Distal
1 yr, 11 mos	0	0	0	23	2	3	0	0
2 yrs, 0 mos	0	0	0	15	1	2	0	0
2 yrs, 2 mos	0	0	0	36	2	0	0	0
2 yrs, 3 mos	0	0	0	18	0	0	0	0
2 yrs, 6 mos	0	0	0	30	0	0	0	0
3 yrs, 8 mos	0	0	0	2	0	0	20	2

three years old and began attending a private bilingual/bicultural Mandarin and English preschool (Ch. *you'eryuan*) within walking distance of his family's apartment. Sonam's apartment building was located near a traditional Tibetan medical hospital, which made this neighbourhood popular among Xining's Amdo Tibetan community. Sonam's preschool class included multiple Amdo Tibetan children. Although some of the preschoolers shared the same *yul skad*, the dominance of Mandarin in the city's education system seems to have motivated the children to speak in Mandarin with one another.

As a toddler, Sonam's dominant language was Amdo Tibetan Farmer Talk. Sonam and his caregivers predominantly used the grammar of their *yul skad*, with some isolated Mandarin loan words. By the end of my field research in the summer of 2018, however, Sonam's language preferences had shifted, and he was speaking mostly in Mandarin. Grammatical patterns in Sonam's talk across developmental time provide insight into the specific trajectory of his language shift from Amdo Tibetan Farmer Talk to Mandarin. From age one year, eleven months to two years, six months, Sonam frequently used his *yul skad's* system of spatial deixis (table 5). He used demonstratives early in his development, with a preference for the proximal demonstrative. This is consistent with crosslinguistic data, which suggest that children produce demonstratives before other deictic markers (Clark 1978; Diessel and Coventry 2020). By age three years, eight months, Sonam's preference for deictic markers had shifted. Sonam continued to prefer the proximal demonstrative, but he now used the Mandarin form. In addition, he never produced the locative adverbs specific to his *yul skad*. His changing production of spatial deixis therefore suggests that he had shifted to speaking mostly in Mandarin before he acquired full knowledge of his *yul skad*'s grammar.[17] This language shift happened eight months after Sonam began preschool, when his social world expanded beyond his household.

Conclusion: Peer Cultures and Language Vitality

In everyday play, children use resources from their immediate social and material environments to create shared cultural practices that iteratively build on the routine behaviours of adults. Language is part of this material environment, providing a foundation of prior utterances that children draw on to shape their unfolding lines of social action. Because children use language to build shared cultural practices with their peers, the language system itself becomes an object of children's collective identification. Languages persist across generations when children interpretively reproduce the cultural practices that employ particular grammatical features and subsequently extend these features to new social contexts. The formation of peer cultures is thus profoundly connected to children's emerging grammatical knowledge.

In rural Tsachen, Dolma and Lhamo adopted their community's existing practices of spatializing kinship, which allowed for the continued vitality of the *yul skad*. For example, Dolma and Lhamo drew on caregivers' uses of spatial deixis to scaffold infants' joint attention. However, the children did not simply reproduce the cultural practices of previous generations. Dolma and Lhamo relied on their knowledge of the potential functions of spatial deixis to create new cultural practices with their related peers. Dolma and Lhamo created novel functions for the *yul skad*'s system of spatial deixis, rooting peer relationships into the village homeland with metonyms. In Tsachen, children dynamically used the grammar of the *yul skad* to build their peer cultures.

In urban Xining, peer relationships also influenced Sonam and Yeshi's language preferences. When Sonam was a toddler, his caregivers spatialized kinship in dyadic play, reproducing an Amdo Tibetan cultural emphasis on the peer group, even in the absence of the immediate, dense kin relationships that characterize Amdo villages. As Sonam grew up, he adapted to the peer culture of his preschool in Xining. Like many preschoolers from minoritized language communities (Fillmore 1991, 342), Sonam shifted to the dominant standard language before he had acquired full grammatical knowledge of his mother tongue.[18] When urban Amdo Tibetan children enter schools, it seems that they are socialized *out* of their pre-existing knowledge of how to use the *yul skad*, halting their trajectory of mother tongue language acquisition. As they form peer relationships outside of their family, urban Amdo Tibetan children use the dominant language of

Mandarin in new cultural practices. They learn to identify with their peers, not only as speakers of Mandarin, but also as non-speakers of the *yul skad*. Chapter 3 examines how, despite pressures to adopt Mandarin in the city, both rural and urban children continue to use the *yul skad* to manage their emotional expression and build identities as Buddhist persons.

Chapter 3

Socializing Compassion: Buddhist Theories of Emotion and Relationality in the Production of Social Difference

ཨོཾ། བྱམས་སེམས་ཅན་གྱི་མི་རིགས་ཡིན།
We are a people of loving compassion.

Tibetan poet *Pema Tashi*

Born in Amdo, Tsongkhapa (1357–1419) was a renowned philosopher who founded the Gelugpa (Tib. *dge lugs pa*) school of Tibetan Buddhism. Tsongkhapa's writings, notably the *lam rim chen mo* ("Great Treatise on the Stages of the Path"), drew from Indic Buddhism to define a series of meditative practices that culminate in enlightenment. Enlightenment marks freedom from the endless cycle of rebirths, which are inherently characterized by suffering. The cycle of rebirths is so infinite that every sentient being has, in at least one lifetime, served as a mother to every other. Among the meditative practices that Tsongkhapa prescribed for the path to enlightenment is the cultivation of altruism (Tib. *byang chub kyi sems*), which unfolds by reflecting on the social attachments that originate in one's relationship to their mother. Cultivating altruism results in the experience of compassion (Tib. *snying rje*).[1] Tibetan philosophy defines compassion as an awareness of the suffering inherent in the lives of all sentient beings (Tib. *sems can*), both human and non-human. As Tsongkhapa advised:

> Imagine your mother very clearly in front of you. Consider several times how she has been your mother numberless times, not only now, but from beginningless cyclic existence. When she was your mother, she protected you from all danger and brought about your benefit and happiness … In various ways she nourished you tirelessly … From the depths of her heart she would rather have suffered herself than have her child suffer. (cited in Powers and Curtin 1994, 2)

By acknowledging a mother's sacrifices for her child, the practitioner gains an experiential understanding of compassion that advances their path to enlightenment. The concept of compassion thus presents a Buddhist philosophical perspective on social attachment and spiritual merit, which both informs Tibetans' collective Buddhist identity and shapes their interpersonal relationships.

In everyday family life in Tsachen and Xining, people build their relationships to others and the natural world in ways that echo canonical writings on compassion. Compassion functions as a recognized emotion that people display in response to the pain or misfortune of others. In everyday conversation, when one witnesses or hears about another's hardship, one is expected to say "*snying rje*" (compassion). This expression of compassion is also associated with verbal displays of love (Tib. *'dang*) and interdependence (Tib. *dgos*) in family relationships. By using these three formulaic expressions, speakers reproduce a Buddhist understanding of the suffering inherent to the karmic cycle of births and rebirths, and implicitly recognize the ways that social attachments from former lives bring people into contact in their present lives. With formulaic expressions of compassion, love, and interdependence, Amdo Tibetan children learn to build their family relationships as well as their moral identities as Buddhist persons.

In this chapter, I examine how Dolma, Lhamo, and Sonam use formulaic expressions of compassion, love, and interdependence to coordinate affect, or the social display of emotion, in everyday family conversations. I integrate literature on language socialization and affect, cultural interpretations of attachment theory, and Buddhist theories of emotion to demonstrate that both rural and urban Amdo Tibetan children rely on sedimented patterns of emotional expression in the *yul skad* to manage their intimate family relationships in real time. By sequencing displays of compassion with touch and movement, Amdo Tibetan children show alignment or disalignment with each other's feeling states, and coordinate social action with explicit reference to Buddhist morality. While children build social attachments through formulaic expressions of emotion, adults also use these affective displays to define a central point of difference between Tibetan and Chinese ethnic identities. Thus, when young Amdo Tibetan children use formulaic language to navigate their interpersonal relationships and express belonging to a Tibetan Buddhist collectivity, they also reproduce an ideology of essentialized social difference.

Affective Stance and Collective Belonging

We build our foundational social attachments by aligning emotional experiences in everyday interaction. Studies from across cultures demonstrate that caregivers and preverbal infants coordinate their feeling states through sound and movement, solidifying an intersubjective attunement that is prior to language (Bateson 1975; Gratier 2020; LeVine and Norman 2001; Takada 2014). Embodied interaction thus provides the foundation for a shared social world, animated by the interpersonal nature of emotional experience. As young children age, language offers them a particular set of resources for coordinating affective stance, or the alignment of social displays of emotion, with others (Cook 2014, 297; Ochs 1996, 410). From this perspective, the locus of emotion lies not in an individual's inner experience, but in a shared, social experience built through communicative resources, including formulaic expressions, grammatical features, and conversational sequences. Experiences of emotion are therefore intertwined with their medium of expression; as young children acquire language, they link their mother tongue to their social attachments and shared emotional experiences.

Ethnographers have found that beliefs about morality and relationality shape the grammatical coordination of affective stance. For example, Clancy demonstrated that the Japanese values of empathy and conformity guided mother-infant interactions in suburban Tokyo. Mothers voiced the feelings of other people, animals, and inanimate objects to help toddlers orient to the unstated emotional states of their interlocutors (1986, 234–5). Mothers' animations of others' emotional states were marked by patterned grammatical features, specific to the Japanese language, that articulated the moral values of empathy and conformity. Similarly, Burdelski (2010) showed how Japanese preschoolers used formulaic language to express politeness and appreciation during shared activities with their peers, while Park (2006) and Song (2009) analysed how Korean-American children used honorific reference and address terms to foster their peer relationships. Fung and Thu (2019) analysed the sequencing of embodied deference routines among Vietnamese children in the Mekong Delta region to show how these children reproduced social hierarchies. Collectively, these ethnographic studies from across cultures demonstrate that children learn to manage their social relationships through formulaic language and that the moral values underlying performances of formulaic language produce collective belonging.

Ethnographic research has also suggested the potential for a community's changing moralities to shift norms of communicative behaviour, influencing, in turn, the grammatical structures of their languages. For example, Schieffelin demonstrated that, among Bosavi speakers in Papua New Guinea, Christian missionization introduced preferences for introspection and sincerity, or a match between an individual's inner emotional state and their social behaviour (2007, 157–8). While pastors emphasized sincerity, Bosavi people held a belief in the opacity of others' minds and, thus, the inability to understand another person's internal state. New Christian beliefs that valued expressing one's inner world in social interaction led to innovations in Bosavi grammar. Specifically, pastors translated Bible passages into Bosavi by using neologisms and expanding the functions of Bosavi evidentiality – an obligatory grammatical category that encodes the source of a speaker's evidence, such as visual witnessing or overhearing. By using evidential morphology to translate passages about others' thoughts and feelings, Bosavi pastors communicated the new Christian value of sincerity, while respecting the Bosavi discomfort with inferring another person's inner experience. These transformations to Bosavi communicative norms suggest that changing beliefs about morality influence the grammatical structures used in everyday talk.

Communicative routines for coordinating affective stance also build enduring expectations about the dispositions of individuals or groups. As Jaffe (2009) argued, affective stance does not only emerge in real-time interaction, but is also sustained across conversational contexts to create recognizable social identities. Metalanguage, or talk about language, is the key channel that links language structures to moral personhood and the typified affective stances associated with social groups.[2] Through metalanguage, speakers quote the words of others, evaluate the moral connotations of others' language use, and prompt one another to produce certain linguistic forms. Metalanguage thus serves as a bridge between the lived experience of shared emotion, the notions of morality that are built in but endure beyond real-time interactions, and the processes of differentiation that create boundaries between social groups.

"Our Children Are Wild": The Metalinguistic Production of Buddhist Morality and Social Difference in Xining

It was an early afternoon in mid-June 2017. I walked down a wide avenue in the northeastern corner of Xining, boxed in by the glossy windows of new high-rise developments that seemed to touch the peaks of the desert mountains behind them. Apart from the towering apartment buildings, this posh neighbourhood featured several multi-storey malls as well as a bustling strip of shops and restaurants. I reached an intersection where a replica Eiffel Tower came into view on my right-hand side. I turned towards it and approached the row of store fronts that stood behind. Most of the stores' thresholds were decorated with red banners, marking the auspicious beginnings of new business ventures. I spotted a sapphire door amid the sea of red banners – the entrance to a restaurant called Blue Barley (Ch. *qinghai lan qingke*), named after the staple grain of Tibetan diets (Tib. *rtsam pa*).

On this afternoon, the Blue Barley restaurant was hosting an English speech competition for Tibetan students in Xining. It was organized by a local, Tibetan-run non-profit that offered English classes in the evenings and on weekends. The students ranged in grade level from elementary school through college. Sonam's cousin Yeshi, who was in Grade 4, was participating in the competition. Sonam and his Ani Tsering Kyi had come to watch Yeshi. I had been invited to participate as a judge.

I grasped the door's golden, circular handle and pushed my way inside, noticing a wide staircase that rose above the ground floor restaurant to open onto a lofted library of Tibetan collections. As I passed through the entryway, I saw Ani Tsering Kyi, Yeshi, and Sonam seated at a booth near the kitchen. Ready for her performance, Yeshi wore a bright pink *chu pa*, or traditional Tibetan overcoat, tied with a thick sash.

I joined the table as the owner of the restaurant approached and graciously offered us tea and snacks. Ani Tsering Kyi and I began to sip sweet milk tea while Yeshi and Sonam snacked on salted popcorn, freshly spun in a stove-top popper. Ani Tsering Kyi and I began to discuss the schools in Xining, and I brought out my notebook to record her words.

Sonam would start preschool in September, and Ani Tsering Kyi was anticipating how the upcoming changes would affect him. She expressed concern that preschool would be too restrictive for Sonam. She explained that Sonam is very precocious, particularly in his language abilities, but is prone to intense emotional states, especially anger. Ani Tsering Kyi used the Tibetan term *sems chung*, meaning "small heart," to describe Sonam's personality. This term connotes a lack of control over the emotional states that move through the body and mind, as well as an underlying carefulness and sensitivity. Sonam's outbursts sometimes involved hitting his cousin Yeshi or his caregivers, which could cause him trouble in school. But, Ani Tsering Kyi added, even Yeshi had struggled in preschool.

"ŋa-tsʰo-kə ɕaji ʳgopo jin-nə-re" (Our children are wild), Ani Tsering Kyi asserted, *"ʳdʑa-ki ɕaji mə-ⁿdʐa"* (not like Chinese children).

Ani Tsering Kyi was characterizing the nature of Tibetan children on the basis of their emotional reactions and contrasting them with Chinese children. She continued speaking, recounting a time when Yeshi had been calling out excitedly in preschool. The teacher scolded her and told her to sit quietly. Ani Tsering Kyi explained that young Tibetan children cannot and should not sit quietly, since it goes against their wild nature.

"ʳdʑa-ki ɕaji ʳgopo min-nə-re-tsaŋ ʱɲəŋdʑi me-kə" (Chinese children are never wild, so they don't have compassion), Ani Tsering Kyi added. With this assertion, Ani Tsering Kyi seemed to imply that the wild traits associated with a "small heart" lead to compassion. She went on to explain that the teacher who told Yeshi to be quiet also had no compassion and did not have any knowledge about children. Chinese relationships, she explained, were not about compassion but instead about the expectation of material benefits (Ch. *guanxi*).[3]

Ani Tsering Kyi continued to rationalize the differences between Chinese and Tibetan children. She explained that, because Chinese children tend to grow up without siblings to play and fight with, they are more reserved and less likely to display their emotional states to others. With this statement about Chinese family structures, she implicitly referenced the one-child policy (Ch. *dusheng zinü zhengce*), which was implemented from 1979 to 2015 and limited each urban Chinese couple to a single child. Tibetan and other minoritized families were allowed two children until 2015, and three children after 2016. Despite these restrictions on family size, many Tibetan parents managed the birth policy by distributing additional children among extended family members.[4]

Ani Tsering Kyi then connected her discussion of family structures to urban Amdo Tibetan children's social isolation. Ani Tsering Kyi explained that, although urban children often live with cousins or siblings, they spend most days in their homes, with no playmates. Siblings or cousins are frequently busy with school, homework, or extracurricular activities, so young children play with toys like stuffed animals instead of each other. Ani Tsering Kyi stated that most children in Xining would prefer to play outside, but, unlike children living in villages, they have no freedom. Parents must supervise them due to safety concerns.

As Ani Tsering Kyi spoke, Yeshi began to pull at her sleeve. She had finished her popcorn and was eager to head upstairs to the library above the restaurant, where the competition would be held. Yeshi stood up and headed for the stairway, and Ani Tsering Kyi, Sonam, and I followed.

Ani Tsering Kyi described the role of emotion in child development, asserting that, as Tibetan children grow up, they undergo a transformation from experiencing emotional volatility, or wildness, to cultivating a stable demeanour of compassion. Ani Tsering Kyi's discussion recalled the Tibetan belief that, while an individual can shape their lived experience of emotion, all emotions have external origins. Tibetan medicine, for example, holds that emotions arise from the movement of substances within the body, in response to one's immediate physical and social environment (Adams 2001, 559). The conception of emotions as separate from the individual mind is also articulated in Tibetan grammar. Emotional states are described with the verb *lang*, meaning "to rise" or "to come upon," or, in Amdo Tibetan, with the direct evidential marker *-kə*, which indicates an involuntary experience.[5] Such links between Tibetan conceptions of emotion and theories of child development evoke Merleau-Ponty's (2010 [1945]) unification of sensation and perception into a "body schema," or "experience of [the] body in the world," that is structured through habitual experience (176). According to Merleau-Ponty, perception matures through the temporal accumulation of embodied experience, to eventually shape the categories that frame subjective interpretations of the external world (35, 189–90). This developmental perspective on perception highlights cultural variability in the experience of the body, an experience that is synthesized from perduring cultural beliefs and real-time human interactions.

The Tibetan belief that emotions enter into individual minds informs local notions of agency and responsibility related to child development, since the ability to control strong emotions represents a skill that children must learn over time. In fact, these understandings of emotional experience are rooted in the Buddhist theory of karma (Tib. *las*), or the cosmic results of human action. While conscious awareness is the natural endowment of all living beings (Tib. *sems can*), the outcomes of karma create additional mental factors, or states of mind that are either virtuous or non-virtuous (Dreyfus 2002, 39–40). Virtuous mental factors protect against the body's shifting emotional states. By allowing one to tame involuntary emotional states, virtuous mental factors support individual mental and physical health, and also promote collective well-being by preventing negative emotions from spreading beyond the individual (Lewis 2013, 329). That is, virtuous mental factors allow individuals to cultivate compassion as an underlying disposition, guarding against negative emotions and interpersonal conflicts (Ozawa-de Silva and Ozawa-de Silva 2011, 99). Ani Tsering Kyi suggested that the wild nature of Tibetan children like Sonam provides them with the opportunity to develop compassion as they progressively gain mastery over their inner emotional experiences.

Given the developmental importance of moving from wildness to compassion, Ani Tsering Kyi expressed anxiety about Sonam's entry into an urban preschool where Chinese teachers did not share Tibetan parents' understandings of children's emotions. Ani Tsering Kyi implied that, in addition to culturally specific notions about social responsibility that shape moral personhood, different kinship structures lend themselves to different trajectories of emotional development. Because Chinese children tended to grow up without siblings, she asserted, they did not develop the same forms of emotional expression as Tibetan children. She extended this observation about the effects of single childhood to urban Tibetan children. Ani Tsering Kyi suggested that scheduled educational activities and a lack of free play caused urban Tibetan children to miss opportunities for peer socialization, leading them to substitute toys for siblings and playmates. Ani Tsering Kyi thus used the concept of compassion to express anxiety about urban children's alienation from a Tibetan Buddhist collectivity, which is modelled in the kinship structures and peer relationships of the rural homeland.

Following Yeshi, Ani Tsering Kyi, and Sonam, I made my way up the staircase that winds above the Blue Barley restaurant's dining room to reach an expansive, single-level Tibetan library. While Sonam and Ani Tsering Kyi took their seats in the audience, Yeshi joined the group of contestants standing in front of the tallest pine bookshelves. The students were beginning to organize themselves into grade levels. Once the competition began, each student would take the stage and tell a personal story to an audience of parents and friends and would be evaluated within their grade category. I moved to the judges table, greeting the two other volunteers – one, the Tibetan organizer of the English-language school, and the other a North American graduate student like me.

Within several minutes, all the contestants had arrived. They walked up the staircase, before filing into the library in order from the oldest college students to the youngest school-aged children. As they settled onto the competition floor, the audience smiled and applauded. The first student in line, a young man, remained standing. The other students moved to a row of seats behind him, as the competition began.

"I am Tenzin from Yulshul," the young man said, indicating his origins in a region at the southwest margin of Qinghai Province. He continued, crafting a retrospective account of how he developed knowledge of compassion through his mother's guidance.

"When I was young, I loved to walk in clover meadows with my mother. When I saw clovers that were blooming, I would pick them. My mother told me that this made the clovers sad because they could not grow anymore. She told me that if I picked the clovers, they would stop growing. No more clovers! *snying rje* (compassion)! Thanks to my mother, I learned the importance of compassion. As a Buddhist, I now know that compassion is the most important human characteristic. For me, being Tibetan means showing compassion. *snying rje*."

As he uttered his last word, Tenzin bowed deeply, his hands held in prayer at his heart. The audience applauded.

When it came time for us judges to deliberate, we chose Tenzin's monologue for the first-place prize for college-aged students. Tenzin had spoken eloquently, with standard English grammar, which was the first evaluation criteria. He had also coherently organized his speech. He articulated a central message that was relevant to the audience of other Tibetan students and family members: his mother's gentle guidance allowed him to experience compassion for all sentient beings.

After the prizes were awarded, Tenzin stood proudly at the front of the room with the winners from each age group. The audience members descended the stairs to exit the building. No longer at the judge's table, I had caught up with Yeshi, Sonam, and Ani Tsering Kyi. As we approached the staircase, Sonam held his hands in a prayer position, faced Tenzin, and called out "*snying rje*." Yeshi, Ani Tsering Kyi, and I began to laugh. Rather than congratulating Tenzin for his prize, Sonam had expressed compassionate pity. Yeshi herded Sonam down the stairs, explaining "*ga-su-ɕu ze-nə-re*" (One says "Congratulations"). Sonam sauntered down the stairs, repeating "*ga-su-ɕu! ga-su-ɕu!*" with each step. As I descended the staircase, I pondered Tenzin's discourse on compassion.

Tenzin's monologue used metalanguage to offer a narrative representation of his socialization to experience and display compassion. By attributing to his mother his knowledge of how and when to express compassion, Tenzin echoed canonical Buddhist writings that locate the origins of compassion in a mother's care for her child. Tenzin had used the formulaic expression of compassion to animate his mother's response to the harm that could befall the clover. By quoting the term *snying rje*, Tenzin marked a narrative moment of revelation, when he realized how to avoid causing harm to other beings. He also modelled for the audience how to interactively display compassion, by ending his monologue with the formulaic expression accompanied by a gesture of prayer. Like Ani Tsering Kyi, Tenzin explicitly identified compassion with collective Buddhist morality. According to Tenzin, *being* Tibetan meant showing compassion.

Studies of caregiver-child interactions across cultures have shown that the forms of moral belonging explicitly articulated in metalanguage are re-instantiated in patterned linguistic resources that endure beyond immediate interactive settings. For example, Ayala Fader's (2006) analysis of family conversations in a Hasidic Jewish community in New York City showed that caregivers' religious beliefs influenced how they responded to children's questions. By emphasizing the divine power of the Torah, they modelled which questions could not be asked by members of their faith. Akira Takada (2013) demonstrated that the cultural value of *omoiyari* (empathy) shaped directive sequences in Japanese parent-child conversations. As young Japanese children gained communicative competence – the ability to use language structures in culturally meaningful ways – they learned to direct joint attention while expressing empathy. Adrienne Lo and Heidi Fung's (2014) analysis of shaming routines in Korean and Taiwanese communities showed how caregivers coordinated affect by evaluating children's behaviour. Even when positioning a child as a target of shame, caregivers displayed affective alignment with them. In everyday talk, local notions of morality thus co-constitute the language forms that frame shared emotional experiences.

Coordinating Compassion: Affective Stance in Real-Time Interaction

In Amdo families, the moral emphasis on compassion emerged in everyday talk as well as explicit metalanguage about Tibetan Buddhist identity. Amdo Tibetan children and adults displayed compassion through formulaic expressions in two discursive contexts. First, speakers offered the expression of compassion (Tib. *snying rje*) – *ʱɲəŋdʑi* or *ʱɲəŋmadʑi* in the *yul skad* – when witnessing or hearing about another's distress. These events of compassionate witnessing could be direct or hypothetical, such as predicting the potential results of human actions. Like Tenzin's mother, who pointed out that the clovers might stop growing if Tenzin continued to pick them, adults often invoked compassion to warn children of the harm they could cause to other beings. Second, speakers expressed interdependence by using the Tibetan terms *dgos* (to need) and *'dang* (to love and depend on). By employing formulaic expressions in these two contexts, families used the *yul skad* to align their emotional experiences in everyday conversation and to build enduring senses of Buddhist morality. As young Amdo children navigated relationships

Figure 8. Dawa and Dolma play outside following the New Year

with their peers and caregivers, they also linked the *yul skad* to these culturally valued affective displays.

It was April 2017 in Tsachen. Two months earlier, in early February, Dolma and her cousin Dawa had celebrated their sixth birthdays during *lo gsar*, the lunar new year (fig.8). According to the Western calendar, the children had turned six years old one month after *lo gsar* in March. In Tibetan communities, however, each new year of life is counted by the passage of the lunar calendar. Lhamo, who would not turn five until the following November, had celebrated her fifth birthday at *lo gsar*.

On that April afternoon, Dolma, Lhamo, and I had finished eating a lunch of rich *'then thug* (pulled noodles). We sat in the courtyard of Dolma and Lhamo's home, snacking on packaged nuts and candies left over from the grand supply we had gathered during the *lo gsar* celebrations. Cousin Dolkar and her mother, Ani Lhari, appeared at the gate on a motorbike.

Ani Lhari called Dolma and Lhamo's Ama to join her for a ride into town to purchase rice and vegetables. As Ani Lhari and Ama packed up several empty rice bags and boarded the motorbike, Dolkar disembarked. The women set off down the dusty alley, and Dolkar waved to them from the gate.

"*a ro!*" (Hey!), Dolkar suddenly turned back to face the courtyard and called to us. She giggled and then began to run up the alley, towards her own home. Dolma and Lhamo laughed and chased after her. I struggled to stand up quickly enough to follow and went jogging after them.

The children had already turned past the bend at the *ma ni khang* (temple) by the time I entered the alley. I rushed ahead, running by the *ma ni khang* and making my way to the row of four houses that stood behind. I spotted Dolma, Lhamo, and Dolkar in a patch of sand outside Dolkar's front gate. Dolkar's grandmother, Ayi Tsomo, sat on a stool and leaned her back against the gate. She held Dolkar's younger sister, Yangmo, on her lap.

"demo?" (Are you well?), I called to Ayi Tsomo with the common greeting heard across Amdo.

"demo demo" (Well, well), Ayi Tsomo responded, as Yangmo bounced gently on her knee.

I heard a sharp call from Lhamo and walked over to where the children were gathered.

Excerpt 3.1: "The Mother Ant Keeps Crying"[6]

"e:: e:: e::!" (Ah ah ah!), Lhamo called from the nearby sand patch.

"ɕaji xtɕik̚ ama xtɕik̚ e:! e:!" (There's one child and one mother. Hey, hey!), Lhamo added, pointing to the ground. As I approached, I saw that the children were focused on a swarm of tunneling ants. With her statement, Lhamo created a kin relationship between two of the ants. Dolma and Dolkar were also busy, crouched down and piling up sand to create small hills around the ants' tunnels. After finishing a sand pile, Dolma reached out with a plastic box and moved towards the pair of ants – one giant, one tiny – that Lhamo had pointed to. The two ants crawled over the lip of the box and entered inside.

"Dolma raŋ-ki ɕe-jak̚ⁿdi ma-ɕi!" (Dolma, you don't do like that!), Lhamo called out protectively. Lhamo then pointed to the box that Dolma held.

"tɕʰə re?" (What's this?), Lhamo added. Before anyone could answer, Lhamo moved towards Dolma, pointing to the ants that were now crawling around inside the box.

"ajə! de-a-ʰti" (Whoa! Keep looking!) Lhamo shouted, again drawing attention to the ants in the box. She inched closer to look inside.

"hə da ji mə-ʳgo-kə-ja" (Eh! Then, you don't need to do that), Dolma scolded. Both girls seemed to be trying to protect the ants from the other's attention.

"e e e" (Ah! Ah! Ah!), Lhamo called as she continued to lean towards the box.

"bətɕʰok̚ma ⁿdi bətɕʰok̚ma" (Here's an ant! An ant!), Lhamo added, pointing to each of the ants in turn.

"har-ra dɨk̚" (Move away), Dolma said, and gently elbowed Lhamo away from the box. Lhamo ignored Dolma and leaned closer.

"raŋ-ki ama de-a ʰti. ⁿdi min-na ⁿde tɕʰu ʰti" (You keep watching the mother. Isn't this [the mother]? There, you look!), Lhamo added. Lhamo seemed to be seeking confirmation from Dolma that the ants were, in

fact, a mother and child. Baby Yangmo whined from Ayi Tsomo's lap as Lhamo continued to talk.

"*e: e: ^{n}di min-nə-e-ra? tɕ^{h}u ^{h}ti.*" (Ah, ah! Isn't this it [the mother]? You look), Lhamo shouted over Yangmo's soft cries. Dolma ignored Lhamo. She crouched down next to Dolkar, now angling the plastic box towards the small sand mounds.

"*rema rema rema*" (Quickly, quickly, quickly!), Dolma said, seeming to urge the ants towards the ground.

"*bu re*" (It's a bug), I added, speaking over Dolma and circling back to Lhamo's rhetorical question.

"*e: e: e:! e::! bətɕ^{h}ok̚ma raŋ-ki de-a ^{h}ti*" (Hey, hey hey! Hey! You keep watching the ant), Lhamo directed Dolma. "*dʑok̚-ko-dʑik̚-la-go*" (It's the one we should put in [the box]), Lhamo added. Lhamo seemed to now be upset that the ants might leave the box.

"*ma-re*" (It's not), Dolma retorted, placing the box on the ground and standing back up.

"*ama! ama! ŋi, ŋi*" (My goodness! I, I –), Lhamo exclaimed. With Lhamo's escalating expression of aggravation, it seemed that the girls were beginning to argue. Ayi Tsomo sensed the mounting tension and interjected.

"*^{n}di ɕi-ra-ta bətɕ^{h}ok̚ma ama goŋmo joŋ-ŋe sipi naŋ-ŋa dzi-^{n}dʑo-nə-re*" (If you do this, the ant's mother will come in the night and go into your stomach), Ayi Tsomo warned. She was drawing attention to Dolma and Lhamo's aggressive stance towards each other. She was also suggesting that they might accidentally hurt the ants. If Dolma and Lhamo did not stop, Ayi Tsomo implied, the mother ant would seek revenge.

"*Ayi!*" Lhamo exclaimed, seeming startled at Ayi Tsomo's implication.

"*ŋe tɕ^{h}u **ba gei** -o*" (I'm giving [this] to you), Dolma quickly interjected, mixing a Mandarin verb into the *yul skad*. Dolma lifted the box off the ground and reached it towards Lhamo. Lhamo ignored Dolma's offering of the box. She looked down towards the ground, eyes fixed on the multitude of other ants moving up and over the sand mounds.

"*^{ɦ}ɲəŋmadʑi k^{h}ə-a!*" (Compassion to him!), Lhamo exclaimed in a high-pitched voice, pointing to a single ant that had moved away from the sand mound. When she uttered the formulaic expression of compassion, Lhamo elongated the final vowel and used an exaggerated pitch contour to communicate heightened affect.[7] Lhamo was displaying compassion for the ant and using prosody to express the intensity of her emotional experience. Lhamo was responding to Ayi Tsomo's warning by shifting the activity to discuss the ants' feelings and behaviours. Next, Dolma aligned with Lhamo's display of compassion, by elaborating on the ants' feeling states.

"*ama joŋmo xi-dep-da-de*" (The mother ant keeps crying), Dolma added. By personifying the mother ant, Dolma was providing evidence for the need to express compassion towards it. She was aligning with Lhamo's affective stance.

"*^{ɦ}ɲəŋmadʑi! bətɕ^{h}ok̚ma t^{h}ok-t^{h}ok-ki ^{n}də.gə*" (Compassion! This is exactly an ant. Like this), Lhamo added. She crouched next to Dolma and pointed inside the box that Dolma held. Lhamo was repeating the formulaic expression of compassion, now with reference to a different ant.

"*k^{h}ər-ki ama ts^{h}el-kə-joŋ-t^{h}a*" (His mother came to look for him), Dolma suggested. Dolma was drawing on Lhamo's display of compassion and explaining the behaviours of the ants with personification.

"*^{n}di? ama? ə? ə?*" (This one? The mother? Uh? Uh?), Lhamo asked, pointing to the large ant inside the box. Dolma did not respond, but placed the box on the ground next to Dolkar. The two ants crawled back over the edge of the box and joined the others in the sand.

"*ajo ajo ajo!*" Dolkar shouted, waving her arms up and down and introducing sound play into the activity sequence.

"*ma-xi-ki*" (It hasn't died), Lhamo said in a low, growling voice, commenting on the ants that had now left the box.

"*moja moja! i:: i::*" Dolkar shouted, continuing to use sound play and wave her arms. Dolma and Lhamo did not take up Dolkar's sound play. Instead, they tried to draw her back into their ongoing activity with the ants. Dolma picked up the box again and moved it towards Dolkar.

"*Dolkar ama ^{n}di naŋ-ŋa ɸdʑok̚-taŋ*" (Dolkar, put the mother in here), Dolma directed. Dolma was suggesting that they find the largest ant and, once again, place it inside the box.

Lhamo immediately interjected, "*e! ma-ji. k^{h}ər-ki ama ^{n}də ^{n}də*" (Hey! Don't. It's his mother, there, there). She pointed to the largest ant crawling up and over the sandhills that Dolma and Dolkar had created. With this directive, Lhamo seemed to be protecting the ants from any potential harm that could come if the children continued to handle them. By naming the mother ant, Lhamo was also recontextualizing Ayi Tsomo's earlier warning that she would seek revenge if her children were harmed.

Dolma dropped the box once again and began to wave her arms, joining in Dolkar's sound play. For the next twenty minutes, the children continued to play in the sand, but they avoided touching or handling the ants.

In the sequential unfolding of their play with the ants, Dolma, Lhamo, and Dolkar coordinated an affective stance of compassion with formulaic language and commentary about the ants' motivations, behaviours, and feelings. By calling out and personifying the ants as a mother and child, Lhamo constituted the ants as a focal point of joint attention. Dolma and Lhamo then issued competing directives to one another, each attempting to shape the trajectory of the unfolding activity. In addition to offering directives, Dolma and Lhamo used exclamations to halt each other's undesired actions. Lhamo's negative affect became particularly exaggerated when she and Dolma argued about how to move the ants into and out of the plastic box.

In response to the children's argumentation, Ayi Tsomo formulated a hypothetical threat: if the children continued to treat the ants and each other this way, the ant's mother would come in the night and enter their stomachs.[8] Ayi Tsomo was predicting the harm to the ants that could result from the children's negative emotional state and suggesting that the mother ant might seek revenge if they inadvertently caused harm to her babies.

In response to Ayi Tsomo's warning, the children shifted their expressions of emotion. Over several turns, they coordinated an affective stance that explicitly displayed compassion. Lhamo initiated this shift by using the formulaic expression of compassion, saying "*ʱɲəŋmadʑi:: kʰə-a*" (Compassion to him). Next, Dolma aligned with Lhamo's affective stance by personifying the ants and describing their emotions and intentions. Lhamo then repeated her formulaic expression of compassion. Finally, Lhamo and Dolma attempted to monitor each other's actions to avoid any harm to the ants. By making reference to Ayi Tsomo's warning that the mother ant might seek revenge, Lhamo directed Dolma and Dolkar to stop handling the ants. Eventually, the children's joint attention moved away from the ants, when Dolma joined in Dolkar's sound play. As the children aligned their affective stance, they solidified a mutual responsibility to express compassion and avoid harm.

Attachment Theory in Cross-Cultural Perspective

While affective stance unfolds in an immediate interactive setting, patterns of verbal interaction also link the social experience of emotion to children's foundational interpersonal attachments. The interplay between affect and relationality in young children's lives has been most thoroughly examined through attachment theory, a psychological paradigm that attends to the emotional states that humans experience throughout social separation and reunification. Developed from experimental research on toddlers' responses to separation from and reunification with their mothers, the Western psychological theory of attachment asserts that children who experience emotional alignment with their primary caregiver build a secure view of the social world (Ainsworth and Bowlby 1991; Ainsworth et al. 2015; Bowlby 1983). Through ethnographic research, anthropologists have critiqued psychologists' assertion that a model of dyadic alignment with a single primary caregiver fosters secure attachment (Allen 2008, 424), instead noting significant cultural variation in how children use affective displays to build interpersonal safety.[9]

More specifically, anthropologists have suggested that local beliefs about interdependence and independence shape verbal interaction as well as the resulting emotional experiences that give rise to attachment patterns (Morelli 2015, 154). For example, Bambi Chapin's (2014) examination of the social lives of Sri Lankan toddlers found that age-based hierarchy influenced their attachment behaviours. In rural Sri Lankan families, higher-status adults were expected to anticipate children's needs and provide for them. Children, as lower-status persons, were expected to be passive receivers of care (71–4). Based on their anticipation of unsolicited care from adults, young children built secure attachments with elders outside of their homes, even in the absence of overt affective alignment. Similarly, Patricia Clancy's examination of mother-infant interactions in Tokyo highlighted how the Japanese concept of *amae*, or dependence on higher-status individuals, was reflected in unfolding affective displays (1986, 217). When toddlers expressed emotions that did not correspond with those of co-present adults, mothers labelled them as "fearful" or "scary" (237). Through such verbal evaluation, Japanese caregivers trained children to conform to elders' expectations about emotional expression. Ethnographic research has therefore demonstrated that diverse models of relationality shape children's emotional worlds, as well as their coordination of affective displays with their caregivers.

In conversation with Merleau-Ponty's phenomenology, culturally specific forms of attachment appear to co-constitute personhood through the synthesis of perception, intersubjective engagement, and habitual action. As Merleau-Ponty asserted, our understandings of the world are "inseparable from subjectivity and intersubjectivity, which establish their unity through the taking up of my past experiences into my present experiences, or of another person's experience into my own" (2010 [1945], 20). That is, any present form of being arises from the integration of experience across time and through interpersonal interaction. Tibetan Buddhist conceptions of personhood similarly emphasize the temporal endurance of intersubjective attunement. In the course of reincarnation, the mental factors created by karma shape the circumstances of our birth, including which mother we are born to. In line with this understanding of reincarnation, displays of compassion directly influence kin relationships, because compassion can increase spiritual merit, leading to more desired incarnations in future lifecycles. Given that caregivers exemplify compassion to their children, the kin relationships in one's present lifetime help to determine the spiritual merits that one can accumulate.

Enacting Compassion in Adult-Child Interactions

In Amdo Tibetan families, formulaic language highlights this connection of compassion to relationality, because expressions of compassion are accompanied by statements about love and interdependence. In rural Tsachen, children's formulaic expressions of compassion were highly dialogic, emerging in the course of free play. In urban Xining, in contrast, adults more explicitly scaffolded young children's displays of compassion. They did so by elaborately discussing the effects of children's behaviour and using prompting questions to elicit children's verbal expressions of compassion. Urban adults not only reflected on the potential harm that could result from children's actions but also commented on the immediate social consequences of children's behaviours. To help children repair and maintain their relationships, adults encouraged children to make declarations of love and interdependence in addition to using the formulaic expression of compassion (Tib. *snying rje*). Specifically, adults prompted children to produce the Amdo terms *go* (Tib. *dgos*), meaning to need or depend on another, and *daŋ* (Tib. *'dang*), meaning to have mutual love and respect for another.

In late October 2016, exactly one week after Sonam's second birthday, I was visiting Sonam's family. The chill that would descend on the plateau in winter had begun to creep over Xining's streets. Ayi Lhamo and I stayed warm on the couch inside the family's living room, while Sonam sat against the far wall on a cushion, snuggled with several stuffed animals. Aphu Lhundhup, Apha, and Ama had left shortly after I arrived. They had gone to perform *skor ba*, or circumambulation, at a shrine nearby the Tibetan medical clinic. After they had departed, calling out the Amdo farewell *tshe ring lo brgya* (long life, one hundred years), Ani Tsering Kyi went into the kitchen to make tea. A few minutes later, she returned from the kitchen and entered the living room, carrying a tray of mugs filled with clear green tea. She placed the tray on the coffee table in front of Ayi Lhamo and me. As Ayi Lhamo and I each grasped a mug and began to sip, Ani Tsering Kyi sat down on a cushion and poured some tea for herself.

As we adults enjoyed the steaming tea, Yeshi came out of her bedroom, carrying a clipboard with several coloured pencils affixed to the top. She sat down next to Sonam against the far wall, and settled in to draw. She picked up three coloured pencils in her right hand, and adeptly mixed the colours together as she moved her hand across the page. As she drew, Sonam stood up and began to spin around in circles. Losing his balance, Sonam plummeted to the cushioned floor below. Yeshi looked up from her clipboard and turned towards him. Sonam then approached Yeshi. He roughly pulled a lock of hair out of one of the braids near her temple. Yeshi whimpered softly, which caught the attention of Ani Tsering Kyi and Ayi Lhamo.

Excerpt 3.2: "You Don't Need Achi"[10]

"*Sonam tɕʰo atɕʰi-kə ʂtɕa tʰen-toŋ-ne Sonam-kə*" (Sonam, you pulled Achi's hair, Sonam did), Ani Tsering Kyi stated as she looked sharply at Sonam. Ani Tsering Kyi was reporting Sonam's negative behaviour to him. Sonam let go of Yeshi's hair, and Yeshi rubbed her temple.

"*hə hə*" (Uh-huh), Sonam grunted. Although Sonam offered a backchannel cue (Goffman 1981, 12) that indicated his active participation, he seemed emotionally unaffected.

"*ama!*" (My goodness!), Ayi Lhamo called, expressing surprise at Sonam's lack of remorse. Ani Tsering Kyi latched onto Ayi Lhamo's exclamation. She was probing further in an attempt to provoke a fuller response from Sonam.

"*atɕʰi mə-ʳgo-ni? awu atɕʰi mə-ʳgo-ni?*" (Don't need Achi? Awu doesn't need Achi?), Ani Tsering Kyi asked. With these rhetorical questions, Ani Tsering Kyi used the formulaic term for interdependence to suggest that Sonam had violated his relationship with Yeshi. Brothers and sisters need one another, and Sonam was acting as if he did not need Yeshi.

"*hə hə*" (Uh-huh), Sonam intoned.

"*mə-ʳgo?*" (Don't need?), Ani Tsering Kyi asked, confirming the meaning of Sonam's backchannel cue. Without waiting for a response, Ani Tsering Kyi turned to Yeshi.

"*na atɕʰi ani-sa tʰur-ra-toŋ-a*" (Achi, follow me then), Ani Tsering Kyi directed Yeshi. Yeshi moved next to Ani Tsering Kyi, as Ani Tsering Kyi stood up from her seat on the floor.

"*hə hə*" (Uh-huh), Sonam repeated, seemingly unaffected by Tsering Kyi's direction to Yeshi.

"*o: na?*" (Oh well?), Ayi Lhamo asked Sonam. Ayi Lhamo was drawing attention to Sonam's unaffected response to Ani Tsering Kyi's actions.

Ani Tsering Kyi then escalated her attempts to draw Sonam into affective alignment. She began to physically choreograph Sonam's separation from Yeshi. Ani Tsering Kyi was creating an exaggerated display of the results of Sonam's action: Yeshi was being excluded.

"atɕ^{h}i ani-kə ^{n}dʑo-kə-dʑak̚-kə-taŋ-ŋa" (Ani made Achi leave), Ani Tsering Kyi asserted, as she turned away from Sonam. Ani Tsering Kyi and Yeshi made their way towards the apartment door.

"o.ta k^{h}e-a atɕ^{h}i me-la" (Well then, it seems he has no Achi), Ayi Lhamo announced. Ayi Lhamo was explicating the negative consequence of Sonam's action. According to Ayi Lhamo, Sonam had caused Yeshi to leave. It was as if Sonam no longer had his Achi.

"'atɕ^{h}i baɪ-baɪ atɕ^{h}i baɪ-baɪ' ze ^{n}dʑo-kə-dʑak̚-kə-toŋ" (Say "Bye-bye Achi! Bye-bye Achi" to make her leave), Ani Tsering Kyi added from the doorway. Ani Tsering Kyi and Ayi Lhamo were collaborating to show Sonam that he had alienated Yeshi from their interdependent relationship.

"hə hə" (Uh-huh), Sonam grunted again.

"atɕ^{h}i mə-^{r}go" ([You] don't need Achi), Ani Tsering Kyi stated. Again, she used the formulaic expression of interdependence. She hesitated, waiting to see if Sonam would dispute her statement.

"mm" (Mm hmm), Sonam added softly. Instead of contradicting Ani Tsering Kyi's assertion, he was remaining complacent in the face of Yeshi's imminent departure. Sonam's dispreferred second led Ani Tsering Kyi to advance her activity of excluding Yeshi.

"ja ja ŋi atɕ^{h}i Yeshi ^{n}dʑo-kə-dʑak̚-kə-taŋ-ŋa" (Okay, then, I made Achi Yeshi leave), Ani Tsering Kyi asserted. *"ani ra atɕ^{h}i ɣɲikə ^{n}dʑo-kə-dʑak̚-kə-taŋ-ŋa"* (Both Ani and Achi left), Ani Tsering Kyi added. She put her hand on Yeshi's back and reached over her shoulder to open the apartment door.

"hə hə" (Uh-huh), Sonam grunted, staring back at them blankly from his position against the living room wall. Ani Tsering Kyi would not end the conversation until Sonam displayed affective alignment in response to Yeshi's unfolding departure.

"na ani e-^{r}go" (Then, do you need Ani?), Ani Tsering Kyi asked. This statement provoked an emotional reaction from Sonam.

"go-a" ([I] need!), Sonam exclaimed, expressing his attachment to Ani Tsering Kyi. He had finally given a preferred second to Ani Tsering Kyi's question, by using the formulaic expression of interdependence.

"go-a?" ([You] need?), Ani Tsering Kyi repeated, using format tying, or the repetition of an earlier language form with modification, to transform Sonam's prior turn into a confirmation-seeking question. By animating (Goffman 1981, 144–5) Sonam's prior utterance with rising intonation, Ani Tsering Kyi suggested that Sonam's expression of interdependence was not fully sincere.

"^{n}di mə-^{r}go" ([I] don't need her), Sonam added, pointing to Yeshi and confirming the implication of Ani Tsering Kyi's question. By using format tying to negate his previous turn, Sonam employed the

formulaic expression of interdependence to verbally exclude Yeshi. Ani Tsering Kyi immediately responded, latching on to Sonam's assertion.

"*ja na atɕ^{h}i go-ne-soŋ*" (Okay, then, Achi, go outside), Ani Tsering Kyi directed Yeshi, while staring at Sonam. She grasped Yeshi's shoulder and gently turned to face her.

"*atɕ^{h}i xok̚ awu-kə tɕ^{h}u mə-^{r}go ze-kə*" (Achi, come. Awu says he doesn't need you), Ani Tsering Kyi said to Yeshi. Ani Tsering Kyi then gently pushed Yeshi out of the apartment door and closed it behind her.

As the door shut, Ayi Lhamo gasped. The display of Yeshi's exclusion had come to a point of culmination. Ayi Lhamo hurriedly directed Sonam to respond.

"*'e-go-a?' ze-kə-ja rema 'go-a' ze*" (She's saying "Do you need me?" Okay, quickly say, "I need you!"), Ayi Lhamo added passionately. Ayi Lhamo seemed to be pleading for Sonam to express his attachment to Yeshi, directing him to respond with the formulaic expression of interdependence. When Sonam did not respond, Ani Tsering Kyi interjected.

"*atɕ^{h}i ^{n}dʑo-soŋ*" (Achi left), Ani Tsering Kyi stated flatly. Now, Sonam gasped, looking up slightly askance.

"***shenme! shenme ! shenme !***" (What! What! What!), Sonam called out in Mandarin. Sonam's affective stance had changed from complacent to flustered.

"*awu 'baɪ-baɪ' ze-toŋ-ja atɕ^{h}i*" (Awu, say "bye-bye" to Achi), Ani Tsering Kyi repeated. Ani Tsering Kyi did not change her own affective stance in response to Sonam's discomfort. Her tone remained flat and assertive.

"***shenme?***" (What?), Sonam repeated, more quietly.

"*'ma-^{n}dʑo' ze-toŋ-ja rema*" (Quickly, say "Don't go!"), Ayi Lhamo instructed. She was modelling for Sonam how to respond to Ani Tsering Kyi and Yeshi. Ayi Lhamo was suggesting that, instead of asking "what?" in Mandarin, Sonam should tell Yeshi not to leave. Sonam did not follow Ayi Lhamo's suggestion.

"***shenme***" (What), Sonam repeated flatly.

"*'daŋ tɕ^{h}e' ze-toŋ-ja rema*" (Quickly, say "I love you!"), Ayi Lhamo added, instructing Sonam to use the Amdo term *daŋ* (Tib. *'dang*) that denotes an emotional experience of love as well as a social experience of interdependence. With vowel elongation, Ayi Lhamo used prosody to mark a heightened affective state.

"***shenme***" (What), Sonam once again repeated flatly. Sonam had offered a dispreferred second to Ayi Lhamo's modelling of the formulaic expression of love. Ayi Lhamo exhaled and giggled softly at Sonam's reticence.

*"'**shenme**' ze-zək"* (You said "what"), Ayi Lhamo added, quoting back Sonam's dispreferred second. Sonam stood up and began to walk in circles.

*"**shenme**"* (What), Sonam repeated one last time. He continued to turn in circles, and pointed his hands up towards the ceiling. Ten seconds later, he was walking towards the apartment door.

"awu-kə atɕʰi Yeshi ʰta-kə-ⁿdʑo" (Awu's going to see Achi Yeshi), Sonam announced. Although Sonam had not performed the formulaic expressions of love or interdependence that Ayi Lhamo had suggested, he was now showing concern for his separation from Yeshi. He was announcing that he was going to find her.

"ai::" (Aww), Ayi Lhamo cooed, displaying her satisfaction with Sonam's shift to orient towards Yeshi.

"a:: atɕʰi raŋ-ki naŋ-ŋa xok̚jaŋ awu-kə go-ze" (Ah, Achi, bring yourself inside! Again, Awu's saying he needs you), Ani Tsering Kyi added. Ani Tsering Kyi interpreted Sonam's move towards the door as a declaration of attachment. She recreated Sonam's action as quoted speech, using the formulaic expression of interdependence.

Yeshi cracked open the door and, laughing softly, came back inside the apartment. Ayi Lhamo, Ani Tsering Kyi, and I also giggled as Sonam bounded over to Yeshi and gave her a hug.

Ani Tsering Kyi and Ayi Lhamo managed Sonam and Yeshi's relationship through Tibetan understandings of affect and attachment. Like Ayi Tsomo, who warned Dolma and Lhamo about the potential harm of their actions, Ani Tsering Kyi initiated the activity sequence by describing how Sonam had hurt Yeshi. Ani Tsering Kyi then performatively excluded Yeshi from the social situation. Ayi Lhamo, Ani Tsering Kyi, and Yeshi collaborated to pretend that Yeshi was leaving and physically moved her out of the apartment. When Sonam did not display the expected response to Yeshi's departure, Ayi Lhamo modelled for him how to verbally express love and interdependence. Sonam first offered backchannel cues, which served as dispreferred seconds, in contrast to the formulaic expressions that Ayi Lhamo was prompting him to produce. When Ani Tsering Kyi asserted that Yeshi had "left," however, Sonam advanced the activity sequence by expressing bewilderment. He repeated "what?" in Mandarin. Ayi Lhamo continued to model for Sonam the formulaic expressions of love and interdependence he was expected to offer. When Sonam moved towards the door to find Yeshi, Ani Tsering Kyi and Ayi Lhamo interpreted his response as affective alignment. Although Sonam had stated that he was "going to see" Yeshi, Ani Tsering Kyi quoted Sonam's words with the formulaic expression of interdependence and directed Yeshi to come back inside to reunite with Sonam. Sonam punctuated the activity sequence by using a hug to repair his relationship with Yeshi.[11]

In their performative exclusion of Yeshi, Ani Tsering Kyi and Ayi Lhamo used metalanguage, especially quoted speech, to shape Sonam's verbal behaviour and respond to his unfolding affective displays. Both Ani Tsering Kyi and Ayi Lhamo explicitly directed Sonam to say that he needed (Tib. *dgos*) and loved (Tib. *'dang*) Yeshi, modelling how to use formulaic language for social reconciliation. When Sonam offered dispreferred seconds, in the form of backchannel cues or inversions of formulaic language, asserting that he did *not* need Yeshi, Ani Tsering Kyi and Ayi Lhamo used metalanguage to assess Sonam's actions as antisocial. Specifically, Ani Tsering Kyi quoted his speech to Yeshi, providing the rationale for her exclusion. When Sonam finally expressed affective alignment with Yeshi's departure, Ani Tsering Kyi and Ayi Lhamo again used quoted speech to positively evaluate Sonam's action. By coordinating the alignment of affective stance through quoted speech, Ani Tsering Kyi and Ayi Lhamo exemplified the role of the *yul skad*'s formulaic language in establishing relationships of love and interdependence. As the shared activity progressed, Ani Tsering Kyi sequenced touch along with formulaic language to strengthen Sonam's attachment to his family members.

A short while after Yeshi had come back inside the apartment, she picked up the clipboard she had left against the wall and retreated to her bedroom. Ayi Lhamo and I were on the couch, still sipping our fragrant green tea. Ani Tsering Kyi was sitting atop a cushion on the floor, on the opposite side of the coffee table. Sonam walked over to her, and she pulled him into her lap. Ani Tsering Kyi began to elicit statements of love and interdependence from Sonam.

Excerpt 3.3: "How Much Do You Love Me?"[12]

"ja na tɕʰo ani daŋ-e-tɕʰe?" (So, then, do you love Ani a lot?), Ani Tsering Kyi asked, gently stroking Sonam's hair.

"tɕʰe" (A lot), Sonam responded, offering a preferred second to Ani Tsering Kyi's question.

"daŋ tɕʰe tɕi.mo.zək̚ daŋ tɕʰe?" (A lot. How much do you love [me]?), Ani Tsering Kyi asked. She was prompting Sonam to intensify his expression of affection.

"apʰa daŋ tɕʰe" ([I] love Apha a lot), Sonam responded. He did not directly answer Ani Tsering Kyi's question. Instead, he expressed love for his Apha, rather than Ani. With this statement, Sonam demonstrated mastery over this formulaic expression. Rather than simply repeating

the structure of Ani Tsering Kyi's question, he reconfigured the formulaic expression with a new referent.

"*apʰa daŋ tɕʰe?*" ([You] love Apha a lot?), Ani Tsering Kyi asked, recycling Sonam's last turn as a rhetorical question.

"*ama daŋ tɕʰe*" ([I] love Ama a lot), Sonam added with a smile. Rather than reasserting his love for Ani, he creatively extended Ani Tsering Kyi's prior use of the formulaic expression of love.

"*ama ra daŋ tɕʰe? ani daŋ tɕʰe-a?*" ([You] also love Ama a lot? Do [you] love Ani a lot?), Ani Tsering Kyi said with a smile, using format tying to craft Sonam's turn into a confirmation-seeking question, and then appealing to Sonam to reassert his love for her.

"*apʰa daŋ tɕʰe ama daŋ tɕʰe aji daŋ tɕʰe*" ([I] love Apha a lot, [I] love Ama a lot, [I] love Ayi a lot), Sonam added, repeating each family member's kin term in a single breath. Sonam had given a dispreferred second to Ani Tsering Kyi's question in the prior turn, because he had not proclaimed his love for her.

"*aji daŋ mə-tɕʰe apʰa daŋ mə-tɕʰe ama daŋ mə-tɕʰe*" ([You] don't love Ayi a lot, [you] don't love Apha a lot, [you] don't love Ama a lot), Ani Tsering Kyi contradicted, using format tying to invert the meaning of Sonam's prior utterance.

"*ani tɕik̚.ko daŋ tɕʰe-a*" ([You] refuse to love Ani), Ani Tsering Kyi added.[13] With this statement, Ani Tsering Kyi clarified why she had contradicted Sonam's previous declarations of love for his family members: Sonam was excluding her from his expressions of affection. Ani Tsering Kyi's tone remained playful, and she smiled as she spoke. Then, Ani Tsering Kyi directed Sonam to hug her, using touch to heighten his display of affective alignment.

"*na rema ani uba-ɕe*" (Then, quickly, hug Ani), Ani Tsering Kyi instructed. "*ʰkepa zək̚ xtɕik̚ doŋ-ŋa-toŋ uba-ɕe. lokwa ɣɲi-kə uba-ɕe-taŋ*" (Give one hug around the neck. Hug with both your hands), Ani Tsering Kyi elaborated. Sonam complied, turning in Ani Tsering Kyi's lap and stringing his arms around her neck.

"*ama ama tɕʰo da xtɕik̚ ɲen-kə-a-ze*" (Wow, wow! You are certainly such a good boy), Ani Tsering Kyi exclaimed. She was expressing approval at Sonam's display of affection for her and his family members.

Ani Tsering Kyi then elaborated on her assessment of Sonam. "*tɕʰo da raŋ-ŋa xtɕik̚ ma-re jin-na*" ([Before] you weren't yourself, right?), Ani Tsering Kyi asked. She was referring to Sonam's previous action of pulling Yeshi's hair, stating that Sonam had behaved out of character. "*Sonam ^{n}di.^{n}dẓa xtɕik̚ ɲen-go*" (Sonam is good like this), she added, praising Sonam's display of love for his family members and defining his expressions of love as an inherent part of his character.

Sonam climbed out of Ani Tsering Kyi's lap and wandered to turn on the television. Sonam's favourite cartoon, *Da Xiong Er Xiong* (Big Bear and Baby Bear), appeared on the screen. Sonam jumped up and down with excitement, and we adults burst into laughter to see his glee. As I watched Sonam's expression of joy, I thought about the connections between the coordination of affective alignment in real-time interaction, the production of enduring kin relationships, and the interface between Buddhist philosophies and social attachment.

Following Sonam's reconciliation with Yeshi, Ani Tsering Kyi initiated a new activity sequence to scaffold Sonam's formulaic displays of love. She sought to realign Sonam's affective displays with an underlying, moral personhood. Ani Tsering Kyi used prompting questions to elicit expressions of love and interdependence. With format tying, Sonam and Ani Tsering Kyi playfully negotiated the target of Sonam's expressions of love. When Sonam declared his love for his family members other than Ani Tsering Kyi, she used interpersonal touch to further prompt an appropriate affective display. Following her directive to Sonam to hug her, Ani Tsering Kyi explicitly assessed Sonam's affective stance in relation to his character. She stated that Sonam was not acting "as himself" when he pulled Yeshi's hair, and she characterized Sonam as essentially good on the basis of his declarations of love for his family members. Ani Tsering Kyi used formulaic expressions in the *yul skad* not only to help Sonam display affective alignment in an immediate interactive setting but also to affirm his moral personhood through his family relationships.

Conclusion: Revealing Compassion through Formulaic Language

This chapter has shown that understandings of compassion undergird beliefs about child development, moral personhood, and relationality in Amdo Tibetan families. Echoing canonical Buddhist writings, Amdo Tibetan adults described children's developmental process of moving from emotional volatility to cultivating compassion. By locating the foundation of this process in the relationship between a child and their mother, Amdo Tibetan adults drew on Buddhist theories of mental states and reincarnation to rationalize the formation of secure social attachments. In addition to supporting individual and collective well-being, experiences of compassion functioned as a marker of moral personhood, grounding an individual in interdependent kin relationships and in a Buddhist collectivity.

Metalanguage linked affective displays of compassion to Tibetan Buddhist identity and mediated the functions of formulaic language in real-time interaction. Through explicit discourse, adults defined Tibetan Buddhist identity through emotional dispositions and affective displays. In the English speech competition, for example, college student Tenzin had recalled learning to express compassion from his mother, and, before the English speech competition began, Ani Tsering Kyi had essentialized Tibetan identities with reference to children's development of compassion out of wildness. This essentialization of affect marked difference as well as belonging, typifying non-Buddhist Chinese identities as lacking in compassion. In real-time interactions, formulaic language co-constituted the ties of affect to identity. Caregivers used prompting questions to help young children use formulaic language, and children creatively repeated or inverted these expressions to show affective alignment or disalignment. Children also introduced these formulaic expressions into activity sequences with peers, shaping their unfolding trajectories of shared play and repairing ruptured kin relationships following everyday transgressions. Because compassion is performed in the medium of the *yul skad*, formulaic language connected the *yul skad* itself to Buddhist morality.

Although this moral socialization through formulaic language linked the *yul skad* to children's shared experiences of emotion in both rural and urban families, adults recognized that urban children continue to face challenges in sustaining cultural and linguistic continuity. Adults explained that, like Chinese children, urban Amdo Tibetan children were isolated from their peers and lacked the security of strong social bonds to their siblings and cousins. They also expressed anxiety about Amdo Tibetan children's entry into Chinese public schools, where teachers did not recognize children's need to experience emotional reactivity in order to develop compassion. Chapter 4 further examines the limits of Amdo Tibetan children's belonging in Xining, as they grapple with the opportunities and losses associated with education policy.

Chapter 4

Learning Standard Language Ideologies: Education Policy and Colonial Alienation between the Homeland and the City

བོད་པ་ཚོ་བོད་ཡིག་སྦྱོང་།
All Tibetan people, study written Tibetan!

Amdo Tibetan song

Situated at the historical boundary between imperial Tibet and China, Xining remains a centre of Tibetan cultural production and religious education. The great Kumbum monastery, founded by a disciple of the Tibetan Buddhist master Tsongkhapa in the sixteenth century, rises onto a mountain slope thirty kilometres south of the city. Since the 1980s, doctors, artists, and scholars have built a vibrant intellectual community within Xining. Xining is home to three universities, two of which offer degree programs in Tibetan. Young adults and families from across Amdo move to Xining to access higher education, seek medical care from the *sman pa* (doctors) at Xining's Tibetan hospital, and enjoy Tibetan restaurants, artisan shops, and bookstores. With these centralized amenities, Amdo Tibetan inhabitants of Xining can access a wider range of culturally relevant services, arts, and cultural products than in their rural homelands.

However, while Tibetans maintain a vibrant presence in Xining, they must navigate a key tension between the resourcing of the city and constraints on urban Tibetan-language vitality. While Tibetan autonomous prefectures, and Hui, Tu, and Salar autonomous counties, surround Xining, the city itself does not have any autonomous status. Because minoritized nationalities in Xining do not enjoy allowances for the use and development of their languages in education or governance, Tibetan children born and raised in Xining cannot access formal Tibetan-medium education. While urban children mostly abandon the *yul skad* for Mandarin after beginning preschool, they also tend to experience more socio-economic mobility than their rural peers, and they graduate high school with access to a wider range of options for postsecondary study in Mandarin. With the relegation of Tibetan-medium education to the rural homeland, and Tibetans' increasing access to urban schooling in Mandarin, education policy has contributed to language shift. In response to the effects of education and urbanization on language shift, Amdo scholars and religious leaders have engaged in fervent discussions about the codification and objectification of the Tibetan language. These intellectual debates, and parents' associated concerns over linguistic assimilation, have contributed to the rise of a standard language ideology that emphasizes a single, correct way of speaking.[1]

In this chapter, I chart the development and consequences of a community-wide standard language ideology that privileges knowledge of literary Tibetan over diverse *yul skad*, positions Amdo Nomad Talk as a prestige variety, and devalorizes code-mixing, or the use of multiple languages in a single context of speaking. I demonstrate that this standard language ideology both arises from and contributes to "colonial alienation," an experience common to communities faced with perduring colonial domination that dissociates the mother tongue from cultural practices and intimate social relationships (Thiong'o 1986, 15). In Amdo, colonial alienation leads children to identify as monolingual rather than multilingual speakers, preventing both rural and urban children from using their full linguistic repertoires and encouraging urban children to shift to Mandarin. To contextualize how this standard language ideology is shaping urban Amdo Tibetan children's trajectories of language shift, I analyse state language policies that have identified entire ethnolinguistic groups with fixed territories and single writing systems. I demonstrate that resulting education policies have intersected with Tibetan intellectuals' rising interest in language standardization to impede rather than support children's multilingualism.

Families instantiate this standard language ideology in everyday talk. Adults praise children for performing allegiance to a literary standard, encourage children to adopt features of Nomad Talk, and characterize Farmer Talk's diverse *yul skad* – including their own mother tongue – as impure and inauthentic. These negative attributions target structural adaptations in the *yul skad* that have resulted from language contact with non-Tibetan communities, and they contribute to a related preference against code-mixing, or the use of multiple languages in a single context of speaking. By examining the effects of this standard language ideology on everyday talk, I show how Amdo Tibetan adults and children shame one another for code-mixing. These shaming practices position children as the agents of language loss and perpetuate colonial alienation from meaningful histories of linguistic hybridity. In the absence of a kin-based peer group, urban children adopt negative attitudes towards the *yul skad* as well as towards code-mixing, and identify as monolingual speakers of Mandarin in line with the state's ideal urban citizen.

Territory, Education Policy, and Colonial Alienation

Linguistic anthropologists have theorized that history shapes how a community defines its standard language.[2] In Amdo, the history of state language policies informs current provincial education practices by mapping language rights and opportunities for socio-economic mobility onto opposing rural and urban territories. Following scholars who define the Chinese state's post-1949 administration of Tibet as an example of settler colonization, I approach these language and education policies as part of a broader goal for territorial dispossession and cultural assimilation (McGranahan 2019, 518).[3] The necessity of Mandarin for socio-economic mobility represents a process of alienation in which Tibetan colonial subjects consent under coercion to linguistic assimilation. Writing of British colonialism in Kenya, Ngũgĩ wa Thiong'o noted that education in English "was crucial to the domination of the mental universe of the colonised" (1986, 17) because children, in particular, internalized the degradation of their mother tongues and associated worldviews after an education in the colonizer's tongue. In Amdo, state language policies and provincial education practices have similarly created colonial alienation by relegating rights to develop minoritized languages to rural places and advancing socio-economic mobility, as well as an associated vision of modernity, solely through urbanization.

Current state-level language policies have emerged from a longer history of efforts to reduce multilingualism and standardize Chinese languages for the purposes of nation building. Like Tibetan, Chinese represents a range of mutually unintelligible language varieties, whose speakers share a single literary language. Each language variety can be further differentiated into topolects (Ch. *fangyan*), or place-based dialects that are mutually intelligible with a regional Chinese language such as Cantonese or Sichuanese.[4] In the early Republican era, political discourse took Chinese linguistic diversity as evidence of the new state's vulnerability to collapse. To modernize and strengthen the nation, reformers modelled an official spoken language on Beijing's dialect, which became known as *Putonghua* (common speech) (Tam

2020, 72; Weng 2018, 611).[5] In the early years of the People's Republic of China (PRC), language standardization remained a political priority. Following evolutionary logics, state discourse asserted that *Putonghua* would naturally supersede existing *fangyan* through development and modernization (Tam 2020, 167; Zhou and Ross 2004, 3).[6] These evolutionary logics of assimilation informed language policies that aimed to promote the new-found standard in the education system, simplify the Chinese script to enhance literacy, and reduce the gap between classical written Chinese and *Putonghua* (Saillard 2004, 164).[7] Language policy in the PRC was thus founded on the notion that the territorial integrity of the nation required a single spoken language, mapped onto a single written standard.

The state extended this vision of standardization to its minoritized nationalities (Ch. *shaoshu minzu*). Beginning in 1949, Beijing employed ethnologists and linguists to codify each *minzu* through a single language, a project that culminated in 1953 in the PRC's first census.[8] Communities with established literary traditions, like Tibetans, had their *minzu* status officially recognized early in the process of codification. Officials did not immediately recognize, but instead deliberated more extensively about, communities that lacked a written standard. Mirroring reforms for Chinese languages, government linguists and ethnologists sought to align the language of each *minzu* with a written standard. To legitimize the categorization of *minzu*, these scholars engineered writing systems for languages that were previously unwritten (Zhou 2003, 101–11).

State efforts to identify each *minzu* through a single written standard erased realities of dense linguistic diversity and multilingualism. Linguists currently recognize 308 languages in China (Eberhard, Simons, and Fennig 2023), a number that stands in stark contrast to the fifty-five designated *shaoshu minzu* (Roche 2019, 493). Yet language rights are narrowly allocated to each *minzu* on the basis of written standards. In 1954, the Chinese constitution asserted each nationality's right to use their recognized standard in official capacities, including schooling and regional governance (Bradley 2005, 10; Zhang 2013, 566–7).[9] Given that language rights are enacted largely through written curricula in schools, as well as government bureaucracy, most minoritized children do not, in practice, access any mother tongue education. Tibetan schools in autonomous regions, prefectures, and counties across China have legal allowances for instruction in written Tibetan. However, diverse spoken languages, including Amdo's multiple *yul skad*, not only lack legal protections but often remain unrecognized as legitimate languages in the first place.[10] State language policy has therefore built a linguistic hierarchy that recognizes language rights based on the extent of standardization and maps these rights directly onto territories.[11]

State language policy has directly informed provincial education policies in Qinghai. Although schools in Qinghai's Tibetan autonomous prefectures provide instruction in written Tibetan, attitudes towards and resources for Tibetan education have shifted throughout the twentieth century. In the first decade of the twenty-first century, Qinghai's schools embraced an assimilationist approach, reducing the scope of Tibetan instruction in most autonomous prefectures. In 2001, Qinghai operated more than 1,000 Tibetan primary schools and 40 Tibetan middle schools. By 2010, the province operated only 434 Tibetan primary schools, although the number of Tibetan middle schools had increased to 66 (Zhang and Tsung 2019, 293). Since 2010, the provincial government has introduced multiple measures to restrict the number of hours of Tibetan instruction in these schools. One initiative aimed for all schools to operate primarily in Mandarin by 2015, with Tibetan offered as a supplementary language (ibid., 294). The stated logic of this initiative was to improve Tibetan children's access to higher education, which offers a wider range of opportunities in Mandarin than in Tibetan. While the initiative was not fully realized, it aligned with many Tibetan parents' beliefs in the potential for socio-economic mobility through Mandarin education. Even in counties like Lungma, where immersion education is still available in Tibetan through high school, the end of the socialist job allocation system has meant that Mandarin-language skills are far more valuable than Tibetan-language skills for market employment (Postiglione 2008, 12–13). Even rural Tibetan parents, who have the option of Tibetan-medium education, often choose Mandarin-medium education for their children, in order to support their opportunities for later work and study (Ying 2023). Positioning Mandarin as a vehicle for academic achievement and socio-economic mobility alienates minoritized children from their mother tongues by breaking the transmission of valued cultural and linguistic practices.

In addition to privileging Mandarin over Tibetan, education policy has ideologically and materially elevated the city above the rural homeland. In Qinghai, schools are centralized in urban areas, which requires rural children to migrate out of villages to continue their education (Yeh and Makley 2019, 4). In Amdo, some rural villages, including Tsachen, operate bilingual preschools in Mandarin and Amdo Tibetan. Previously, some primary schools were also located in villages. However, with the School Consolidation Policy (2001), rural primary schools were closed and moved to county seats. Secondary schools were moved to prefecture seats, the next administrative unit above the county. Scalar patterns thus shape access to education in Qinghai, because each level of education is consolidated into a larger administrative unit (Grant 2018b, 544). Parents must therefore choose either to board their children in primary and secondary schools, or to move out of their village homeland and rent an apartment in the closest county- or prefecture-level seat. Because most universities are located in Xining, young adults must move once again if they wish to continue their education after they graduate high school.

Policies that consolidate schools in urban centres lead students to internalize the state's emphasis on modernization through urbanization. Surveys of Tibetan high school and college graduates suggest that few wish to pursue traditional livelihoods in farming or nomadism, and most hope to settle in a major city on the Tibetan plateau, such as Lhasa or Xining (Postiglione 2009, 503; Washul 2018, 494). In these cities, young adults can find stable market employment, but their work requires Mandarin language and literacy skills. The highest-achieving young people can also travel, study, and work in central China's cities. These cities offer cosmopolitan lifestyles and a broader range of professional opportunities but are physically, culturally, and linguistically dissociated from Tibet. Aspirations for urban living reveal colonial alienation, as youth have looked away from their rural origins and linguistic heritage in order to achieve belonging.

Tibetan Language Standardization as Renaissance and Resistance

In the 1980s, following the Cultural Revolution, urban centres in Tibet, including Lhasa and Xining, experienced an artistic, intellectual, and religious renaissance. With the rebuilding of monasteries and establishment of schools, the plateau saw a massive increase in Tibetan-language publications, including school books, religious materials, and literature, as well as new media such as popular music (Prins 2002, 33). With these cultural products circulating across the plateau, intellectuals and religious leaders became particularly interested in creating a standard language that represented the unity of Tibet's three major regions (Tib. *chol kha gsum*) of Amdo, Kham, and U-tsang. In response, authors and musicians adopted the literary language as the primary medium for cultural expression. Popular music from this period borrowed and adapted lyrics from new authors, whose works drew on their knowledge of classical Tibetan literature and poetry (Morcom 2018, 132–4). Tibetan authors engaged in extensive debates regarding the standardization of the literary language, arguing that classical Tibetan should be modernized in order to express contemporary emotional experiences and create a lexicon for new products, practices, and ideas (Maconi 2008, 189). Popular music, performed and produced in cities, echoed scholars' interest in modernization. By the 1990s, popular music employed a literary register and "presented a modern, prosperous image of Tibet ... grounded in urban centers of power" (Morcom 2018, 136). By creating cultural products in literary Tibetan, artists and authors articulated resistance to the forced assimilation that had been especially prominent during the Cultural Revolution, and they reclaimed the Tibetan literary language as a carrier of culture during an era of economic reform. Despite these motivations for cultural sovereignty, however, efforts for language standardization mirrored the language ideologies underlying state language policy. Both Chinese and Tibetan language reformers sought to create a single written standard that would advance ethnonational unity and modernize their communities by overcoming the spoken linguistic diversity characteristic of rural areas.

Tibetan efforts for language standardization emerged not only in response to the ideologies articulated in the state's language policy, but also from a longer-term history of mobility, both physical and socioeconomic, through education. In traditional models of Amdo Tibetan education, families generally sent one son to study Buddhism, through literary Tibetan (Tib. *chos skad*), in a nearby monastery. Monasteries served as cosmopolitan hubs of governance, education, and cultural exchange among Buddhists from different regions.[12] As early as the Qing dynasty (1636–1911), some elite Amdo Tibetan families also sent their children to boarding schools in Chinese cities, where they were educated in Chinese and trained to serve in government positions (Postiglione 2009, 485). During the Republic of China (1912–49), non-religious schooling for Tibetans expanded in Amdo, as well as in central China. In 1913, the Republic of China established a boarding school for Mongolian and Tibetan students in Beijing that operated in Chinese (Leibold 2019, 5). In this era, the provincial and central government explicitly advocated linguistic and cultural assimilation. For example, Qinghai's provincial government mandated that all Amdo Tibetan monasteries operate primary schools that offered at least one hour of instruction in spoken and written Chinese per day (Haas 2013, 211–16). While, during the Republican decades, education served as a tool to incorporate borderland communities into the nation, elite Tibetans embraced these expanded opportunities for secular study.

With the subsequent transition to Communist rule, beginning in 1949, and the Cultural Revolution (1966–76), however, opportunities for Tibetan secular education contracted. As Pema Bhum describes in his memoir of schooling in Amdo's Chentsa County (Tib. *gcan tsha*; Ch. *jianzha xian*), students surreptitiously copied banned Tibetan books – notably, the treatises of the *dag yig* and *sum cu pa* that are foundational to the study of written Tibetan – in order to keep Buddhist grammatology alive (Bhum and Hartley 2001). Opportunities for monastic education were largely eliminated, as religious institutions were ravaged. In the late 1970s, however, the Communist Party began to reassess its education policies for minoritized nationalities. Following the death of Mao Zedong, Chairman Deng Xiaoping created a vision of reform that included provisions for the economic development of China's borderlands, including state sponsorship for Tibetan education both within Tibet and in central China.

Reinforcing China's colonial domination of Tibet, the most elite academic opportunities for Tibetans remained in central China. In 1984, a joint agreement between the government of the Tibet Autonomous Region and China's central Ministry of Education encouraged rural Tibetan families to send their children to ethnic boarding schools (Ch. *neidiban*) located in sixteen different provinces and municipalities (Leibold 2019, 6).[13] These schools, which operated entirely in Mandarin, aimed to place graduates in prestigious government positions; they differed from earlier patterns of Tibetan access to secular Chinese education by serving rural students instead of children of the elite. The highest-achieving students from rural families within the Tibet Autonomous Region continue to participate in *neidiban*, with the promise of socio-economic mobility outweighing concerns over children's separation from their families and homelands (Postiglione 2009, 497). Although *neidiban* education dislocates Tibetan children from their homelands, most graduates eventually return to Lhasa or another urban centre within greater cultural Tibet (505–8). Few return to their rural homelands.

Alongside increased opportunities for Tibetan students in central China, education in Tibetan areas expanded after the Cultural Revolution. In the 1980s and 1990s, the Tibet Autonomous Region invested heavily in its own provincial education programs. In 1989, the Tibet Autonomous Region was the first Chinese province or region to offer pathways of secondary education entirely in the Tibetan language. Despite the success of this high school program, it was discontinued in 1997 (Zenz 2010, 308). As in Amdo, by the early twenty-first century, education policies within the Tibet Autonomous Region had shifted once again to prioritize assimilation to Mandarin. Today, earlier gains in opportunities for Tibetan-language study in the Tibet Autonomous Region have largely disappeared.

Since the 1980s, Qinghai's provincial education policies have offered more sustained opportunities for Tibetan-language development than those of the Tibet Autonomous Region. Following the Cultural Revolution, former monks, who had been forced to give up their monastic lives, used their expertise in literary Tibetan to teach in Qinghai's burgeoning public schools (Zenz 2010, 300–1). In 1982, Qinghai's Department of Education mandated the introduction of bilingual education in Tibetan and Mandarin at the primary and high school levels (ibid., 295). While this mandate was initially complicated by a lack of qualified teachers and teaching materials, the development of Tibetan-language departments in Qinghai's universities facilitated the creation of Tibetan-language tracks of study at all levels of education. For example, Qinghai University for Nationalities (Ch. *Qinghai minzu daxue*) in Xining had initiated a Tibetan-language major as early as 1956. Until the late 1970s, however, this degree mainly served Han Chinese and Hui Muslim students seeking government positions within Qinghai (Zenz 2010, 298–9). By the early 1980s, the program received its first intake of Tibetan students who had completed their primary and secondary education in Tibetan, allowing for this cohort's specialization and professionalization in Tibetan language and literature. By the year 2000, the university had created a separate Tibetan Language Department that mostly served ethnic Tibetan students who would go on to use their training in Tibetan-language primary and secondary schools (ibid.). These positive developments in Tibetan-language education resulted from the advocacy of Amdo Tibetan teachers and government officials, who continue to work tirelessly to create a pipeline of Tibetan schooling from primary schools to universities. As a result, literacy rates in Tibetan-speaking areas have increased exponentially since the late twentieth century (Thurston 2018b, 205). Lungma County, in particular, has benefited from foundational planning for Tibetan-language education and continues to operate primary and secondary schools with Tibetan-language tracks.

Tibetan successes in the realm of formal education have been overshadowed by colonial alienation, because they depend on the institutional support of the state. With the most elite academic opportunities accessible only through Mandarin, and only in urban areas, Tibetan is relegated to a secondary status. The upward socio-economic mobility experienced by Tibetan graduates of elite Chinese schools perpetuates notions of rural backwardness that stand in opposition to urban modernity, entrenching the division between rural and urban Tibetan life worlds. Tibetan scholars' attempts to elevate the status of their languages within the state's education system, and to enhance the quality of rural education, have been met by ambivalent allowances for bilingual education from the state and have solidified Tibetan linguistic identities around a single written standard. An ideal of monolingualism, either in Mandarin or in standard Tibetan, is promoted both in state discourse and in Tibetan arts, literature, and education. As a result, Amdo children's opportunities for mother tongue development remain constrained to the village homeland, the family, and the rural peer group.

"Our Only Option": Defining Standard Tibetan

The central conflict between desires for socio-economic opportunity and linguistic survival is realized in a community-wide standard language ideology. Apart from targeted efforts to increase access to Tibetan-language education, concerted activism that frames Tibetan language development as a fundamental right expanded in 2008, following a series of protests against China's broader human rights violations across the Tibetan plateau (Roche 2021b, 71). Since 2008, language activism has dovetailed with explicit calls for language standardization from Tibetan intellectuals, artists, and religious leaders. The standard language ideology articulated by these high-status Tibetans identifies written Tibetan as a carrier of a singular, pure culture, because it serves as the medium of monastic and secular Tibetan education.[14] Specifically, religious leaders and celebrities have promoted the value of "purity" associated with written Tibetan through debates and messaging on social media (Lhagyal 2021, 358). These campaigns encourage audiences to speak pure Tibetan (Tib. *pha skad gtsang ma*) by substituting new vocabulary items, elaborated in written standards, for Chinese loan words.[15]

The community-wide standard language ideology perpetuated in campaigns for purity has also contributed to the valorization of Amdo Nomad Talk over Amdo Farmer Talk. The sound system of Amdo *'brog skad* (Nomad Talk) retains more similarities to literary Tibetan than other spoken varieties, specifically the presence of voiced initial and final consonants (Hartley 1996, 38). Through is sonic connections to literary Tibetan, the qualities of purity and authenticity are also associated with Amdo *'brog skad*. In addition, because its speakers historically participated in year-round migrations, Amdo *'brog skad* is imagined to be free of structural interference resulting from prolonged language contact with settled, non-Tibetan speakers. This belief also holds that *rong skad* (Amdo Farmer Talk's diverse *yul skad*) diverged from the literary standard due to farming communities' interactions with non-Tibetan peoples. By manifesting literary Tibetan in the speech of nomads, Amdo's standard language ideology creates a linguistic hierarchy that devalues most of Amdo Tibetan's spoken varieties. Children in Tsachen encounter this standard language ideology in their everyday lives at home and school, but they continue to develop their family and peer relationships through the *yul skad*. Children from Tsachen living in Xining or other cities, however, face pressures in school to speak the dominant language of Mandarin, while also encountering negative attitudes towards their mother tongue within their own families and communities.

On a sunny day in September 2016, I leaned against the white tiled archway, warmed from the afternoon sun, that marks the entry way to the local university in Xining. I was waiting to meet Rinchen, a relative of one of my Tibetan teachers in New York City. Rinchen and I had been in touch prior to my arrival in Xining, on the social media platform WeChat. I had learned that, by chance, Rinchen had spent two years living abroad while her husband worked as a visiting scholar. Rinchen and I were planning to meet in person for the first time and share tea at a nearby café. From the university's entrance, I gazed across the road and towards the mountains that rise along the city's far edge. Rinchen's figure passed in front of the rising mountains, as she crossed the street to join me. We greeted each other and, leaving the university campus behind us, entered a café whose entryway featured a neon coffee cup that blinked dully against the plateau sun.

Rinchen ordered us a pot of tea while I found a table near a panel of windows that looked back on the university campus. In the distance, I could see the outdoor basketball court, where several foreign students were competing against their local peers. By the time Rinchen had sat down to join me, with our pot of tea in hand, I was bubbling over with excitement to tell her about my research interests. I had a pen and notebook ready to record any important ideas about language, culture, and children that might emerge in the course of our conversation.[16]

"I came to Xining to see how Amdo Tibetan children from Tsachen are learning their *yul skad*," I explained. Rinchen opened the clay-coloured teapot to reveal bright, white jasmine flowers blooming in the hot water. She smiled as she poured us each one cup of the delicate *huacha* (scented tea).

"Each *yul skad* is so different!" I added. I then elaborated on several of the linguistic features of Tsachen's *yul skad* that I had recorded on my most recent trip to Lhamo and Dolma's home and that I had not encountered in the speech of Amdo Tibetans living in New York City.

"Yes, this is the problem for us Tibetans," Rinchen replied. "We don't have one language. We have one writing system, but many languages."

I had encountered similar attitudes throughout my years of speaking with Tibetan people living in India and New York. Speakers of Tibetan languages often explicitly framed linguistic diversity as a problem to be overcome rather than as a source of cultural meaning. However, these explicitly articulated language ideologies contrasted with the place-based meanings that Amdo Tibetan speakers created in the course of everyday language use.

"Why is this a problem?" I asked, trying to tease out Rinchen's personal interpretation of Tibetan linguistic diversity.

"Because," Rinchen said, pausing to take a sip of her tea. "Because, without one language, like English or Chinese people have, we have no way to have common understanding."

"Our Amdo *'brog skad* sometimes sounds like our writing, but other than that we have many differences between our speaking and our writing," Rinchen stated. I knew from previous studies that, with the phrase "sounds like our writing," Rinchen was alluding to the fact that speakers of Amdo *'brog skad* pronounce many of the consonant clusters that are represented in Tibetan spelling. Also, colloquial *'brog skad* uses some words and phrases that are more commonly found in literary Tibetan than in other spoken varieties.

"Kids from different places can't speak with each other here in Xining. This is why it is so important for kids to learn how to read and write," Rinchen continued.

"Is it important for them to learn the *yul skad*?" I asked.

"Because each *yul skad* is different, we have to have them read," Rinchen replied. "For Tibetans, this is our only option."

"For my own sons, we decided to teach them *bod yig* (written Tibetan) with books and games. Because they go to school here in Xining, otherwise they would only learn Mandarin," Rinchen said, alluding to the state's education policy.

"Did you ever consider sending them to study Tibetan in your homeland?" I asked. I knew that Rinchen's older son was in high school, and her younger son was starting his last year of preschool. Some Amdo Tibetan parents who worked in Xining chose to have their children live with relatives in the rural homeland in order to access Tibetan-language education. I was aware, however, that highly educated Tibetan parents like Rinchen rarely chose this option.

"We never considered this because we want our kids to have a choice about where to go to university," Rinchen explained. "If they go to school in Tibetan, then they can only become rural teachers, and the number of students who want to be teachers is more than the number of jobs. This way, if we teach them [at home] to read in Tibetan, they can still understand Tibetan culture ... If they study Mandarin and English then they can have more choices in their lives, and they can still learn Tibetan culture if they read in Tibetan." Rinchen's explanation not only exemplified the competing pressures for socio-economic mobility and linguistic survival, but also reinstantiated the devaluation of Tibetan language diversity.

In Amdo, public campaigns for language standardization have concerned not only modernizing the classical literary language but also bringing spoken languages into line with this written standard (Thurston 2018b, 204). Rinchen explicitly reproduced this ideology. She identified written Tibetan as the only reliable medium for fostering shared understanding among Tibetan children – in her words, the "only option" for preventing language shift to Mandarin. She also described Amdo *'brog skad* as a prestige variety through its sonic similarities to written Tibetan, and described the presence of Amdo's diverse *yul skad* in Xining as a problem. While portraying written Tibetan as a pathway for language vitality, she expressed an essentialist ideology that mirrored the Chinese state's language policy. Rinchen identified the national identities of "English" and "Chinese" through single, named languages and suggested that Tibetans should develop a similar standard to ensure linguistic survival in a modern world. Adults' explicitly stated investment in a single standard, however, contradicts children's lived experiences of building their social worlds through their mother tongue. Negative attitudes towards children's intuitive uses of language pose particular challenges to child speakers in the city, who lack the opportunity to create alternative, affective associations between their *yul skad* and their peer relationships. As a result, urban children learn to perform their Tibetan identity through the written language and literary speech registers in limited social contexts, but shift to speaking Mandarin in everyday talk.

lu-taŋ: "Sing"

On a mid-afternoon in May 2017, I was riding a bus back to Xining from Tsachen. Around noon, the bus creaked into the station in East Xining. As I disembarked, I pulled a soft fabric scarf over my nose to protect myself from the late spring dust that swirled around the parking lot. I made my way to the sidewalk and turned right to enter a café, nestled behind a poplar tree, that served hungry travellers. I had just finished the nearly five-hour-long trip from Tsachen to Xining.

Early that morning, Akhu Norbu had delivered me to the bus station in Tsachen's county seat on a motorbike. Now, I would meet Sonam and his Ama, who had graciously offered to drive me from the bus station to my small apartment next to the university.

As I entered the café, Sonam bounced up and down from a nearby table, calling out "*Ani demo!*" (Hi, Ani!). I walked between the crowded stools, accidentally knocking into a red-robed Tibetan monk. I apologized as I sunk onto the stool next to Ama.

Ama had ordered a platter of steamed buns filled with potato (Ch. *baozi*) for the table. The dumplings sat in front of us, still snuggled in their bamboo basket for steaming. Sonam reached for one and dipped it into a small pool of thick chili oil that Ama had spooned onto his plate. Ama inquired about the journey from Tsachen. I assured her that the road had been safe. Then, I pulled out my cellphone, and located a video of Lhamo to show to Ama and Sonam, to ensure them that their family members were well.

I pressed play, and Lhamo appeared on my phone screen in a pink dress and matching wide-brimmed sun hat. She stood next to the *khang* in the family living room, her arms gently waving by her sides.

"*wopa-tsʰo, woʳjik̚ dʑoŋ*" (All Tibetan people, study written Tibetan), Lhamo's voice belted from the phone. She was singing a traditional Amdo Tibetan song. Her figure continued to wave its arms on the phone screen, her whole body now swaying with the beat of her voice.

"*wopa-tsʰo, dendʐel ɕe*" (All Tibetan people, unite), Lhamo's voice continued. Sonam leaned over the table to get a closer look.

"*ɲen-kə, ɲen-kə,*" (Good, good), Ama called out, clapping with pleasure to see her young relative's performance. Lhamo's voice continued to radiate from my phone's speakers, as she reached the final verse.

"*ŋa-tsʰo tsʰaŋma tɕʰimtsʰaŋ xtɕik̚ jin*" (We are all one family), Lhamo's voice called, as the video came to a stop. Ama continued to clap. As Sonam leaned further over the table, Ama directed him to sing. "*lu-taŋ, lu-taŋ*" (Sing, sing!), Ama said, smiling towards Sonam.[17] Sonam stood up on his stool. Ama gasped in surprise, but before she could reach across the table to help Sonam sit down, he had launched into a dramatic performance.

"*wopa-tsʰo, woʳjik̚ dʑoŋ!*" (All Tibetan people, study written Tibetan), Sonam called out. He was repeating the first verse from Lhamo's song. Ama stood up from her chair and circled around the table to help Sonam down to safety, while the monks seated next to us laughed and applauded.

With this didactic song, Sonam and Lhamo reinforced a standard language ideology that defines Tibetan belonging through the literary language. The lyrics of the song suggest that Tibetan identity must be consciously cultivated through the study of written Tibetan. Although standard language ideologies like those articulated in the song aim to create new speakers through identification with a common code, they also regiment language use in ways that must be learned through explicit instruction (Bourdieu 1991; J. Milroy 2001, 537). Standard languages are, in fact, imagined, perfectly uniform varieties that cannot accommodate the dynamic structural changes that occur through everyday talk (J. Milroy 2001, 531). While formal instruction in a literary language can help foster shared identities, the fixity posited by standard language ideologies can contribute to language shift by discouraging speakers from using a given code in a range of social contexts and in a variety of forms of talk.

Although Lhamo and Sonam performed an orientation towards a fixed standard language, they also showed the capacity to creatively move between language varieties. The song lyrics were written in the grammar of literary Tibetan, rather than the children's *yul skad*. In other contexts of everyday talk, Sonam and Lhamo use their *yul skad*. By performing literary Tibetan in song, Sonam and Lhamo therefore demonstrated the ability to differentiate between language varieties and their associated contexts of use. Lhamo had switched out of her *yul skad* to perform the song lyrics in standard literary Tibetan. Prompted by Ama, Sonam then isolated the lyrics from Lhamo's song, which had been playing on my phone, and repeated them to recreate Lhamo's performance.

In addition to demonstrating knowledge of how to regiment language varieties by their appropriate contexts of use, Sonam's performance hints at the values that characterize rural and urban children's speech. Using Lhamo's performance as a model, Ama prompted Sonam to recreate her demonstration of linguistic allegiance. Lhamo's speech served as a legitimate standard. By isolating the song lyrics, Sonam recognized this standard. Following Ama's suggestion to sing, Sonam performed what linguistic anthropologists Charles Briggs and Richard Bauman (1992) termed "recontextualization," or the embedding of a segment of talk in a new social context. Sonam took Lhamo's song from the rural homeland and performed it in a bustling restaurant in Xining. By recreating Lhamo's performance, Sonam momentarily defied the expectation that urban children enact language shift to Mandarin. He did so by bolstering an imaged standard language, as he repeated the song lyrics that were composed in literary Tibetan and voiced by his rural relative. Through Sonam's recontextualization of Lhamo's song, he defined literary Tibetan as the variety that should be used in formal performance, and he identified his rural relative's speech as a model of the standard language. Both Ama and Sonam therefore reproduced a hierarchy of linguistic value that positioned the speech of rural children above the speech of urban children.

Standard Language Ideologies in Action: Code-Mixing and Shaming Routines

The ability to regiment language varieties to particular social contexts is intimately tied to the practice of code-mixing, or the use of multiple languages in a single social context. With code-mixing, participants mark social and linguistic boundaries and use code variation to highlight specific values such as authenticity, common heritage, or place-based identities (Ferguson 2016, 157). Despite the forms of social and linguistic knowledge that are built through code-mixing, Amdo's standard language ideology positions code-mixing and other markers of language contact as impure and inauthentic. Indeed, as noted earlier, Amdo Tibetan Nomad Talk is revered as a prestige variety because speakers believe it to be free from the influence of non-Tibetan languages. By producing a hierarchy of value that positions literary Tibetan above spoken varieties, Nomad Talk above Farmer Talk, and rural speech above urban speech, Amdo's standard language ideology devalues language contact on multiple scales. Amdo Tibetan families reinforce negative attitudes towards language contact through assessments of code-mixing in everyday talk.

In both rural and urban Amdo Tibetan homes, adults and children monitor the boundaries between the Tibetan and Chinese languages by shaming one another for code-mixing. When children use both their *yul skad* and Mandarin in a single sentence, overhearers often pejoratively label their speech. Adults and other children call code-mixed speech *ra-ma-lik̄* (Neither goat nor sheep), highlighting the notion of impurity ascribed to code-mixing. They also use the rhetorical question "*tɕʰo ʳdʑa re-ba*" (Are you Chinese?), rejecting code-mixed speech from legitimate inclusion in Tibetan language practices.[18] These two statements serve as routinized shaming practices that reproduce Amdo's standard language ideology. Children's reactions to these statements provide insight into why and how this standard language ideology contributes to language shift.

On a mid-afternoon in late October 2016, I had just finished lunch in Lhamo and Dolma's home in Tsachen. Several of the girls' neighbours had joined us for the meal. Cousins Dawa and Dolkar sat on the *khang*, chewing hunks of brittle *go re* (Amdo bread), and little cousin

Tashi wandered around outside in the courtyard. I was continuing to savour the rich salted *am dʑa* (Amdo tea) that Ama had served me with our meal. Ama had cleared our dishes from the table next to the still-heated stovetop. As Ama was wiping down the table, Dolma rummaged through a nearby drawer, pulling out several stacks of white paper. Dawa joined her, reaching over her shoulder to grab a sheath as several pages floated onto the floor. Lhamo scooted over to take possession of the stray papers as Dawa and Dolma carried their piles over to the now-clean table.

The four children lined up, one next to the other, on one side of the table. They reached over each other – arms crisscrossing with excitement – to accumulate personal piles of paper. Ama and I glanced at each other and giggled at the children's exuberance. Once all the children seemed satisfied with the paper they had amassed, they began a coordinated play activity. Dolma picked a single piece out of her pile and began to fold it. The other children creatively followed Dolma's movements, folding their papers into more and more elaborate configurations. As the activity progressed, they negotiated how to fashion the paper into new, imaginative shapes.

Excerpt 4.1: "You Have a Goat's Mouth!"[19]

"Lhamo, ⁿdi.gə ɕatok̚ li-dʑi-re-ja. jin-na?" (Lhamo, we'll make a hat like this. Right?), Dawa suggested to Lhamo. As he spoke, he showed her the cone-like shape he had created through meticulous crinkling and folding.

"ɕatok̚li-dʑi-ma-re-ja ***feiji feiji*** *"* (We won't make a hat. An airplane, an airplane), Lhamo responded, using the Mandarin word for "airplane." Lhamo's own piece of paper was folded in half, horizontally.

"ŋi mtsʰodʑu li-dʑi" (I'll make a boat), Dawa decided.

"ɣnamdʑu ze-nə-re" (One says "airplane"), Ama called from the kitchen. Ama was correcting Lhamo's use of the Mandarin loan word for "airplane" by offering the Amdo Tibetan equivalent. The children seemed to ignore Ama's correction.

"ŋa-tsʰo ***feiji*** *li-dʑi* ***feiji*** *da"* (We'll make an airplane. An airplane, then), Dolma added. She did not acknowledge Ama's correction but followed Lhamo's prior use of the Mandarin word.

Then, latching onto Dolma's utterance, Dawa reiterated his previous decision to make a boat, saying, *"ŋa-tsʰo-gə mtsʰodʑu li-dʑi"* (We'll make a boat). He pointed to Dolma, adding, *"ŋa-ɣɲi-gə mtsʰodʑu li-dʑi jin-na"* (We two will make a boat, right?). Dawa was emphasizing his interest in making a boat and forming an activity pair with Dolma.

After Dawa spoke, Dolkar jumped in with another solution to the problem of who should make which shape. "*ŋa-ts^{h}o ɣnamdʑu li-dʑi*" (We'll make an airplane), Dolkar suggested, pointing between herself and Dolma. Unlike Dolma and Lhamo, Dolkar used the Amdo Tibetan word for "airplane." Then, she shifted her pointer finger to Dawa and Lhamo, saying, "*ak^{h}ə-ɣɲi-gi mts^{h}odʑu li-a*" (You two make boats). Dolkar was attempting to mediate between the different children's ideas about who should make which shape. However, not all the children accepted her solution. Dolma folded her paper horizontally, starting to make an airplane.

"*ŋa mts^{h}odʑu li-mə-xi-a*" (I don't know how to make a boat), Dawa said, seeming resigned after his former enthusiasm over the idea of making a boat.

Dolma chimed in hurriedly, latching onto Dawa's utterance as she moved the activity sequence forward and showed her mastery over the task of creating an airplane: "*tɕ^{h}e-tɕ^{h}u da **feiji** li-mə-xi-a!*" (You all don't know how to make an airplane then). She looked with narrowed eyes at Dawa's unfolded sheet while she held up her finished airplane.

"*ɲi mts^{h}odʑu li-a*" (I'll make a boat), Dolma resolved, as she began to fold a new piece of paper. Ama walked out of the kitchen and stood across the table, opposite the children.

"*ama! ra-ma-lik̚ ɣnamdʑu ze-nə-re*" (My goodness! Neither goat nor sheep. One says "airplane"), Ama declared. She was explicitly shaming Dolma for continuing to use the Mandarin word for "airplane."

Before the children seemed to register Ama's admonition, Lhamo latched on, eager to claim her place in the game by making an airplane. "***feiji** da **feiji** li-go-a!*" ([I] want to make an airplane, then, an airplane!), Lhamo called out.

Because Lhamo had ignored Ama's correction for a second time, Ama focused her attention on Lhamo. "*ŋo-ts^{h}a rama k^{h}a tɕ^{h}o*" (Shame. Like a goat's mouth!), Ama scolded Lhamo. Although her words were harsh, Ama's tone was gentle and joking. But then the other participants took up Ama's shaming routine.

"*Lhamo da ŋo-mə-ts^{h}a*" (Lhamo's not ashamed, then), Dolma claimed, using format tying, or the recycling of a prior turn with transformation, to escalate Ama's reprimand. "*rama k^{h}a!*" (Goat's mouth!), Dolma added, repeating Ama's pejorative label.

Beset by the other children, Lhamo became overwhelmed. She began to wail, threw her unfolded paper onto the table, and ran outside to the porch. Perhaps because Lhamo was, like Sonam, prone to strong expressions of emotion, Ama and the other children ignored her. They continued to fold their papers, as I wandered out to the porch, where cousin Tashi had come to crouch next to Lhamo to comfort her.

By shaming the children for using code-mixing, Ama reinforced a standard language ideology that labels admixture as impure and that associates children's speech with language shift. Ama first corrected Lhamo's use of the Mandarin loan word ***feiji*** (airplane) with a standard Amdo Tibetan equivalent. As the children continued to negotiate which shape to make, Dolkar used the Amdo Tibetan word for "airplane," *ɣnamdʑu*, but Dolma and Lhamo continued to use the Mandarin loan word, ***feiji***. In response, Ama labelled Dolma's speech as *ra-ma-lik̚*. She then repeated her correction, stating that the normative term for "airplane" should be the Amdo Tibetan word. After Ama joined the children at the table, Lhamo's repetition of the Mandarin loan word became the focus of shaming. Ama used the routinized phrase for shame, *ŋo-tsʰa*, and described Lhamo as having "a goat's mouth." Even though Dolma had used the same loan word in her previous turns, she expanded on Ama's negative evaluation of Lhamo. Dolma used format tying to state that Lhamo was not ashamed, and she repeated Ama's teasing statement that Lhamo has "a goat's mouth." After becoming the target of this shaming activity, Lhamo became distressed. She not only stopped speaking, but she began to cry and left the activity entirely. Despite the light-hearted tone of Dolma and Ama's shaming activity, Lhamo was clearly emotionally affected. Lhamo's reaction suggests that children may seek to avoid becoming the target of shaming routines by attempting to censor their code-mixing.

Such negative attitudes towards code-mixing represent a historically specific reinterpretation of multilingualism on the Tibetan plateau. As late as the early years of this century, the use of Mandarin alongside Amdo Tibetan served as a marker of education (Thurston 2018b, 200). Before the 1980s, many Amdo authors had produced writings in both Chinese and Tibetan, sometimes representing code-mixed speech in textual form. With the rise of language standardization efforts, however, intellectuals began to critique code-mixing in literature, identifying it as a form of pollution (Maconi 2008, 195). The interpretation of code-mixing as a threat to the purity of the Tibetan language has been solidified through activism against Chinese state policies that promote monolingualism. This facet of Amdo's standard language ideology is present across multiple modes of language production, from artistic expression to everyday talk with young children.

Despite the motivation to ensure cultural survival through a common literary language, standard language ideologies contribute to language shift. When children are dissociated from their intuitions about how to use language, they experience a broader conflict between their attempts to build social relationships in everyday talk and to perform a valued cultural identity. The emphasis on a single written standard devalues children's diverse forms of communicative competence, including code-mixing and the ability to regiment language varieties according to social context. In addition to erasing the linguistic knowledge that young children are creating and reformulating in their everyday talk, Amdo's standard language ideology focuses attention on *children's* speech, bringing children's code-mixing under greater scrutiny than that of adults.[20] Although Lhamo became the target of the shaming routine, she was not the only participant using code-mixed speech. In fact, in both rural and urban homes, *adults* frequently code-mix. Yet, in Amdo Tibetan communities, the surveillance of children's code-mixing intersects with a rural/urban divide to identify urban children as the primary agents of language shift.

The Social Consequences of Standard Language Ideologies

In everyday talk in families, adults and children alike use both Mandarin and the Amdo Tibetan *yul skad*. However, as demonstrated in chapter 2, young urban children begin to abandon their *yul skad* in favour of Mandarin when they enter preschool and form relationships with peers outside of their homes. Shaming routines that target code-mixing encourage children to identify either as speakers of the *yul skad* or as speakers of Mandarin. Urban children largely to choose to identify with Mandarin, and adults explicitly label them as Mandarin speakers. When urban children adopt this linguistic identity, they also express a distance from the *pha yul* (homeland) that contributes to the stark division between rural and urban cultural worlds.

From August 2017 until May 2018, I had been away from Amdo. I was back living in New York City, continuing to analyse the data that I had collected in 2016–17. In the summer of 2018, I had the opportunity to return to Amdo. In the time I was away, some important changes had taken place. In March 2018, in Tsachen, Lhamo and Dolma had welcomed baby sister Yangkyi into their family. In September 2017, in Xining, Sonam had started preschool. Just one month later, his baby cousin Sherab was born.

On a warm and sunny Saturday morning in June 2018, I was visiting Sonam's home in Xining. Cousin Yeshi was away, participating in one of the multiple English speech competitions held through her local public school. Ama and Ani Tsering Kyi had accompanied her, leaving Ayi Lhamo and Aphu Lhundhup at home with Sonam and Sherab. I sat on the sofa next to Ayi Lhamo, who held baby Sherab facing outward on her lap. That morning, Aphu Lhundhup was particularly talkative. He began to discuss how Sonam was faring after beginning preschool.

Excerpt 4.2: "I Won't Go to the Homeland"[21]

"*kʰə-a gen-na ⁿdʑo-go* ***you'eryuan*** *-na ⁿdʑo-go*" (He has to go over there, to the preschool), Aphu Lhundhup explained, gesturing towards the boundary of the gated apartment complex where Sonam's bilingual English-Mandarin preschool was located. His use of the Mandarin word for "preschool" did not invite any attention from Ayi Lhamo or Sonam.

"*kʰə-a ʳdʑaʰke zək̚ma-lʰəb-na ɕipa-kə ⁿdi.ⁿdʐa mə-go-ki-a*" (If he doesn't learn any Chinese, the other children won't understand him), Aphu Lhundhup observed, defining knowledge of Mandarin as essential to Sonam's social relationships.

"*ɕoŋ.la.ta ə-tɕʰu ⁿde-ni kʰor-kʰor ɕe ⁿde-na kʰorjul ⁿdə.ⁿdʐa mə-xa-kə*" (So, when they go around, then the environment isn't good like that), Aphu Lhundhup elaborated. He was evaluating the social context of urban Xining, stating that it had negatively affected Sonam because he had to learn Chinese in order to be understood by others.

Aphu Lhundhup continued to articulate the social consequences of urban living for Sonam. "*kʰə-a go-a ʰtsʰe-ne ɕipa-ki ʰtsʰe-ki-soŋ-ŋa*" (When he plays outside, when the children go to play), Aphu Lhundhup explained, "*kʰə-ʳkə ʰtsʰe tsʰaŋma ʳdʑa tak̚-tak̚re*" (their play is all exactly Chinese).

"*kʰə-a ʳdʑajik̚ma-tʰon-na ⁿdʑo-sa me-la*" (If he doesn't know written Chinese, he will have nowhere to go), Aphu Lhundhup said with concern.

"*kʰə kʰəmo re-a*" (He's alone, then), Aphu Lhundhup concluded. By stating that Sonam was "alone," Aphu Lhundhup was articulating urban adults' common concern that their children lack social connections because of their minoritized ethnolinguistic identity.

Up to that point in the conversation, Sonam had been sitting quietly on the floor, holding two beanie babies, one in each hand. Maybe because he became uncomfortable with Aphu Lhundhup talking about him, Sonam joined our conversation.

"*apʰu* ***ni bie dasheng yidian*** " (Aphu, don't talk so loudly), Sonam requested, elongating the final vowel in Aphu's name to express irritation. He spoke in Mandarin, except for his use of the Amdo Tibetan kin term to address Aphu Lhundhup.

"ja" (Okay), Aphu Lhundhup responded, acknowledging Sonam's statement.

He continued, with a slightly lowered voice: *"ze.na.ta ŋa-tsʰo jul-va ⁿdʑo pʰajul-va ⁿdʑo, kʰə-a kʰorjul-ki laka xa-kə"* (Then, if we go to our land, to our homeland, everything in the environment is good for him).

"tsʰaŋma woʳke ɸɕe-no ⁿdi ɸɕe-na kʰə jaŋ woʳke ɸɕe" (Because everyone speaks Tibetan, he will also speak Tibetan), Aphu Lhundhup elaborated. He explicitly linked the homeland's desirable environment to the presence of Tibetan speakers. Aphu Lhundhup also suggested that Sonam does, in fact, speak his *yul skad*. By stating that Sonam speaks Tibetan in the homeland, Aphu observed that Sonam uses different languages in different contexts. Perhaps feeling excluded from the discussion, Sonam interrupted.

"ni bie dasheng yidian ni bie dasheng yidian" (Don't talk so loudly, don't talk so loudly), Sonam repeated, holding his hands over his ears for dramatic effect. Aphu Lhundhup didn't stop talking. Instead, he tried to draw Sonam into our conversation.

"o.ta pʰajul-va ⁿdʑo-dʑi?" (Oh, then, will [you] go to the homeland?), Aphu Lhundhup asked Sonam.

"pʰajul mə-ⁿdʑo" ([I] won't go to the homeland), Sonam stated, flatly and stubbornly, using format tying to negate Aphu Lhundhup's question. Aphu Lhundhup chuckled slightly.

"Tsachen ⁿdʑo-la akʰə-tɕʰo ʰtsʰerok̚ jo" (If [you] go to Tsachen, all our playmates arethere), Aphu Lhundhup said, coaxingly. He named the village and used the first-person plural pronoun, *akʰə-tɕʰo* (our), to characterize Sonam's playmates, highlighting collective belonging in the homeland.

"bu yao wo yao wo gege" ([I] don't want [them]. I want my older brother), Sonam retorted. He had switched from the *yul skad* into Mandarin to reject his playmates in Tsachen. Instead, he said, he wanted his "older brother." I knew from previous conversations with Ani Tsering Kyi that Sonam was using this Mandarin kin term to refer to a Han Chinese neighbour and playmate whom he had met at preschool.

"do-a do-a akʰə-tɕʰo tɕʰimtsʰaŋ tsʰaŋma jo-no" (Wait, wait, all our family is there), Aphu Lhundhup protested. Sonam refused to acknowledge the positive facets of the homeland that Aphu Lhundhup was listing.

"bu yao wo yao wo gege" ([I] don't want [them]. I want my older brother!), Sonam repeated, now raising his voice markedly.

"aləi" (Oh), Aphu Lhundhup said, resigned. It seemed as if Aphu Lhundhup had given up on trying to convince Sonam to express appreciation for the homeland. Sonam, however, escalated his complaints about the conversation.

"***chao si le***" (It's so loud!), Sonam protested again. He used a dramatic Mandarin phrase to emphasize his irritation with Aphu Lhundhup's conversation. "***wo yao wo gege***" (I want my older brother!), Sonam repeated.

Aphu Lhundhup responded by trying once again to convince Sonam to express a desire for the homeland. "*^{n}dʑo-la Tsachen ^{n}dʑo-na ak^{h}ə-tɕ^{h}o awu Dawa atɕ^{h}i Dolma*" (If you go to Tsachen there's our Awu Dawa and Achi Dolma), Aphu Lhundhup said, his voice almost pleading as he named Sonam's relatives. Sonam, however, refused to acknowledge Aphu Lhundhup's statement.

"*ap^{h}u* ***chao si le chao si le*** *!*" (Aphu, it's so loud, it's so loud!), Sonam shouted. Ayi Lhamo took in a sharp breath to mark her disapproval.

Aphu Lhundhup then scolded Sonam: "*k^{h}a rok̚do (.) ^{n}də.gə ji ɲen-nə-ma-re*" (Be quiet. Doing like this isn't good). Sonam did not accept Aphu Lhundup's request to be quiet. He had become irate.

"*na ŋi k^{h}a rok̚* ***shuo****! o! tɕ^{h}i tɕ^{h}its^{h}ək* ***shuo****? ap^{h}u!*" (Then, I said be quiet! Oh! What are you saying? Aphu!), Sonam shouted. He used the Mandarin verb for "say" in his Amdo Tibetan utterance. In his state of heightened emotion, Sonam had switched back to using the *yul skad*. Aphu Lhundhup responded with curiosity.

"*ap^{h}u ɸɕe-ko-no mə-t^{h}un-nə-re?*" (Don't [you] agree with what Aphu is saying?), he asked Sonam.

"***chao si le***" (It's so loud), Sonam repeated, his voice now lowered.

"***chao si le****?*" (It's so loud?), Aphu Lhundhup repeated, intoning a question. "*ap^{h}u ɸɕe-ko-no e-ko-kə?*" (Do [you] understand what Aphu is saying?), Aphu Lhundhup added.

"*mə-ko-kə*" ([I] don't understand), Sonam said flatly.

Aphu Lhundhup and Ayi Lhamo chuckled, possibly because Sonam had, in fact, switched into the *yul skad*, while Sonam stomped out of the living room.

Aphu Lhundhup's monologic description of the challenges of urban living focused on the seemingly impenetrable dominance of Mandarin. Without knowledge of Mandarin, Aphu Lhundhup explained, Sonam would "have nowhere to go" – that is, would have no future opportunities – and would be "alone" in Xining. Although Sonam's future opportunities and peer relationships depended on his knowledge of Mandarin, Aphu Lhundhup did acknowledge Sonam's continued understanding of the *yul skad*. He explained that Sonam speaks in Tibetan when visiting the rural homeland. Despite this acknowledgment of Sonam's multilingual capacities, Aphu Lhundhup did not entertain sustained multilingualism in the *yul skad* and Mandarin as a realistic possibility for Sonam's future.

Perhaps feeling excluded, or even embarrassed because his Aphu was talking about him, Sonam interjected into Aphu's monologue. Sonam first used Mandarin to request that Aphu Lhundhup speak more quietly. Even when Aphu Lhundhup ceded to this request, however, Sonam escalated his commands. In response, Aphu Lhundhup tried to include Sonam in the conversation, asking if Sonam would visit the homeland. Sonam answered flatly, in the *yul skad*, "I won't go to the homeland." Sonam's rejection of the homeland led Aphu Lhundhup to remind Sonam that his relatives are there. Sonam then switched into Mandarin, rejecting his relatives in favour of his urban *gege* (older brother). By using the Mandarin kin term for his peer, Sonam located his desired relationship clearly within the Mandarin-dominant environment of Xining. He reinforced the opposition between the city and Tibetan homeland that Aphu Lhundhup had established.

Next, Sonam escalated his Mandarin commands to Aphu Lhundhup to be quiet. He shouted at Aphu Lhundhup, "It's so loud," leading Ayi Lhamo and Aphu Lhundhup to reproach him. In response, Sonam used code-mixing to continue to yell at his Aphu. Aphu Lhundhup attempted to de-escalate the conversation by asking if Sonam understood what he was saying. Sonam stated that he did not understand Aphu Lhundhup. The form of his talk suggested otherwise. Sonam had switched out of Mandarin and into the *yul skad*. He had taken the verb from Aphu Lhundhup's question, *ko* (to understand), and negated it. Sonam therefore demonstrated the capacity to use the *yul skad*, while explicitly denying his understanding.

In real-time interaction, multilingual speakers adjust their code choices to meet the expectations of their audiences. Participants "build on their own and their audience's abstract understanding of situational norms to communicate metaphoric information about how they intend their words to be understood" (Gumperz 1982, 61). Sonam used code choice, as well as the content of his talk, not only to reject the rural homeland and his extended family, but also to metaphorically communicate his identity as an urban speaker of Mandarin. Sonam first used Mandarin to issue his commands for Aphu Lhundhup to be quiet, juxtaposing Amdo Tibetan and Mandarin only when Aphu Lhundhup did not comply with his request. Sonam used Mandarin to assert his desire to remain in the city and to express his wish for his urban "older brother." Through these linguistic choices, Sonam grounded his sense of belonging in the city and suggested that others should identify him as an urban speaker of Mandarin.

When urban children identify as Mandarin speakers, they reveal fragile bonds to their families and communities, rejecting the forms of collective belonging that are rooted in the village homeland and the *yul skad*. Minoritized children's identification with a dominant language can have profound effects on family relationships.[22] Although adults label children's code-mixing as the cause of language shift, children's linguistic choices reveal more complicated struggles for identity. To assert their belonging in the city, children may enter into explicit conflict with caregivers or refuse to engage in family activities. When Sonam emphasized his knowledge of Mandarin, he demonstrated an understanding that his family values a standard Amdo Tibetan language, that his *yul skad* does not conform to this valued standard, and that his *yul skad* is out of place in urban Xining. Urban children like Sonam learn to perpetuate a social and linguistic opposition between the homeland and the city, internalizing difference from their rural peers and from their adult family members.

Conclusion: Standard Language Ideologies and Social Differentiation

While education policy has bridged rural and urban worlds by facilitating and encouraging migration, it has also entrenched the social, economic, and linguistic divide between children in the homeland and those in the city. As Tibet remains under a settler colonial regime, Xining represents the boundaries of sustained mobility for most Amdo Tibetans. Structural inequalities and biased hiring practices restrict many Tibetans from obtaining stable employment in urban centres in central China (Fischer 2013, 37; Washul 2018, 495). While those children born in the rural homeland may one day move to Xining for higher education, they lack opportunities for migration throughout the Chinese nation. In contrast, while those children born in Xining may visit the homeland, their futures are unfolding with an increased orientation towards higher education and market employment in China's urban centres. Young children who are raised in Xining, as opposed to young adults who move there to access higher education, have the best chance of eventually moving throughout mainland China. Success in the contemporary Chinese education system requires young children to be physically removed from their rural homelands and schooled in Mandarin, resulting in "the dissociation of the sensibility of [children] from [their] natural and social environment, what we might call colonial alienation" (Thiong'o 1986, 17).

Education policy has also contributed to the rise of a standard language ideology by mapping written languages onto this rural/urban divide. Amdo Tibetan communities have responded to constraints for meaningful language development by adopting a historically specific standard language ideology that emphasizes knowledge of written Tibetan, that frames the speech of rural nomads as the most authentic, and that prohibits code-mixing. This standard language ideology is contributing to urban children's identification as speakers of Mandarin, even when their everyday language use reveals continued grammatical and pragmatic knowledge of the *yul skad*. Furthermore, this standard language ideology discourages all Amdo Tibetan children from identifying as multilingual speakers, and targets children, rather than adults, as the agents of language shift. With their everyday talk under scrutiny, children seem to adopt negative attitudes towards multilingualism that prevent them from using their full linguistic repertoires. This standard language ideology, which arises from colonial alienation, further dissociates children from their intuitive knowledge of their *yul skad* and the cultural practices built through it.

Language shift in Xining is not inevitable. It is motivated by everyday linguistic choices, informed by the interaction between standard language ideology and education policy. The construction of a single standard language always creates boundaries between groups of people. The boundaries between rural and urban identities, and between children and adults, unfold in the context of desires for full participation in China's market economy. This aspiration for socio-economic mobility currently reproduces colonial alienation, which manifests in urban children's rejection of both the homeland and the *yul skad*. Despite the challenges of forging Tibetan belonging in Xining, urban children's speech continues to show forms of cultural and linguistic knowledge that adults often overlook. Although this chapter has described a seemingly irreversible progression of urban language shift, chapter 5 shows the potential for Amdo Tibetan caregivers to support flexible, multilingual language practices in the city.

Chapter 5

Reading in the City: Literacy as Belonging in Urban China

སེམས་ཀྱིས་ཤེས།
Knowing from the heart-mind.

Amdo Tibetan saying

In 2008, on the anniversary of the 10 March 1959 uprising in Lhasa, more than 150 protests broke out across the Tibetan plateau (Barnett 2009, 8). In the context of international scrutiny over China's human rights record, Tibetan protestors saw an opportunity to demand meaningful political autonomy, as well as the repatriation of the Dalai Lama to Lhasa, their imperial and spiritual capital. As an outgrowth of the 2008 protests, human rights discourses gained traction among Tibetans within the People's Republic of China (Robin 2016). In particular, public protests and social media campaigns demanded state resources to develop Tibetan language in media, education, and governance. While the 1980s had seen a burgeoning of efforts for Tibetan language standardization and the expansion of Tibetan-medium education, language activists after 2008 explicitly framed the dominance of Mandarin as a threat to Tibetan linguistic survival (Roche 2021b, 71). As was charted in chapter 4, essentialist understandings of language articulated in both Chinese state policies and Tibetan language planning promote a single written standard and devalue the diversity of spoken Tibetan languages as well as everyday practices of code-mixing. Through these standard language ideologies, written Tibetan has become emblematic in two senses: as claimed by China, it is emblematic of Tibetans' integration into the Chinese state along with other minoritized nationalities; as claimed by Tibetan activists, it is emblematic of an autonomous nation experiencing territorial dispossession by the Chinese state. By mirroring the state's emphasis on language standardization as a marker of national identity, however, demands for language rights have further entrenched a dichotomy between the Tibetan and Chinese languages that erases the long histories of bilingualism and cultural hybridity that continue to influence children's code choices.

The application of human rights discourse to concerns over language vitality since 2008 has carried two primary consequences. First, language activism has expanded, unfortunately exacerbating the criminalization of advocacy efforts. For example, in 2010, in the city of Rebgong (Tib. *rebgong*, Ch. *tongren shi*), more than 1,000 Tibetans protested a proposed education reform in Qinghai that called for defining bilingual education as primary instruction in Mandarin, with Tibetan taught as an additional subject. Protests against this reform spread throughout Amdo and reached as far as the renowned Minzu University of China (Ch. *zhongyang minzu daxue*) in Beijing. Beginning one year later, a series of self-immolations rocked the Tibetan plateau, with statements from protestors naming the protection of Tibetan language as a primary concern (Barnett 2012, 54; Roche 2021b, 72). Protests over language reforms resurfaced in Rebgong in 2012 and 2015, and in the Tibet Autonomous Region in 2018. Demonstrating the state's escalating suppression of language activism, Tashi Wangchuk, a Tibetan man from Yulshul Tibetan Autonomous Prefecture in western Qinghai, was sentenced to five years in prison in 2015 on charges of inciting separatism, following the publication of a *New York Times* article that featured his language advocacy efforts (Buckley 2021). While Tashi Wangchuk's case received particular attention in Western news media, ethnic Tibetans continue to be disproportionately arrested for inciting separatism within China – a charge that now encapsulates language activism (Dui Hua Foundation 2020; Roche et al. 2023, 36).

As a second consequence of framing language as a human right, urban Tibetan families who seek to develop their children's knowledge of literary Tibetan now face the possibility of social marginalization within a majority Han community. In the absence of formal education in Tibetan, urban parents must informally organize learning activities for their own children. However, in light of negative attitudes towards minoritized languages, even informal support for children's development of Tibetan literacy can be interpreted either as backwardness – an unwillingness to integrate into the modern city – or as an implicit call for separatism. Urban Amdo Tibetan parents wish for their children to fully participate in city life by building peer relationships and excelling in the education system, but they also hope that their children will learn to read and write in Tibetan. To balance these competing goals, parents coordinated a variety of informal educational activities, including curated social media channels where children read and spell in Tibetan, bilingual speech competitions in English and Tibetan, and reading groups hosted by parent volunteers.

These educational activities supported children's use of multiple languages and literacies, but some did not focus on Tibetan at all. In this chapter, I show how one activity group, "I Read," encouraged acceptance of multilingualism within the constraints posed by standard language ideologies and the possibilities of social censure associated with Tibetan language activism. "I Read" was organized by several Amdo Tibetan parents in Xining, including Sonam's aunt, Tsering Kyi, and Rinchen and Tsomo, both Tibetan scholars at the local university. About ten children who attended a bilingual English/Mandarin preschool participated in the group. Each week, one parent served as a volunteer teacher and guided the children through collaborative reading of Chinese and English picture books. Despite the absence of Tibetan books, parents used Tibetan theories of learning focused on repetition to guide their lessons. While a Tibetan cultural framework of knowledge shaped the unfolding of reading activities, young children attended to symbolic forms – images in picture books, sound segments in words, and the sequential organization of talk – to blur the boundaries of the English and Chinese languages. By analysing the turn-by-turn unfolding of collaborative reading activities, I argue that, despite its focus on Chinese and English literacy, "I Read" provided opportunities for Tibetan belonging in Xining by helping preschoolers establish peer relationships in and through multilingual, multimodal language practices.

Sound, Image, and Sequencing: Anchors for Metalinguistic Knowledge in Literacy Activities

Although "I Read" excluded written Tibetan from its lessons, children built their identities as multilingual speakers in the course of collaborative reading. Specifically, children used texts as a basis to elaborate metalinguistic knowledge about multiple codes while sharing in common experiences of language. "Metalinguistic knowledge" refers to conceptions of languages, including their functions, forms, and boundaries, that are built through analogous linguistic representations such as talk, writing, and sound play. In the course of language acquisition and socialization, reflexive linguistic representations that articulate this knowledge, known as "metalanguage," are "indispensable both for a creative assimilation of the mother tongue and for its final mastery," because the meanings of language forms are inherently tied to their social functions (Jakobson 1980, 91). While speakers openly reflect on the referential meaning of language through the content of talk, other types of metalanguage allow participants to elaborate on social and contextual meanings (Silverstein 2001). In face-to-face interaction, for example, participants' shared orientation to diverse symbolic forms serves as a foundation for coordinating metalinguistic knowledge, demonstrating that language is not separate from context but is an inherent part of the material setting in which interactions unfold.

Metalinguistic knowledge resides not in the mind of the individual speaker but in the social coordination of cognition. Approaching cognition as "a public, social process" (C. Goodwin 2000, 1491) allows researchers to track the moment-by-moment transformation of knowledge itself – that is, the shared forms of meaning elaborated in interaction – as well as the shifting identification of participants as knowledgeable or unknowledgeable. Metalinguistic knowledge emerges from transparent reflections about language and also from the elaboration of meaning across multiple modalities, such as sound, text, gesture, and image. By creatively moving between modalities, participants engage in a "process of building something new through decomposition and reuse with transformation of resources placed in a public environment by an earlier actor" (C. Goodwin 2018, 3). Analyzing metalinguistic knowledge through the coordination of social cognition can reveal how young children build understanding through their immediate social relationships and interactions. As Vygotsky argued, knowledge is not developed independently, but is first "refracted through the prism of the child's environment … pass[ing] through another person" (1978, 30).

While all interaction involves a process of developing shared understanding through selective attention to multimodal resources, previous ethnographic studies have documented multilingual children's particular creativity in transforming taken-for-granted understandings of language boundaries by reassembling sounds, words, and speech styles. For example, Polly Björk-Willén (2007) showed how children in a multilingual Swedish preschool used shadowing, or the replication of features of immediately prior turns, as well as code-mixing, to secure roles as participants in play activities. In order to claim space in an unfolding play trajectory, young children repeated one another's alternation of language forms, adopting features from languages that they did not speak but that were being used by their peers. In a similar ethnographic setting, Asta Cekaite and Polly Björk-Willén (2013) demonstrated that Swedish preschoolers also established forms of language expertise not directly linked to their mother tongues. Children used correction and word searching to construct identities as speakers of Swedish, a lingua franca that represented *none* of the children's first languages. A continent away, in California, Amy Kyratzis (2017) analysed how two preliterate children in a Spanish-English bilingual preschool pretended to read to one another by linking codes to particular images in picture books. Asta Cekaite and Ann-Carita Evaldsson (2019) emphasized that, as multilingual children coordinate social relationships in real-time, they redefine their communities' language ideologies by refusing to identify with a single code. Together, these ethnographic studies suggest that, by reusing and elaborating on prior turns at talk, children build linguistic identities that transcend both the language ideologies of their communities and the boundaries between discrete codes.

During the literacy activities in "I Read," sounds, images, and sequencing provided salient symbolic focal points for children to coordinate their metalinguistic knowledge. Volunteer teachers used repetition – a culturally accepted method for learning to read and write – by linking spoken words to images in picture books. Children used images to collaboratively establish joint attention, as well as to wonder about and converge on agreed-upon word meanings. With word searching and repetition, children demonstrated authoritative knowledge of which language forms belong to English or Chinese, establishing their identities as speakers of both languages. At the same time, the children used sound play to exaggerate similarities between English and Chinese, blurring the very boundaries that they seemed to establish through word searching. During the sequential organization of sound play, children drew on prosody – patterns of stress, intonation, and rhythm in language – to mark the boundaries of turns and display attention to each other's previous utterances.[1] With prosody, children built common emotional experiences and established metalinguistic knowledge that supported their identities as multilingual speakers.

Because adults in Xining emphasized the importance of literacy, reading activities represent a particularly relevant forum for examining the constitution of children's metalinguistic knowledge. In discussions about "I Read," adult volunteers articulated essentialist views of written languages that equated literacy with communicative competence and erased the complexity of their community's multilingual repertoires. Along with a focus on learning through repetition, adults associated static social values with standard languages, which informed their choice to run lessons in English and Chinese and guided their organization of reading activities. Specifically, adults directed reading activities through prompting questions, and they reserved code-mixing in spoken Amdo Tibetan almost exclusively for managing children's behaviours outside of the main activity sequence. Despite adults' emphasis on standard written forms, children creatively located equivalencies in sound and meaning across Chinese and English and used their multilingual competence to claim authority to direct the sequential organization of talk.

sem tɕə xe: "Knowing from the Heart and Mind"

It was a late Thursday afternoon in February 2017. I sat at Rinchen's kitchen table, sipping hot and bitter green tea. Together, Rinchen and I were poring over a hefty book, *Bod Kyi Yul Skad Rnam Bshad* (Commentary on Tibet's Dialects) by renowned scholar Dondrup Tsering (2011). I had asked Rinchen for her help in deciphering the text, since it included many technical vocabulary items that I could not locate in any of my Tibetan dictionaries. As we worked through the text together, I also realized that, while I possessed intermediate Tibetan reading-comprehension skills, I was a beginner when it came to reading out loud.

I was struggling over a passage that described the tendency for nomads' speech to resemble the pronunciations of written Tibetan. Rinchen stopped me to point out that I was shifting my own pronunciation of the word *skad* (speech).

"*ʰkɛt*" (Speech), Rinchen intoned.

"*kɛt*" (Speech), I responded. As soon as I spoke, I realized that I had left out a sound in the word's initial consonant cluster. While some varieties, like the central Tibetan *spyi skad* (common language) spoken in diaspora, drop initial consonants, Amdo Tibetan does not. This initial consonant also indicates an important detail in the word's written form: the presence of a superscribed letter *sa*.

"*sa ka-tak̚ ʰka ta ʰkɛt*" (*sa* attaches to *ka* to make *ska, da skad*), Rinchen said. Rinchen's method of spelling out loud specified that the consonant *sa* was attached on top of the consonant *ka*, which changes its pronunciation to *ʰka*. Once the final consonant, *da*, is added, the vowel changes to make the full word *ʰkɛt*, transliterated from written Tibetan as *skad*. When she spelled, Rinchen had omitted a final verb, *ϕdʑak̚*, used in the style of spelling common in Amdo. Perhaps drawing on my central Tibetan pronunciation from the previous turn, Rinchen had spoken each syllable using the conventions common in central Tibet and diaspora. Although standard language ideologies posit a one-to-one relationship between text and talk, Rinchen's speech demonstrated that the dialogic co-construction of meaning inherently involves the mixing of language varieties, even in the seemingly transparent act of spelling out loud.

"*sa ka-tak̚ʰka ta ʰkɛt*" (*sa* attaches to *ka* to make *ska, da skad*), I repeated.

"Very good!" Rinchen called out cheerfully in English. Rinchen's encouraging tone resembled the ways she spoke to children in the sessions of "I Read" that I had participated in over the past several months.

"You have to repeat," Rinchen said. "*sa ka-tak̚ʰka ta ʰkɛt*" (*sa* attaches to *ka* to make *ska, da skad*), she modelled, mirroring how the repetition should unfold.

"*sa ka-tak̚ʰka ta ʰkɛt*" (*sa* attaches to *ka* to make *ska, da skad*), I responded.

"Yes!" Rinchen called out in English.

Next, Rinchen elaborated on her positive evaluation, using metalanguage to describe the proper way to learn to spell.

"If you keep repeating the word correctly, you will know it from your heart and mind. You won't even have to think about how to spell or read anymore. In Tibetan, we say '*sem tɕə xe*,'" she explained.

"*sem tɕə xe*," (Knowing from the heart and mind), I repeated, smiling. I was familiar with the Tibetan concept of *sems* (pronounced *sem*), which refers to the locus of a person's consciousness. Rinchen had wisely translated *sems* into English as "heart and mind," which emphasized the dual elements of feeling and cognition evoked by the Tibetan term. Rinchen was suggesting that one can cultivate deep, inner knowledge within the *sems* through proper practices of repetition. These reading practices were not simply a matter of rote memorization. Rather, a reader dissected a word into its smallest meaningful units, analysed each of these units, and poetically explained how they fit together.

When they "know from the heart and mind," Tibetan readers use repetition to build affective connections to texts through culturally specific embodied practices. Anthropologists have noted the significance of repetition to the study of canonical texts in multiple ethnographic settings, including Qur'anic schools in Cameroon (Moore 2006), grassroots Confucian revivalist movements in China (Zeng 2022), and *doctrina* classes in a Catholic, Mexican heritage community in Los Angeles (Baquedano-López 2000). Across these communities, repetition facilitates learners' development of communicative competence. Despite the common functions of repetition across cultures, the details of embodied practices such as prosody, turn-taking, and segmentations of text are unique to each interactive setting and are shaped by culturally specific theories of learning. In Xining, Amdo Tibetan lay teachers adapted repetition – a practice also found in the study of Tibetan Buddhist canonical texts – to help learners memorize the sonic and textual forms of words and to facilitate broader metalinguistic knowledge. In Tibetan Buddhist monastic education, learners generally pass through three stages of knowledge – hearing, thinking, and meditating (Tib. *thos bsam bsgom gsum*) – by memorizing textual sequences before interpreting and analysing them (Lempert 2012, 33–4). While "knowing from the heart and mind" employs repetition, it departs from this monastic model of learning by integrating the analysis of form and meaning together. Texts serve as a foundation for developing the learner's knowledge of language structures and meanings, which are found across speech and writing, rather than as an authoritative source of cosmology.

As they practice "knowing from the heart and mind," learners can therefore bridge multiple codes as well as multiple modalities. In my courses at the local university in Xining, I encountered teaching methods that interpreted Chinese textual forms through practices of repetition similar to "knowing from the heart and mind." As a foreign student, I had joined a department of language learners from countries as diverse as the United States, South Korea, and Germany. Our instructors were Tibetan and Chinese graduates of the university. All instructors emphasized the importance of repetition in learning to read and write. Tibetan teachers of the Chinese language, however, brought to their lessons unique perspectives informed by the complex, composite syllables encoded in Tibetan writing. These instructors used repetition of the individual components of Chinese characters to explain more elaborate language structures and to make reference to Tibetan culture. In Xining, Tibetan teachers thus built a syncretic learning practice that blended Chinese and Tibetan norms of repeating and perfecting language segments.[2] The metalinguistic knowledge that emerged from these lessons encompassed writing and speech as well as the Tibetan and Chinese languages.

The morning after reading with Rinchen, I walked over the frosted ground on the university campus, grabbing a hot tea at the canteen on the way to my Chinese classroom. Warming my hands against my metal thermos, I entered the university hall, found my classroom, and took my seat. The classroom was unheated, despite the late-winter chill. Due to my limited knowledge of how to read and write standard simplified characters, I had been placed, along with five other foreign students, in the elementary Chinese class. Our classes covered the basics of stroke order and proper hand writing, skills that my courses in New York City had overlooked in favour of proficiency in conversational Mandarin. Our instructor, Lhari Tso, was an Amdo Tibetan woman raised in Tsholho Tibetan Autonomous Prefecture. She was bilingual in Amdo Tibetan and Mandarin and had attended bilingual Tibetan-Mandarin schools prior to entering university. After successfully writing the university entrance exam (Ch. *gaokao*) in Chinese, she had joined the local university with a major in Chinese literature five years earlier. She had recently graduated and taken a job in our department for foreign students.

Although Lhari Tso was instructing us in Chinese, she drew from Tibetan Buddhism to craft her lesson. The textbook chapter for that day, which focused on food items, included a seemingly mundane list of words whose characters encoded deeper metaphorical meanings. For the first part of class, Lhari Tso instructed us to write the Chinese character for "tea" (茶) 108 times – an auspicious number in Buddhism. It is said that 108 represents the wholeness of the universe, which is why the *ma la* (rosary) around Lhari Tso's wrist was strung with 108 beads. The Chinese character for "tea" is made up of three components. The radical meaning "grass" sits above components that correspond to the characters meaning "people" and "tree." After we had finished the exercise, Lhari Tso showed us that we could decipher the symbols for the numerals ten and eight within the strokes. In fact, we could add up marks showing eighty (the number ten times the number eight) and twenty-eight (the numbers ten plus ten plus eight) to equal 108. Lhari Tso explained that the sacred number manifested itself in this character because of the significance of tea to Tibetan culture. Along a branch of the Silk Road where Himalayan outposts west of Lhasa once reached to meet cities in southwestern China, Tibetans had traded horses in exchange for Chinese tea.[3] When tea was introduced to Tibet, it developed into regional specialities, including the rich butter tea of central Tibet (Tib. *bod ja*) and the salted milk tea of Amdo (Tib. *am ja*). In addition to referencing Buddhist philosophy in her lesson, Lhari Tso connected contemporary tea culture to historical connections between Tibet and China.

Lhari Tso's unconventional decomposition of the character's components encouraged learners to build imaginative, affective connections to the word *cha* (tea). She meticulously described how multiple meanings could be read into the character in the process of piecing together its components. The day before, Rinchen had similarly decomposed and recomposed the sound units of the written Tibetan word *skad* (speech). While Rinchen's discussion of spelling had been limited to Tibetan, Lhari Tso used her interpretation of the Chinese character's strokes as an opportunity to reference the history of Tibetan and Chinese economic relations. When thinking across modalities of text and sound, the method of "knowing from the heart and mind" allowed learners to interpret multiple meanings in language structures, locate similarities between Tibetan and Chinese, and connect cultural history to language forms. This forging of links across text, sound form, and meaning represents a contemporary practice of linguistic hybridity. Although standard language ideologies emanate both from the Chinese state and from within Amdo communities, syncretic reading practices locate Tibetan identities in histories of inter-ethnic contact and provide opportunities to transgress language boundaries.

Urban Belonging through Multiple Literacies

Given their interest in supporting children's educational achievement, adults in Xining acknowledged the importance of literacy in both Chinese and Tibetan. With Chinese literacy, children can advance in the education system, and with Tibetan literacy, children can connect to an anchor of common Tibetan heritage. The politicization of Tibetan language activism, however, complicated adults' efforts to organize instructional activities in written Tibetan. With Tibetan language activism framed by the Chinese state as separatism, promoting opportunities for learning Tibetan could further entrench their children's social marginalization in a majority Han Chinese city. As a result, urban Tibetan parents found alternative avenues to assert the importance of multiple literacies.

The presence of English in Xining – in private bilingual schools, in speech competitions, and as a required foreign language in public schools – provided an acceptable forum for developing multiple literacies.[4] International guests to Xining – including tourists, foreign exchange students, and Christian missionaries, who often focused evangelization efforts on minoritized communities – contributed to an infrastructure of English learning through bilingual private schools, individual tutoring, and city-wide speech competitions.[5] With support from foreign teachers in Xining and contacts abroad, urban Amdo Tibetan youth can, in rare circumstances, study in the Western world. While the spread of English to China's urban centres is arguably an outgrowth of interlocking forms of colonization realized through globalization, this process also challenges the evolutionary logics of Chinese state discourses that privilege monolingualism in Mandarin. In opposition to the dominance of Mandarin, Amdo Tibetans adults framed English as a politically neutral, urban, and cosmopolitan language. More specifically, to subtly resist pressures for linguistic assimilation to Mandarin, Amdo Tibetan adults drew on the belief that English is inclusive and carries the potential for mobility.

dʐa kʰaŋ: "Teahouse"

It was Christmas Eve, 2016, in Xining. Although the local university did not close for Christmas, December 24th happened to fall on a Saturday, our weekly holiday. Tsering Kyi had invited me to tea with our friends Rinchen and Tsomo. Like Richen, Tsomo is a professor in the Tibetan language department at the local university. Both Tsomo's and Rinchen's children attended the bilingual English/Mandarin preschool that Sonam would join the following September. Familiar with the significance of Christmas for North Americans, Rinchen had initiated the tea so that we could have a small celebration while I was away from my homeland.

Although the arid climate meant that it rarely snowed in Xining, about two inches of sparkling powder dusted the ground on that evening. I was making my way from my shared apartment to a *ja khang* (teahouse, pronounced *dʐa kʰaŋ*) next to the university. I slipped along the glittering glass tiles that covered the walkway near the university's gate. Steadying myself against the gate, I turned left to reach the row of storefronts immediately east of the university. Owned by a Tibetan family, the teahouse was located in a cozy, vine-covered loft above a bookstore. The bookstore primarily featured literary Tibetan works and hosted events with Tibetan artists, authors, and intellectuals. I pushed open the door and climbed up the stairs to see Tsering Kyi, Rinchen, and Tsomo seated at a table in the corner.

As I settled in, saying "*demo*" (hello) to the group of women, Tsering Kyi poured me a cup of sweet, Indian-style milk tea. I noticed a pile of picture books next to the teapot on the table in front of me. I picked up the first one, admiring the cover, and realized that it was a Mandarin translation of a famous American children's book that names animals of different colours. I glanced back towards the stacked books and saw the original English version. I remarked out loud at how beautiful the books were. Although I had read this book many times as a young child, I did not know that it had been translated into Mandarin. Rinchen explained that she and Tsomo had ordered the books from an online retailer and that, along with Tsering Kyi, they were planning to start an after-school reading group for preschool-aged children. Intrigued by the direction that the conversation was taking, I asked the women if I could record our discussion. I turned on my field-recorder as we continued to speak.

"*ʱwetɕa-gi ɕaji tɕʰimo ^{n}dendʐel-ɕe-na lʰob-nə-re*" (Books teach children how to connect with each other), Tsering Kyi explained in Amdo Tibetan. She then elaborated: "*^{n}di.^{n}dʐi xepa ɸɕitsʰok la pʰantok jo-nə-re*"

(This knowledge is good for society). With these statements, Tsering Kyi asserted the social and moral benefits of reading, for individual children as well as for the collective well-being of communities.

Tsering Kyi began to talk about the unique qualities of the picture books in front of us. *“^{n}di.^{n}dʐ̩i ^{ɦ}wetɕa naŋ-na rimo jo-na xa-kə, ^{n}di tsaŋ ɕaji ga-nə-re”* (It’s good that there are pictures in the books, because children enjoy them), she remarked. She then provided more specific evidence, by describing her children’s interest in picture books: *“Yeshi rimo dʐ̩i ga-nə-jod-tsaŋ rimo jo-no-gi ^{ɦ}wetɕa ^{h}ti ɕik̚-ki ga-nə-re”* ([My daughter] Yeshi loves to draw, so she really likes to read picture books).

“Plus, with books like this, kids can get more practice reading before they start Grade 1,” Rinchen noted, switching to English. Rinchen portrayed picture books as preparatory materials for the more intensive reading that children would master beginning in first grade. In traditional Tibetan and Chinese schooling practices, there were no picture books. Instead, children learned to read and write largely through rote memorization. The pictures in Tibetan and Chinese primary school textbooks tended to associate a single word with its referent, rather than provide narrative context to stories.

“Yes, if we had more books like this in Tibetan, or cartoons in Tibetan, then children would be more interested in learning Tibetan,” Tsomo explained, also in English. Tsomo had moved to topic of conversation from focusing on the general benefits of picture books to pointing out the need to further develop children’s enthusiasm for reading in Tibetan.

Tsering Kyi switched into Amdo Tibetan to add that, lately, her nephew Sonam had been watching Mandarin cartoons all day long. Tsering Kyi suggested that the television, and not only his preschool friendships, were leading him to speak more Mandarin than Tibetan.

“da xiong er xiong?” (Big Bear and Little Bear?), I asked, invoking the name of a Mandarin cartoon series and recalling the many times I had seen those two characters bounding across the television screen in Tsering Kyi’s apartment. All three women nodded and laughed.

Because the conversation had turned towards the lack of resources for learning written Tibetan, I asked if the reading group would include any Tibetan books. I assumed that, as a forum for encouraging their children’s interest in reading, the parents would aim to build opportunities for their children’s early study of written Tibetan. The women’s responses suggested otherwise.

“We will mostly read in English, which is why the group is called ‘I Read,’” Rinchen explained. She switched to English, mirroring the language of choice for the reading group.

"English is a language for everyone," Tsering Kyi added, using English for the first time in this conversation. She then switched back to Amdo Tibetan: *"^{n}di.^{n}dʐi ɕuŋl^{h}ob-gi ɕaji ɲam-gi l^{h}ob-nə-re"* (This way, the children from preschool can learn together). Tsering Kyi was focusing on the importance of children maintaining their peer relationships outside of preschool. Rinchen switched into English to reiterate this point.

"The most important factor is for them to be together outside the school, and English is inclusive," Rinchen added. Then, Rinchen picked up the books and placed them in her bag, to give us room on the table to order food. Before we ordered, I confirmed that I would be welcome to attend "I Read" once the weekly meetings began.

When discussing their plans for "I Read," Tsering Kyi, Rinchen, and Tsomo integrated two explicit goals: supporting children's peer relationships and ensuring their readiness for entering public schools. These goals responded to moral anxieties about children's loss of peer relationships in the city, while skirting the institutionalized forms of linguistic exclusion that marginalize Amdo Tibetan children from their urban peers. Rather than framing literacy as a technical skill, these women described reading picture books as a way for urban children to establish and maintain friendships with their classmates. For example, Tsering Kyi stated that reading helps children develop interpersonal skills that are "good for society." Alongside the women's discussion of reading as a prosocial activity, Rinchen noted the importance of preparing children to perform well in mainstream public schools. Although Rinchen expressed interest in supporting children's entry into urban Chinese schools, this milestone is accompanied by anxiety over the resulting transition away from peer-group socialization and language shift to Mandarin.[6] By framing literacy skills as a collective social benefit, Tsering Kyi, Rinchen, and Tsomo offered a community-based response to the absence of culturally and morally responsive urban education but avoided explicitly advocating for the development of Tibetan-language education.

The women's conversation also revealed ideologies about the social value of each code, demonstrating the logics that informed their decision to operate "I Read" in English and Chinese. Tsering Kyi described English as "a language for everyone," and Rinchen labelled English as "inclusive," marking English as a symbol of pluralism in urban China. The women did not characterize Chinese literacies so explicitly. However, they did compare resources for developing Chinese and Tibetan literacies, noting that Chinese picture books and cartoons pique children's interest. Tsomo commented on the relative lack of resources for Tibetan reading and writing, which displayed her concern over ruptures in the transmission of Tibetan literacy to future generations. When I asked if the group would include any Tibetan books, however, Rinchen and Tsering Kyi responded by refocusing our discussion on the social context of the reading group. By discussing discrepancies in resources for Tibetan and Mandarin literacy development, they noted the dominance of Mandarin without overtly critiquing the subordination of Tibetan.

Although Rinchen, Tsomo, and Tsering Kyi chose not to include Tibetan books in "I Read," they framed English language learning as a remedy to their children's marginalization in Xining. Their children could study English as a second language, along with their non-Tibetan peers. By focusing on a language other than Mandarin, the Amdo Tibetan parent organizers challenged education policies that frame assimilation to Mandarin as an inevitable result of modernization. As M A and Darren Byler (2022) similarly found in an ethnography of private English training schools in Urumqi, the capital of the Xinjiang Uyghur Autonomous Region, the global hegemony of English offered opportunities for Uyghur students to counter the singular dominance of Mandarin as well as the stigma of bilingualism that labelled Uyghurs as deficient speakers of Mandarin. The dynamics of language oppression that dissociated Uyghur students from their mother tongues, and excluded them from full participation in employment and education, actually encouraged them to learn English. Unlike Uyghurs in Urumqi, Amdo Tibetans in Xining, at the time of my research, did not regularly experience detention, arrest, or forced disappearance on the basis of mother tongue language use or the organization of social and educational activities. Nonetheless, state language and education policies promoting assimilation to Mandarin intersected with the overt criminalization of language activism to limit urban children's opportunities for and interest in Tibetan reading and writing. By constructing English as a cosmopolitan yet foreign language, the parent organizers of "I Read" agentively created space for literacy to serve as resistance to assimilation.

Collaborative Reading: Between Standardization and Hybridity

While the values associated with the standard languages of English and Mandarin motivated Rinchen, Tsomo, and Tsering Kyi to organize "I Read," children's actual reading practices defied standard language ideologies. About ten preschoolers from Sonam's private bilingual English/Mandarin preschool regularly attended "I Read." Four of the regular attendees were Amdo Tibetan, four were Han Chinese, one was Hui Muslim, and one was a member of the Tu nationality (Ch. *tuzu*). Each week, one parent volunteered as a teacher and led the children through a series of activities including picture book reading, singing, and drawing. "I Read" was held in a meeting room at the Tibetan bookstore/café where I had met Richen, Tsering Kyi, and Tsomo on Christmas Eve. By participating in "I Read," preschoolers reinforced the friendships they built in the classroom, practised the Chinese reading skills they will need when they enter public school, and discussed topics viewed as essential for children's social and emotional development.

Each week, the volunteer teacher chose picture books with a common narrative theme. While each week focused on a unique theme, the activities incorporated into each lesson emphasized individual words and phrases. The teachers coordinated the children's engagement with picture books by identifying images and encouraging the children to find associated words. The teachers then identified key words in written English and written Chinese, highlighted the individual sound components of these words, and helped the children repeat the words together. The activity of decomposing the internal elements of words and finding equivalencies across languages mirrored the Tibetan practices of "knowing from the heart and mind" that Rinchen and Lhari Tso had introduced to me. During these guided word repetitions, children used prosody to playfully negotiate the meaning of individual words and determine which could be included in the spoken English and Mandarin languages.

By late May 2017, "I Read" had been meeting for several months. Each Wednesday evening, the young students filed up the hardwood stairs of the Tibetan bookstore/café, passed the rows of tables where university students sat sipping rich, sweet tea, and entered a glistening, glassed-in meeting room. Although the chairs in the meeting room were so high that the children's legs swung precariously above the ground, the children seemed unaffected by the ill-fitting furniture. They would bolt into the meeting room and scramble onto the chairs so the lesson could begin as quickly as possible.

One Wednesday in May, Rinchen was leading the group as the volunteer teacher. It was a small class, with only six children and two parents in addition to myself and Rinchen. Zangmo, age seven and about to start first grade, was the oldest child. Zangmo sat at the head of the table, across from teacher Rinchen. Ribu and Migmar, both six years old, sat to Zangmo's left. On Zangmo's right sat Janet and Gracie, who were both five, and six-year-old Joshua. Joshua and Janet, who were Han Chinese, used the English names they had been given in preschool. Gracie was the only Tibetan child who chose to use the English name given by her preschool teacher. I sat not at the table, but against the side wall with Joshua's and Ribu's mothers.

Because the weather in Xining was starting to warm up, Rinchen had chosen to focus the lesson on picture books about spring. The first book was titled *Spring Is Here*. As Rinchen turned each page, she revealed a new animal creeping out of a forested hiding spot and into a sun-drenched meadow. Rinchen was prompting the children to correctly identify the written names of the animals by repeating them in English and Mandarin. She turned to a page that featured an image of a turtle, alongside animals that had emerged in previous pages, and asked how to translate the English word "turtle" into Mandarin.

Excerpt 5.1: "What Is 'Turtle'?"[7]

"***ranhou na ge*** turtles turtle ***shi shenme ya*** ?" (Then, those "turtles," what is "turtle"?), Rinchen asked, as she turned the open picture book to face the children seated around the table.

"***tuzi***" (Rabbit), Zangmo suggested in Mandarin. Zangmo was drawing on the similarity between the sound form of the English word "turtle" and the Mandarin word for rabbit. Both words share similar features in their first syllable. When Rinchen had pronounced the English word "turtle" in the prior turn, she had even used a falling pitch contour, which loosely matched the lexical tone of the Mandarin word *tuzi* (fig. 10–11).

"Huh?" asked Rinchen, initiating a repair to demonstrate that Zangmo had provided an incorrect answer.

"***tuzi***" (Rabbit), said Gracie, repeating Zangmo's turn to collaboratively locate the correct answer. From the sidelines, I laughed gently with the mothers, because both Gracie and Zangmo were equating rabbits and turtles.

"Turtle," Rinchen repeated in English, elongating the word's first vowel to add emphasis. With vowel elongation, Rinchen used prosody to mark the continued need for a correct answer. Zangmo latched onto Rinchen's utterance.

"***xiao tuzi***" (Bunny), Zangmo suggested. Zangmo drew on her own and Gracie's prior utterances, using format tying, or the repetition and modification of an earlier language form. She elaborated on her initial answer, providing more specificity about the type of rabbit she had identified.

"No," Rinchen asserted, in English. Her pitch rose and then fell sharply. Rinchen was marking a more explicit repair to interrupt the children's equation of the Mandarin word *tuzi* (rabbit) with the English word "turtle."

"***tuzi shi shenma ya***. *Ra?*" (What is "rabbit." Ra?), Rinchen asked. Inverting the target code from her previous question, Rinchen prompted the children to locate the English equivalent of *tuzi*.

"Rabbit!" Gracie called, making bunny ears with her fingers next to her temples. Gracie drew on Rinchen's pronunciation of the first syllable of "rabbit" in the immediately prior turn to provide the correct answer. She also used gesture to emphasize her knowledge of the word's meaning.

"Oh, rabbit," I added from the sidelines, overlapping Gracie's turn. I was showing approval of Gracie's correct answer and trying to encourage the other children to participate.

"Yeah," Rinchen added, praising Gracie's demonstrated knowledge and concluding the sequence of word searching.

Young children's ability to sequentially build and amend their shared knowledge provides evidence of the dialogic nature of learning (Kyratzis and Johnson 2017, 3). In this sequence, participants relied on each other's prior turns to orient to shifting focal points, which they defined largely through prosody rather than content. Initially, Rinchen formulated a question about the meaning of the English word "turtle," exaggerating the segmentation of the word's two syllables. By emphasizing each sound segment, Rinchen grounded the interactive sequence in the same form of repetition advocated by the learning theory "knowing from the heart and mind." In response, the children recycled sound features from one another's utterances to bridge the two languages of English and Mandarin. First, Zangmo drew on sonic similarities between the English word "turtle" and the Mandarin word *tuzi* (rabbit), specifically the common first syllable and pitch contour. Zangmo used these shared features to suggest that the words have a common meaning. Gracie repeated Zangmo's assertion, and Zangmo used format tying to elaborate her answer into a related form, *xiao tuzi* (bunny). Rinchen responded to Gracie and Zangmo's incorrect answer by recycling it into a repair, asking them to locate the English equivalent for *tuzi*. When Gracie provided the correct answer, "rabbit," by drawing on Rinchen's prior pronunciation of the word's first syllable, Rinchen praised her. Rinchen then advanced the word-searching sequence by returning to her initial question of the Mandarin equivalent for "turtle."

"***na*** turtle ***shi shenme ya*** ?" (Then, what is "turtle"?), Rinchen continued. As she spoke, Rinchen moved her finger to point at the picture of the turtle in the book, clarifying her intended referent among the present animals.

"turtle ***shi na zhong hen man shangmian you na ge qiao*** " (Turtle is the kind that moves slowly with a shell on top), Rinchen explained, drawing her finger across the turtle's shell in the picture book.

Zangmo called out, overlapping Rinchen's turn, "*a* ***woniu***!" (Ah, snail!). There was no snail in the image.

Without waiting for Zangmo to finish, Ribu chimed in,

"***wo zhidao wo zhidao***!" (I know, I know!), latching onto Zangmo's turn.

"***woniu***" (Snail), Zangmo repeated, answering for Ribu and latching onto his turn.

"***woniu***" (Snail), chimed in Ribu, reiterating Zangmo's answer as he latched onto her turn.

"***woniu***" (Snail), added Gracie, latching onto Ribu's turn and agreeing with Zangmo and Ribu. Each child relied on the prior turn to locate the word *woniu*.

Rinchen paused with a slight smile on her face and looked down towards the open picture book in her hand. She pointed to the turtle. She was using a visual cue in the picture book to indicate that the children's answer, "snail," was not correct. Ribu advanced the children's shared understanding.

"***bu shi a wugui***" (Ah, no it's turtle), Ribu concluded.

"Ah," said Rinchen, overlapping Ribu's answer and nodding to demonstrate her approval.

Zangmo latched onto Ribu's turn. "***wugui wugui***" (Turtle, turtle), Zangmo said, using repetition to emphasize her knowledge of the correct answer.

As Zangmo repeated the Mandarin word for "turtle," Rinchen reached across the table towards Ribu. She was displaying her approval of Ribu's contribution as the first, correct iteration of the Mandarin word for "turtle."

"Very good!" Rinchen called and raised her right hand near Ribu.

"***wugui***" (Turtle), Zangmo repeated once more as Ribu stood up.

"Yay! Yes," called Rinchen, latching onto Zangmo's turn. Rinchen's hand met Ribu's in a high-five.

All the participants laughed as Rinchen and Ribu completed their high-five. Rinchen sat back down and turned to the page to continue reading *Spring Is Here*.

The children relied on Rinchen's prompting questions, as well as visual cues, to collaboratively equate the English word "turtle" with the Mandarin word *wugui*. Rinchen initiated the prompting sequence, using the image in the picture book to state that the animal in question moves slowly and has a shell. Based on this explanation, Zangmo, Ribu, and Gracie incorrectly identified the meaning of "turtle" as *woniu* (snail). They repeated one another's immediately preceding turns, collaboratively locating the answer. After Zangmo, Ribu, and Gracie incorrectly identified *woniu* as the Mandarin word for "turtle," Rinchen formulated a repair by relying on a visual cue – the image of the turtle in the picture book – to guide the children towards the correct answer. Ribu was the first to correctly provide the Mandarin word for turtle, *wugui*. Then, Zangmo repeated Ribu's answer, claiming her own knowledge of the Mandarin equivalent. Rinchen performatively high-fived Ribu and used an English exclamation to mark Ribu's answer as correct. The sequenced closed with laughter, as the participants collectively recognized Ribu's achievement.

In this sequence, the children built intersubjective, metalinguistic knowledge that simultaneously constituted and destabilized the boundaries between English and Mandarin. The children's uses of repetition recall findings about children's enactments of agency in collaborative reading activities in other communities. For example, Burdelski and Evaldsson's study of preschoolers' storytelling strategies suggested that the reuse of prior turns at talk allowed individual children to claim their right to actively participate as narrators (2019, 2–3). As the children in "I Read" drew on the sound form and content of prior utterances to establish an agreed-upon answer to Rinchen's prompting questions, they also crafted identities as knowledgeable speakers of English and Mandarin.

The children did not build metalinguistic knowledge simply by associating single words with English and Mandarin. Instead, they used prosody and images to interpret shared referential meanings. While Rinchen's guiding questions remained rooted in single, standard language forms, the children collaboratively focused on sounds and meanings that could belong to both Mandarin and English. By establishing agreement over word meanings, they also ratified one another's identities as multilingual speakers and managed their personal authority to display knowledge in real time. The children's intersubjective attunement through turn-taking and repetition drew on prosody to establish a common affective experience, a process that was intertwined with their enactments of linguistic hybridity and their claims to knowledge of multiple codes.

Code-mixing in Sequence: Constraining the Functions of Amdo Tibetan

Although the children in "I Read" challenged standard language ideologies when they used prosody to cross language boundaries, English and Mandarin remained the primary codes used by both the volunteer teachers and the children. In addition to the absence of Tibetan books, participants rarely used spoken Amdo Tibetan during collaborative reading activities. Both the teachers and children used code-mixing between English and Mandarin in prompting questions and in sequences of collaborative reading. The teachers only rarely used Amdo Tibetan, largely to direct the Tibetan children's behaviour outside of the main activity sequence.

On that Wednesday in May 2017, I was contentedly watching the conversations unfold in "I Read." After receiving a high-five from volunteer teacher Rinchen, Ribu sat back down in his seat, smiling. The jovial laughter from the other participants died down. The group had finished reading *Spring Is Here*. Rinchen took out a ukulele and led the children in a song titled "I Can Sing a Rainbow." In a perfectly choreographed transition, Rinchen finished the song, put down the ukulele, and pulled out a book with a rainbow on the front cover. It was titled *A Sunny Day*. Rinchen read the title, then opened to the first page of the book. She pointed to a dark raincloud cloaking half of a yellow sun. A vibrant rainbow slipped out beneath the cloud. Rinchen began to ask the children to identify the different elements of the image.

Excerpt 5.2: "'Bow' Means 'Sunshine'"[8]

"Rainbow," said Rinchen. She elongated the vowel in the word's second syllable, letting her tone fall like the arching rainbow in the picture. Over eleven turns, Rinchen and the children repeated the word "rainbow," emphasizing the boundary between the word's two syllables. Overlapping these repetitions, Zangmo used format tying to expand the word "rainbow" into a narrative description.

"rainbow rainbow ***wo jian guo*** rainbow" (Rainbow, rainbow, I've seen a rainbow), stated Zangmo, using the current activity of word repetition to recall a past experience.

"Rainbow, rainbow, rain" Rinchen continued to repeat, overlapping Zangmo. Then, Joshua used format tying to recycle Zangmo's statement, also departing from the other children's continued word repetition.

"***wo ye jian guo*** rainbow" (I've also seen a rainbow), Joshua added. While the other participants continued to repeat the two syllables of the word rainbow, Joshua began to repeat his utterance.

"***wo jian guo*** –" (I've also seen –), Joshua added, as Zangmo overlapped him.

Interrupting Joshua, Zangmo stepped into the role of the teacher, attempting to explain the meaning of the word's second syllable. "bow,

bow ***shi taiyang de yise***" (Bow, bow means "sunshine"), Zangmo said. With this turn, Zangmo took on the authoritative role of decoding the sound components of the English word "rainbow." Zangmo analysed the second syllable by providing a Mandarin equivalent. However, Zangmo had incorrectly defined the English word "bow" as *taiyang* (sunshine). She had also initiated a shift in the activity sequence away from word repetition. Rinchen stepped in to moderate the activity sequence.

"*da tɕ^{h}o jar laŋ ^{n}de-ni jar laŋ ɸdʑok̚^{n}de-ni*" (Okay, you get up there. Get up and stand there), Rinchen said, switching into Amdo Tibetan and pointing to the ground next to her chair. Zangmo stood up and walked towards Rinchen.

"*tɕ^{h}o ^{n}de ɸɕe ɸɕe-jaŋ* ***taiyang shi shenme***. sun" (You said this, this way, "sunshine" is what? Sun), Rinchen added. Rinchen was reclaiming her authority as the teacher by mixing Amdo Tibetan and Mandarin. Without waiting for Zangmo to answer, Rinchen had provided the English equivalent, "sun."

"Sun," Zangmo repeated, still standing and facing Rinchen.

"Sunny!" shouted Joshua from his seat, overlapping Zangmo. Joshua had drawn on the sound form of "sun" to offer an additional interpretation of the English word, transforming it into "sunny."

"Sunny?" repeated Ribu, overlapping both Joshua and Zangmo. The other children seemed unaffected by the somewhat harsh tone Rinchen was taking with Zangmo. They were simply responding to the content of her question.

"Sunny?" Rinchen asked again, now shifting to address Joshua and Ribu. "Sunny ***jiu shi qingtian de yise***" (Sunny means "sunny,"), Rinchen clarified, differentiating the Mandarin words for "sun" or "sunshine," *taiyang*, and "sunny," *qingtian*. She had switched out of Amdo Tibetan, distinguishing her activity of word searching with Ribu and Joshua from her activity of scolding Zangmo.

"***qingtian***" (Sunny), Zangmo repeated quietly. Rinchen's next turn suggested that Zangmo should not have participated in this repetition.

"Okay, *tɕ^{h}i mə-ɲen*" (Okay, you're not good). Rinchen began to scold Zangmo, again switching into Amdo Tibetan.

"Ah," Zangmo added passively as a backchannel cue, demonstrating her reception of Rinchen's words.

"*aləi k^{h}a rok̚ɲen-a-do*" (Okay, sit and listen quietly), Rinchen added, directing her in Amdo Tibetan to wait for her turn to speak.

"Ah," said Zangmo.

"***yinwei***" (Because), Rinchen said, now switching between Mandarin and English to address the class as a whole, "we are going to, you are going to be, a Grade 1 student, huh?"

"Huh?" I added, gasping slightly to mirror Rinchen's emphasis on the category of "Grade 1 student."

"You have to learn to listen to teacher, okay?" Rinchen explicated, in English.

"Okay," said Zangmo, mirroring Rinchen's code choice.

"And follow teacher, okay?" Rinchen added.

"Okay," Zangmo answered. Rinchen latched onto Zangmo's turn to continue her explanation.

"This is the rule of our class," Rinchen added. She then repeated the content of her turn in Mandarin.

"***zhe shi women yi ge zunshou de yi ge*** rule ***shi zhe li*** ok?" (This is our one thing to follow. This rule here, okay?), Rinchen reinforced.

Zangmo did not answer but began to cough.

"Okay? Very good, very good. Okay, okay, okay. Rainbow," Rinchen continued, refocusing the children's attention on the word "rainbow." Zangmo turned around and took her seat, as Joshua initiated another repetition.

"Rainbow," said Joshua. The other children continued to repeat after him.

In the course of collaborative reading, Rinchen used code-mixing between English, Mandarin, and Amdo Tibetan to establish distinct activity frames. When prompting word searches, Rinchen interchanged English and Mandarin as matrix languages. In this particular sequence, Rinchen initiated a repetition of the word "rainbow." The children joined her, using prosody to mark syllable boundaries, thus focusing joint attention on each of the word's sound components. Zangmo and Joshua then departed from the shared task of word repetition by using the word "rainbow" to launch descriptions of their past experiences of seeing rainbows. As is common in young children's organized reading activities (Johnson and Avetisian Cochran 2021), Zangmo took on an authoritative role, mirroring the teacher's displays of knowledge for her peers. In a practice that recalled the community's particular emphasis on "knowing from the heart and mind," Zangmo decomposed the English word, describing the equivalent Mandarin meaning of its second syllable.

Rinchen then switched into Amdo Tibetan, marking a shift in the activity frame by directing Zangmo to stand in front of her. Although Rinchen publicly addressed Zangmo, she used a code that was not understood by the non-Tibetan children. She reserved Amdo Tibetan for utterances in which she explicitly scolded Zangmo, establishing a dyadic exchange with Zangmo amid the multiparty reading activity. Rinchen switched back to Mandarin to correct Zangmo's interpretation of the word *taiyang* (sunshine). Next, she used English to rationalize her decision to scold Zangmo, explaining that she will soon enter Grade 1. With the category, "Grade 1 student," Rinchen established Zangmo's responsibility to show respect for the teacher's authority and implied that the other children would share this responsibility when they, too, entered public school. To mark the end of the scolding activity, Rinchen repeated, in English and then Mandarin, that listening to the teacher was the "rule" of the class.

By demarcating the functions of English, Mandarin, and Amdo Tibetan, Rinchen revealed beliefs about the social values of each code. Rinchen established the public role of English and Mandarin by using these codes to manage the unfolding of collaborative reading sequences and to assert her expectations for children entering public school. By moving out of Amdo Tibetan to engage with the full group of children, Rinchen excluded Amdo Tibetan from the main activity sequence of collaborative reading, relegating it to a semi-private, dyadic exchange. Rinchen's contrasting uses of these codes also underlined adults' explicit rationalization for operating "I Read" in English and Mandarin. By establishing English and Chinese as the target written languages, and associating spoken English and Mandarin with group activities, Rinchen suggested that these codes should be used publicly and inclusively. In nearly all collaborative reading activities, English and Chinese language forms provided the foundation for establishing shared meaning. However, in rare instances, Rinchen made Amdo Tibetan into an object of joint attention.

Reading Tibetan Culture in English Picture Books

On the first Wednesday in April 2017, the early spring air had not yet warmed in Xining. I had forgotten to bring gloves on the short walk from my shared apartment to the bookstore/café, so I rubbed my palms together to guard against the cold, descending dusk. I reached the café's entrance, walked up the stairs, and entered the meeting room where "I Read" would take place. As I moved through the glass doors, I blew into my open hands to warm them. I took a seat against the back wall and waited for the children and their parents to arrive.

Over the next several minutes, Janet, Gracie, Ribu, and Joshua came bounding up the stairs with their mothers. They entered the room and began to colour on a whiteboard behind me with black dry-erase markers. Their mothers settled into the chairs next to me, as Rinchen, her son Tenzin, and neighbour Zangmo arrived together. Rinchen would be leading the class again that day. She took a seat at the head of the table and called the children to gather around. She pulled out a stack of books from her oversized purse. She fanned the books out on the table and selected one titled *A Good Meal*.

Rinchen opened the first page and began asking the children to name the plethora of food items floating above a picnic basket in the picture. The children first established reference to a hunk of Swiss cheese.

Excerpt 5.3: "A Thousand Years of History"[9]

"***na zhe shi shenme***" (Then, what is this?), Rinchen asked in Mandarin. Rinchen moved her finger from the cheese to point at a container of yogurt.

"***suannai***" (Yogurt), responded Gracie, in Mandarin. Rinchen latched onto her answer.

"***suannai dui bu dui***" (Yogurt, right?), Rinchen said, acknowledging Gracie's correct response.

"Uh-huh," Gracie added in approval.

"Yogurt," added Rinchen, providing the English equivalent.

"Yogurt," I chimed in. Rinchen then marked a shift in the line of talk by switching into Amdo Tibetan.

"*ɕo ɕo*" (Yogurt, yogurt), said Rinchen. For this food item alone, Rinchen provided an equivalent Amdo Tibetan term (Tib. *zho*). She then switched back into English – "Yogurt." However, before moving to the next image of a rosy red apple, Rinchen launched into an elaborate discussion about yogurt.

"*e::* ***zangyu na ge suannai ye shi*** *ɕo* ***jiu shi*** yogurt" (Eh, in Tibetan that "*suannai*" is "*ɕo*," which means "yogurt"). Rinchen was clarifying the lexical item across Mandarin, English, and Amdo Tibetan.

"*ɕo*" (Yogurt), Ribu repeated, overlapping Rinchen's turn.

"*ɕo*" (Yogurt), I added, now overlapping Ribu. While Rinchen, Ribu, and I were focusing on the image of the yogurt, Gracie sought to advance the activity sequence to the next food item.

"Apple," added Gracie, in English. Rinchen, however, was still attending to the image of the yogurt. She latched onto Gracie's utterance, discussing the yogurt that she had referred to in her prior turn.

"***youdian jia na ge***" (Looks a little bit like that), Rinchen said. With the qualifier *youdian* (a little bit), Rinchen implied that the image did not perfectly depict Tibetan yogurt, which is never packaged. Gracie latched onto Rinchen's statement, still attempting to move the group's focus to the next image.

"Apple," Gracie repeated. Rather than taking up Gracie's turn, Richen continued with an account of her reasons for focusing on the yogurt.

"***qian nian de lishi dui bu dui suannai de lishi***" (A thousand years of history, right? The history of yogurt), Rinchen added, hinting at the cultural significance of yogurt to Tibetans. Traditionally made from the milk of *'bri* (female yak), this rich yogurt is a staple in the diets of both Tibetan farmers and nomads. In Xining, Tibetan women sold large barrels of Tibetan yogurt on street corners, and some trendy tourist shops offered ice cream made from the milk of *'bri*. Rinchen then shifted back to the sequence of naming food items.

"Okay, apple! Apple," Rinchen said. The children continued to decode the names of the food items in English and Mandarin until Rinchen turned the page to display an elaborate picnic scene in a crowded city park.

As in the other conversations in "I Read," Rinchen established an activity sequence involving picture identification and collaborative word searching between English and Mandarin. However, she initiated a minor shift in the activity sequence by providing the Amdo Tibetan word for "yogurt." One child, Ribu, took up Rinchen's emphasis on the yogurt by repeating the Amdo Tibetan word *ɕo* (yogurt). While Gracie sought to continue to the next food item, Rinchen used Mandarin to account for her continued focus on the yogurt, explaining that yogurt has a thousand years of historical significance to Tibetans. She used a seemingly mundane food item as a symbol of Tibetan cultural identity. While Rinchen was asserting a place for Tibetan language and culture in the class, she did so primarily through the channels of Mandarin and English. She did not explicitly encourage all the children to repeat the Amdo Tibetan word, and she did not use Amdo Tibetan to explain the word's meaning or guide the children's repetitions.

Therefore, although the volunteer teachers in "I Read" used English to help the children develop academic skills while subtly resisting the dominance of Mandarin, they also confirmed the displacement of Amdo Tibetan in the city. Rinchen switched into Amdo Tibetan only to shift the trajectory of an unfolding collaborative activity. For example, by using Amdo Tibetan to scold Zangmo, and then switching to Mandarin and English to explain the class rules, Rinchen established Amdo Tibetan as a private, non-inclusive language. Also, while Rinchen fleetingly introduced the Amdo Tibetan word for "yogurt," she shifted back into Mandarin to rationalize its cultural significance. She did not use any Amdo Tibetan sound forms as a basis for sustained repetition. By excluding Amdo Tibetan from public reading activities, Rinchen reinforced its difference from the cosmopolitan codes of English and Mandarin.

Conclusion: Literacy and Agency in Xining

Amid the suppression of Tibetan language advocacy, urban adults used English to quietly support bilingualism and counter the monolithic status of Mandarin in Xining. By using English as an alternative lingua franca to Mandarin, "I Read" advanced a vision of urban, multi-ethnic inclusion that was distinct from Tibetan language activism. Although the volunteer teachers' uses of code-mixing relegated Amdo Tibetan to the background of shared activities, they used Tibetan cultural frameworks of knowledge to guide collaborative reading sequences. The volunteer teachers drew on the theory of *sems kyis shes* (pronounced *sem tɕə xe*) – "knowing from the heart and mind" – to help children connect the sound forms of words to their meanings. The teachers' engagement with Amdo Tibetan culture remained almost entirely limited to English and Mandarin explanations, but they nonetheless created opportunities to link picture books to symbols of Tibetan identity. As Duranti and Ochs suggested in a study of Samoan-American reading practices, code choice cannot be taken "as a privileged key to how cultures interface in the literacy activities of a person or of a community" (1997, 170). That is, literacy activities can support cultural continuity in minoritized language communities, even when they take place through the medium of a more dominant code. In "I Read," for example, urban adults read Tibetan culture into Chinese and English texts by using the guiding framework of "knowing from the heart and mind" to organize literacy activities.

Furthermore, although the adults who organized "I Read" explicitly aimed for the participants to develop literacy in English and Chinese, the children transcended the boundaries between these two codes through their embodied reading practices. When children responded to the volunteer teachers' prompting questions, they used prosody to develop shared metalinguistic knowledge of English and Mandarin that emphasized commonalities in sound, structure, and meaning. They also used sounds and images as the basis for format tying, sequentially elaborating on language forms to co-operatively construct narratives and sound play. While the children relied on each other's words to coordinate shared understandings, they also claimed independent knowledge of language structures and meanings. By offering both complementary and contradictory answers to one another's prior turns, the children agentively established their identities as speakers of both English and Mandarin. Sound, image, and sequencing served as resources for the children to constitute shared learning experiences and assert their multilingual identities through displays of metalinguistic knowledge.

Because living languages are dynamic and changing systems, how participants orient to codes affects language vitality. Standard language ideologies that value literary languages over diverse spoken codes often overlook the forms of dynamic change that support children's continued uses of minoritized languages. "I Read" was conceived through a standard language ideology that positioned standard English as a counterpart to standard Mandarin, and the program emphasized knowledge of written English and Chinese. By organizing "I Read" as a forum for enhancing multi-ethnic preschooler's social relationships and early reading skills, urban Amdo Tibetan adults demonstrated their agency in responding to constraints on language activism and pressures for assimilation. Despite the group's explicit orientation to standard literary languages, Amdo Tibetan child learners co-created knowledge of multiple languages during sequences of collaborative reading. Young children agentively forged belonging through multimodal, dialogic engagement with texts, demonstrating the continuity of linguistic hybridity in contemporary Amdo.

Conclusion

lok wa: "Return"

It was early July 2018. That morning, I had shared a taxi with Akha Norbu, whose summer holiday from university had just begun, to travel from Xining to Tsachen Village. Sonam and Yeshi were also on summer holiday and had arrived in Tsachen a few days earlier with their families.

Seated in the back of the taxi, I looked out the window as we crossed the last pass on the winding mountain highway. Its peak was adorned with hundreds of prayer flags, marking its sacred nature. As the road opened onto the barren highland desert that rises above Tsachen, we stopped to gaze at the seemingly endless expanse of golden sand, before descending the narrowing street that leads to Tsachen's *rdzong* (town centre) (fig. 9). Then, we followed the road straight through the town. After traversing a quick two-kilometre-long stretch of gravel beyond the town's periphery, the taxi turned and began to lumber down the narrow alleys of Tsachen Village.

As we rounded the bend near Dolma and Lhamo's household, the two girls came running out of the gate to greet us. Before the car had fully stopped, they had managed to tug open the taxi's back door, as they shouted "*ʱkora ɕe! ʱkora ɕe!*" (Let's do *skor ba* [circumambulation]!). Excited to join in the girls' suggested activity, I jumped out of the taxi and followed the children as they ran off towards the *ma ni khang* (temple).

By the time I arrived at the *ma ni khang*'s gate, Lhamo and Dolma were already darting in quick circles around the temple's perimeter. Several older women were performing *skor ba* more slowly, tugging to spin the weighty prayer wheels built into the temple's exterior as they walked. I joined the older women's circumambulation route. By the time I had performed three circumambulations, considered to be the

Figure 9. The desert highland near Tsachen Village

minimum number needed to accumulate spiritual merit, I already felt tired. I sat down on the temple steps. Shortly after, the girls collapsed on the ground next to me, giggling and out of breath.

As we sat on the steps, I glanced up to see Sonam and Yeshi approaching the temple gate. Dolma also looked up, her eyes wide with curiosity.

"ŋa-zo dewa-ki ma-re-pa" (I guess they're not from our village), Dolma pondered, and began to walk towards the gate. Lhamo ran to catch up with Dolma. By the time the girls reached the entryway, Sonam was gripping the metal bars of the gate, climbing over as Yeshi steadied him from behind.

To my surprise, Dolma greeted Sonam and Yeshi in Mandarin, calling out ***"xiao pengyou! xiao pengyou!"*** (Little friend! Little friend!) as she waved. Dolma and Lhamo seemed not to recognize Sonam and Yeshi, who had not visited Tsachen village since the *lo gsar* (new year) holiday in late January. As I arrived at the gate, I explained that Sonam and Yeshi were their relatives, the grandchildren of Ayi Lhamo's cousin. My explanation seemed to spark Dolma's memory of Sonam and Yeshi's pasts visits to Tsachen, and she nodded.

"jiejie ni lai wan" (Older sister, come to play), Dolma said in Mandarin, and ran off towards the temple. Lhamo and Yeshi followed Dolma. Now accompanied by Yeshi, Dolma and Lhamo resumed their rapid, playful circumambulation, while I carried Sonam over to the temple's steps. After several more circles, the girls came to join me and Sonam to sit on the steps. In hesitating Mandarin, the girls discussed the locations of their schools – Dolma and Lhamo's in Tsachen Village, and Yeshi's in

Xining. After several moments, Lhamo took off running in circles again, and Dolma and Yeshi followed her.

While the children seemed unphased by their encounter, I was not. Over the past two years, I had watched Sonam gradually shift to speaking more and more Mandarin rather than his *yul skad*. I had watched adult family members label the speech of young children, in both the *yul skad* and Mandarin, as "Chinese." I had seen adults state that, like other urban children, Sonam and Yeshi had lost their knowledge of the Amdo *yul skad*. This mid-summer meeting suggested to me that, when Sonam and Yeshi used Mandarin, they were adapting their language use to others' expectations. Their code choices responded to a broader, community-wide identification of urban children as monolingual speakers of Mandarin. When Dolma recognized Sonam and Yeshi as outsiders, as children not from their village, she also made it explicit that the village is where the *yul skad* is grounded. I wondered what would happen for Dolma and Lhamo, when, in a few years' time, they too would depart the homeland of Tsachen to begin Grade 1 in a boarding school in Lungma County.

In this ethnography, I have shown that young children make choices in their everyday interactions that shape their trajectories of language acquisition and influence the vitality of their mother tongues. These choices dialogically unfold in the immediate social settings of real-time talk but are simultaneously rooted in political histories that sediment associations between linguistic features, collective moral values, and social identities. In the course of language acquisition and socialization, children adopt linguistic identities that will allow them to belong to their families and communities. In situations of migration and colonization, however, children encounter mismatches between the ways of speaking in their families and those that are valued in their broader communities. Studies of adults' lived experiences have demonstrated the consequences of these mismatches. As they grow up, children shift to prefer a dominant language and lose their pre-existing knowledge of their mother tongues. From studying adults' retrospective accounts, we know that language shift can rupture social relationships and fragment one's sense of self. Although we have access to adults' transparent and explicit descriptions of their shifting linguistic identities, we lack similar insights into lived experiences of language shift as it occurs across developmental time in early childhood. This book has addressed this gap in existing scholarship by charting the contrasting language-learning trajectories of rural and urban Amdo Tibetan children. It has demonstrated that, while adults often acknowledge the social and emotional challenges faced by child speakers of minoritized languages, they tend to overlook the forms of cultural knowledge that young children draw on to inform their everyday language choices.

Amdo, Tibet, serves as an important site for examining young children's processes of identity formation amid language shift. Located at the historical border of Tibet and China, Amdo's linguistic diversity has arisen from long-term migration and resulting language contact. This book has suggested that contemporary children's language use is shaped by Amdo's political history, because listeners associate features of children's speech with the forms of language contact that have accompanied coerced migration. In addition to the Chinese state's military interventions, which, throughout the second half of the twentieth century, drove many Tibetans into exile, Amdo has experienced internal political conflicts catalyzing other forms of displacement. In the twenty-first century, Chinese state-led development campaigns have spurred on rural-to-urban migration in Amdo and contributed to the encroachment of the state's official language, Mandarin, on Amdo's diverse mother tongues. Despite pressures to adopt Mandarin, Amdo Tibetan children continue to reproduce the culturally meaningful, place-based distinctions that have traditionally formatted the Amdo Tibetan language into diverse *yul skad*. With the increased flow of Amdo Tibetans from their rural homelands to Xining, children are integrating new language varieties into a central cultural logic that associates Tibetan places with distinctive ways of speaking. From this perspective, urban children's language shift to Mandarin represents cultural continuity, as children are associating this new language with Amdo Tibetan lives in the city.

Although meaningful cultural logics underly urban Amdo Tibetan children's adoption of Mandarin, language shift is not an inevitable outcome of migration. As outlined in the preface, Khangmo, an Amdo Tibetan child born in exile in India and living in New York City, adopted her mother's native Amdo Tibetan in addition to English. China's policies regarding language education and urban development pose considerable challenges for the vitality of Tibet's spoken languages. Currently, China's constitution contains some provisions for Tibetan language education in rural autonomous counties and prefectures. Despite these legislated language protections, policies for school consolidation and urbanization have displaced Amdo Tibetan children from their rural homelands. Unless their families move with them to the county seats that host primary, middle, and secondary schools, rural children must live at school as boarding students. When they enter primary school, even rural Amdo Tibetan children lose access to the social contexts of village life that have supported their continued use of the *yul skad*.

Those families privileged enough to move to Xining and participate in urban China's public education system willingly give up their children's rights to any education in Tibetan.

In February 2023, the United Nations Committee on Economic, Social and Cultural Rights expressed alarm over the approximately one million Tibetan children living away from their families in Chinese state-run boarding schools. The committee called for the Chinese state to "abolish immediately the coerced residential (boarding) school system imposed on Tibetan children and allow private Tibetan schools to be established" (Committee on Economic, Social and Cultural Rights 2023, 13). China's efforts to modernize its borderlands through urbanization have constrained secular Tibetan-language education and, combined with religious repression, have actively undermined opportunities for Tibetan children's language socialization in their mother tongues both at home and in school. Amdo Tibetan communities will continue to adapt to changing state policies. However, in the current historical moment, young Amdo Tibetan children are increasingly dissociated from the dense kinship ties that are established through their mother tongue. Continuing on this pathway may lead children's early experiences of language acquisition and socialization to result in the loss of Amdo's diverse *yul skad* and associated cultural worlds.

Appendix: Annotated Transcriptions

Glossing Conventions

Morpheme glossing follows the Leipzig Glossing Rules (Max Planck Institute for Evolutionary Anthropology 2015), with modifications for unique morpho-syntactic units in Amdo Tibetan Farmer Talk. Morpheme abbreviations are listed below.

1	*first person*
2	*second person*
3	*third person*
ABL	*ablative*
ADJ	*adjectival*
AUX	*auxiliary*
CAUS	*causative*
COND	*conditional*
COP	*copula*
CVB	*converb*
DA	*direct article*
DAT	*dative*
DE	*direct evidential*
DEM	*demonstrative*
DU	*dual*
EGO	*egophoric*
EPIS	*epistemic*
ERG	*ergative*
EXCL	*exclamation*
FOC	*focus*
FUT	*future*
GEN	*genitive*

IA *indirect article*
IE *indirect evidential*
IMP *imperative*
INS *instrumental*
LOC *locative*
NEG *negative*
NMLZ *nominalizer*
OBL *oblique*
PFC *perfect*
PROG *progressive*
PRS *present*
PST *past*
Q *question*
QUOT *quotative*
RES *resultative*

Suprasegmental features and turn-taking are marked using conventions from conversation analysis (Jefferson 2004):

[ ] indicates overlapping talk
= indicates latching
(.) indicates brief pause
: indicates vowel elongation
? indicates slight rising tone
! indicates slight falling tone
↑ indicates substantial rising tone
↓ indicates substantial falling tone
(( )) provides contextual details
( ) provides additional clarity regarding referents

Excerpt 2.1: "Look at Achi"

Context: Lhamo [L] (age 5 years, 7 months), Dolma [D] (7 years, 3 months), and Tenzin [T] (3 years, 5 months) play in the courtyard of their home in Tsachen. Ama [A] and Ani Khangla [AK] sit on the steps. Ama holds baby Yangki [baby Y] (age 3 months), and Ani Khangla holds baby Tashi [baby T] (age 3 months). Lhamo, Dolma, and Tenzin form a circle with Ama and Ani Khangla. The participants use spatial deixis to discuss the kin relationship between the two infants. Amdo Tibetan words are in italics. Deictic markers are bolded.

1 D *da k^hə-ɲə k^hə-ɲə-a ^{h}ta-ki-joŋ ani*
then 3-DU 3-DU-DAT look-CVB-CAUS ani
Ani, make them look at each other ((pointing and waving at baby T))

2 AK *ja ja*
ok ok
Okay, okay ((moving body orientation towards baby Y))

3 D *wumo awu-a ^{h}ti*
girl awu-DAT look\IMP
((to baby Y)) Girl, look at Awu

((L moves towards T with arms outstretched and pinches his cheeks. Eight seconds elapse, as both L and T move back towards the others.))

4 D *atɕ^{h}i **gen!***
achi **over_there**
((to baby T)) Achi, **over there**!

((baby T moves head towards baby Y))

5 D *tɕ^{h}o-ɲə ^{h}ts^{h}e-a-de-a*
2-DU play-CVB-stay-EMP
You two keep playing

6 L ***gen** ^{h}ti-da-kə*
over_there look-PROG-DE
(baby Tashi) is looking **over there**

7 L *a::-ze k^hər-ki k^hə-a k^hər-ki awu ra ze*
a::-QUOT 3-ERG 3-DAT 3-GEN awu COP QUOT
Hey, she'll say he's her Awu

8 L *^{n}**di**-a k^hər-ki atɕ^{h}i ^{n}**di**-a k^hər-ki* (.)
this-DAT 3-GEN achi **this**-DAT 3-ERG
This one ((pointing to baby T)), his Achi, **this** one, he –

((D, A, and AK begin to laugh at the infants.))

9 L *aləi! ^{n}də.gə-ne*
EXCL like_this-then
Wow! Like this, then

10 L *kʰə-a lo xtɕik͡tʰon-na-ta atɕʰi zer-nə-re*
3-DAT year one arrive-COND-CVB achi say-FCT-FCT
When she's a year old, she'll be called "Achi" ((pointing to baby Y))

11 L *ⁿ**di**-a lo xtɕik͡tʰon-na awu zer-nə-re=*
this-DAT year one arrive-COND awu say-FCT-FCT
When **this** one's a year old, he'll be called "Awu" ((pointing to baby T))

12 AK *=kʰə-a awu ze-nə-ma-re*
3-DAT awu say-FCT-NEG-FCT
He won't be called "Awu"

13 AK *kʰə nuwo re ɲima kʰaxi=*
3 younger COP days several
He's younger by several days

((Baby Y cooes, and baby T turns his head in response.))

14 D *=a:: **gen** ʰti*
EXCL **over_there** look\IMP
Hey, look **over there**! ((pointing to baby T))

15 D *awu atɕʰi-a ʰti-a-toŋ*
awu achi-DAT look-CVB-IMP
Awu, look at Achi ((holding baby T's arm to reorient his body))

16 AK *atɕʰi-a ʰti-a-toŋ-ja*
achi-DAT look-CVB-IMP-EMP
Look at Achi

17 D *atɕʰi **gen**! (.) awu Tashi ((giggles))*
achi **over_there** awu Tashi
Achi, **over there**! Awu Tashi ((giggles))

18 baby T *hi::*
hi::
((Baby T exhales audibly, and the other participants laugh.))

19 AK *hi:: **gen***
hi:: **over_there**
"hi::" **over there**

Excerpt 2.2: "The One Where We Had Chased the Cats"

Context: Lhamo [L] (age 5 years, 7 months), Dolma [D] (7 years, 3 months), and I [S], are playing outside in Tsachen Village. The girls are picking dandelions and blowing off the seed heads. Lhamo and Dolma discuss where to find the most dandelions. They use spatial deixis to coordinate shared movement. Amdo Tibetan words are in italics. Deictic markers are bolded.

1 L *ani* ***gen*** *-na* *jo-pa*
ani **over_there**-LOC COP-EPIS
((to S)) There must be some (dandelions) **over there**, Ani ((pointing past bend in road))

2 L ***gen***-*ni* ***jar*** *koŋwa* ^{n}*dʑo-ra* *jo-pa*
over_there-ABL **up** house go-PRT COP-EPIS
Let's go **over there**, to the house **up there**, there must be (some)

3 L ^{n}***di***-*ni* ***jar*** *koŋ* ***gen*** *-na* *jo-pa*
here-ABL **up** house **over_there**-LOC COP-EPIS
From **here**, the house way over **up there**, there must be (some)

4 D ***gen***-*na* *jo-nə-ma-re*
over_there-LOC COP-FCT-NEG-FCT
There aren't any **over there**

5 L *jo-ki-a (.)* ***gen*** *ker-ker-wo*
COP-DE-EMP **over_there** white-RED-NMLZ
((pointing to distant house)) There are! **Over there**, what about those white ones?

6 L ***gen*** *min-ne*
over_there COP\NEG-Q
Aren't those (dandelions) **over there**?

7 D *kə* *ma-re!*
that NEG-COP
That's not (them)!

8 L *ŋa ^{n}dʑo ʰta*
1 go look
I'll go look.

((L runs towards the distant house. For twenty-five seconds, D ponders where to locate the dandelions))

9 L *wase! hor.dʑu maŋ.ŋa jo-ki-a*
EXCL dandelions many COP-DE-EMP
Wow! There's so many dandelions!

10 D *^{n}dʑo!*
go\IMP
Let's go!

((D takes S's hand and runs towards L.))

11 D *ani kʰər-ki ɕob-taŋ-jo-ki*
ani 3-ERG take-AUX-PFC-DE
Ani, she's already picked all of them

12 D ***gen**-ni ta maŋ-nə-re-ja*
over_there-ABL EMP many-FCT-FCT-EMP
Hey, there's a lot **over there** ((pointing away from L))

13 D ***har**-ra akʰə-tɕʰo ^{n}dʑo-sa jo-la*
up_there-LOC 1-PL go-NMLZ COP-EPIS
Up there, there must be a place for us to go

14 D *lam zək̚-ke ʈʂaŋmo zək̚^{n}di.mo*
road IA straight DA like_this
There's a straight road, like this,

15 D *akʰə-tɕʰo milu da-ki-jo-no*
1-PL cat chase-CVB-PFC-NMLZ
the one where we had chased the cats ((drawing on left hand with right fingertips))

16 D *ʰkor-ʰkor ^{n}di.ni.ta da maŋ.ŋa jo-no*
round-RED then EMP many COP-NMLZ
Round and round, then there's (a road) with many (dandelions)

17 D *ⁿdʑo ta!*
go\IMP EMP
Let's go, then!

Excerpt 2.3: "Let's Go, Yeshi!"

Context: Sonam [S] (age 2 years, 5 months) is in his apartment with Ani Tsering Kyi [AT], Ayi Lhamo [AL], and me. Cousin Yeshi [Y] is in her bedroom. Ani Tsering Kyi looks at a car catalogue with Sonam and uses spatial deixis to include Yeshi in her play with Sonam. Amdo Tibetan words are in italics. Mandarin words are bolded and underlined. Deictic markers are bolded.

1 AT *ŋi-kə awu ra ŋi-ɣɲi-kə* **<u>che</u>** *-a ʰta rema*
1-ERG awu and 1-DU-ERG **<u>car</u>**-DAT look quickly
Awu and I, let's both look at the **<u>cars</u>**, quickly

2 S *awu* **<u>che</u>** *ʰta*
awu **<u>car</u>** look
Awu (will) look at **<u>cars</u>**

3 AT *awu-kə* **<u>che</u>** *(.) awu* **<u>che</u>** *gaŋ re?*
awu-GEN **<u>car</u>** awu **<u>car</u>** which COP?
Awu's **<u>car</u>**. Which is Awu's **<u>car</u>**?

4 AT *ani ɕol-a-toŋ*
ani tell-CVB-IMP
Tell Ani

5 S ***ⁿdi***
DEM
This one ((pointing to a black SUV in the catalogue))

6 AT *ani* ***ⁿdi*** *si-kə* **<u>che</u>** *re*
then **DEM** who-GEN **<u>car</u>** COP
Then, whose **<u>car</u>** is **this**? ((pointing to a red sedan in the catalogue))

7 S *ani-kə*
ani-GEN
Ani's

8 AT *ani-kə* **<u>che</u>** *re*
ani-GEN **<u>car</u>** COP
It's Ani's **<u>car</u>**

9 S *^{n}**di** awu-kə che*
DEM awu-GEN **car**
This, Awu's **car** ((pointing to a red sedan in the catalogue))

10 S *^{n}**di** awu-kə che (.) ^{n}**di** awu-kə re-ja*
DEM awu-GEN **car** **DEM** awu-ERG COP-EMP
This, Awu's **car**. Hey! This one's Awu's

11 AT *awu daŋ atɕ^{h}i-kə che*
awu and achi-GEN **car**
Awu and Achi's **car**

12 AT *^{n}**di** ap^{h}a-kə che re-la?*
DEM apha-GEN **car** COP-EPIS
Isn't **this** one Apha's **car**? ((pointing to a black SUV in the catalogue))

13 S *ma-re awu-kə re*
NEG-COP awu-GEN COP
No! It's Awu's!

14 AT *o:: awu-kə re awu-kə re*
oh awu-GEN COP awu-GEN COP
Oh, it's Awu's, it's Awu's

15 AT *^{n}**di** tɕ^{h}i re*
DEM what COP
What's **this**? ((pointing to the SUV's tire))

16 S *^{n}**di** awu-kə che re*
DEM awu-GEN **car** COP
This is Awu's **car**

17 AT *^{n}**di** che -kə ^{h}korlo zək̚ re-ja ze-go*
DEM **car**-GEN wheel DA COP-EMP say-need
You should say, "**This** is the **car**'s wheel"

18 S *^{h}korlo*
wheel
Wheel!

((AT and S continue a question-and-answer sequence for one minute, twenty seconds. AT turns a page in the catalogue, marking a new line of play.))

19 AT *a:: awu l^{h}odʐa-na ^{n}dʑo-kə tɕ^{h}i* ***<u>che</u>*** *^{h}kor-re*
EXCL awu school-LOC go-PRT 2\ERG **<u>car</u>** drive-PRT
Ah! Awu, to get to school, you drive the **<u>car</u>**!

20 AT *atɕ^{h}i Yeshi* ***^{n}de*** *ts^{h}ok̚-kə-dʑɨ-taŋ*
achi Yeshi **there** sit-PRT-CAUS-IMP
Have Achi Yeshi sit **there** ((pointing to the passenger's seat))

21 AT *awu* ***^{n}de*** *ts^{h}ok̚-taŋ*
awu **there** sit-IMP
Awu, sit **there** ((pointing to the driver's seat))

22 AT *awu* ***<u>che</u>*** *^{h}kor-re atɕ^{h}i l^{h}odʐa-na ^{n}dʑo*
awu **<u>car</u>** drive-PRT achi school-LOC go\IMP
While Awu's driving the **<u>car</u>**, he says, "Achi, let's go to school!"

23 AT *rema xok̚ ^{ɦ}we k^{h}ər-ra xok̚ ze-na*
quickly come\IMP bag carry-PRT come\IMP say-COND
"Come quickly! Come and bring your schoolbag!"

24 S *mm mm*
mm hmm ((smiling and nodding))

25 AT *awu* ***<u>che</u>*** *^{h}kor*
awu **<u>car</u>** drive
Awu, drive the **<u>car</u>**!

26 AT *atɕ^{h}i naŋ-ŋa ^{n}dʑo-ja l^{h}odʐa go-na soŋ*
achi inside-LOC go-EMP school door-LOC go\IMP
"Achi, go inside! Go into the school!"

27 AT *bi:: bi:: t^{h}on-taŋ-a zer-toŋ-a (.) jin-na?*
beep beep arrive-PST-EMP say-IMP-EMP COP-COND
Beep beep! Say "We arrived!" Right?

28 S *ə: ə:*
eh eh
Eh eh

((Ten lines omitted, AT advances the storyline))

29 AT ***gen*** *da ts^{h}ə da.kə ts^{h}ə ze-ta*
over_there PRT what all.those what say-PRT
What about all those, **over there**? ((pointing to the back seats))

30 AT *awu-kə ʰkor-taŋ*
awu-ERG drive-IMP
Awu, drive

31 AT *apʰa ⁿ**de** tsʰok̚-kə-dʑɨ-taŋ*
apha **there** sit-PRT-CAUS-IMP
Make Apha sit **there** ((pointing to the right-hand back seat))

32 AT *ama ⁿ**di** tsʰok̚-kə-dʑɨ-taŋ*
ama **here** sit-PRT-CAUS-IMP
Make Ama sit **here** ((pointing to left-hand back seat))

33 AT *ama tsʰaŋ ⁿdʑo-ze awu-kə* ***che*** *ʰkor*
mom house go-QUOT awu-ERG **car** drive
"Let's go to Ama's house!" Awu's driving the **car**.

34 AT *zər-zər-zər-zər-zər*
zoom-RED-RED-RED-RED
Zoom zoom zoom zoom zoom!

35 S *Yeshi:: ⁿdʑo*
Yeshi go\IMP
Yeshi! Let's go!

((Y comes out of her bedroom and into the living room when her name is called.))

Excerpt 3.1: "The Mother Ant Keeps Crying"

Context: Dolma [D] (age 6 years, 1 month), Lhamo [L] (4 years, 5 months), and Dolkar [DK] (approximately 2 years, 6 months) are playing in the sand near Dolkar's house. I [S] watch them. Dolkar's grandmother Ayi Tsomo [AT] is sitting nearby and holding Dolkar's baby sister, Yangmo [Y]. Dolma, Lhamo, and Dolkar play with ants, moving them into and out of a plastic box. Ayi Tsomo intervenes when the girls begin to argue. Amdo Tibetan words are in italics. Mandarin loan words are bolded.

1 L *e:: e:: e::! ɕaji xtɕik̚ ama xtɕik̚ e:! e:!*
EXCL child one mother one hey hey
Ah ah ah! There's one child and one mother. Hey, hey!

2 L *Dolma raŋ-ki ɕe-jak̚ ^{n}di ma-ɕi*
Dolma self-ERG do-NMLZ this NEG-do\IMP
Dolma, you don't do like that!

3 L *tɕʰə re ajə! [de-a-ʰti]*
what COP EXCL stay-CVB-look\IMP
What's this? Whoa! Keep looking!

4 D *[hə] da ji mə-ʳgo-kə-ja=*
EXCL then do NEG-need-DE-EMP
Eh! Then, you don't need to do that

5 L *=e e e bətɕʰokm̚a ^{n}di bətɕʰokm̚a*
EXCL ant this ant
Ah! Ah! Ah! Here's an ant! An ant!

6 D *har-ra dɨk̚*
away-LOC move
((to L)) Move away

7 L *raŋ-ki ama de-a-ʰti (.)*
self-ERG mother stay-CVB-look\IMP
You keep watching the mother.

8 L *[^{n}di min-na ^{n}de tɕʰu ʰti]*
this COP\NEG-Q there 2 look\IMP
Isn't this (the mother)? There, you look!
[((Baby Y whines.))]

9 L *e: e: [^{n}di min-nə-e-ra? tɕʰu ʰti]*
EXCL this COP\NEG-FCT-Q-FCT 2 look\IMP
Ah, ah! Isn't this it (the mother)? You look

10 D *[rema rema rema]*
quickly quickly quickly
Quickly, quickly, quickly!

11 S *[bu re]*
bug COP
It's a bug.

12 L *e: e: e:! e::! bətɕʰokm̚a raŋ-ki de-a-ʰti*
EXCL ant self-ERG stay-CVB-look\IMP
Hey, hey, hey! Hey! You keep watching the ant

13 L *dʑok̚-ko-dʑik̚-[la-go]*
put-NMLZ-put-CVB-need
It's the one we should put in (the box)

14 D *[ma-re]*
NEG-COP
It's not.

15 L *ama! ama! ŋi ŋi=*
EXCL EXCL 1\ERG 1\ERG
My goodness! I, I –

16 AT *=ⁿdi ɕi-ra-ta bətɕʰok̚ma ama goŋmo joŋ-ŋe*
this do-CVB-PRT ant mother night come-CVB
If you do this, the ant's mother will come in the night

17 AT *sipi naŋ-ŋa dzi-ⁿdʑo-nə-re=*
stomach in-LOC enter-go-FCT-FCT
and go into your stomach

18 L *=aji!=*
ayi
Ayi!

19 D *=ŋe tɕʰu* ***ba*** ***gei-*** *o*
1\ERG 2 **AUX** **give**-EMP
I'm **giving** (this) to you

20 L *ʱɲəŋmadʑi:: kʰə-a*
compassion 3-DAT
Compassion to him!

21 D *ama joŋmo xi-dep-da-de*
mother ant cry-VZR-CVB-stay
The mother ant keeps crying

22 L *ʱɲəŋmadʑi (.) bətɕʰok̚ma tʰok-tʰok-ki ⁿdə.gə*
compassion ant just-RED-ADJ like_this
Compassion! This is exactly an ant. Like this

23 D *kʰər-ki ama tsʰel-kə-joŋ-tʰa*
3-GEN mother search-CVB-come-PST\DE
His mother came to look for him

24 L *ⁿdi? ama? ə? ə?*
this mother eh eh
This one? The mother? Uh? Uh?

25 DK *ajo ajo ajo*
((sound play))

26 L ((growls)) *ma-xi-ki*
NEG-die-DE
((growls)) It hasn't died

27 DK *moja moja! i:: i::*
((sound play))

28 D *Dolkar ama ^{n}di naŋ-ŋa ϕdʑok̚-taŋ=*
Dolkar mother here in-LOC put-IMP
Dolkar, put the mother in here

29 L *=e! ma-ji (.) kʰər-ki ama ^{n}də ^{n}də*
EXCL NEG-do 3-ERG mother there there
Hey! Don't. It's his mother, there, there

Excerpt 3.2: "You Don't Need Achi?"

Context: Sonam [S] (age 2 years) is playing in the living room of his apartment with his cousin Yeshi [Y] (7 years). Yeshi's mother, Ani Tsering Kyi [AT], and the children's grandmother Ayi Lhamo [AL] are sitting nearby with me. Sonam pulls Yeshi's hair. Ani Tsering Kyi and Ayi Lhamo respond by choreographing Yeshi's exclusion. Mandarin loan words are bolded.

1 AT *Sonam tɕʰo atɕʰi-kə ʂtɕa tʰen-toŋ-ne Sonam-kə*
Sonam 2 achi-GEN hair pull-PST-FOC Sonam-ERG
Sonam, you pulled Achi's hair, Sonam did

2 S *hə hə*
Uh-huh

3 AL *ama!*
EXCL
My goodness!

4 AT *atɕʰi mə-ʳgo-ni awu atɕʰi mə-ʳgo-ni*
achi NEG-need-Q awu achi NEG-need-Q
Don't need Achi? Awu doesn't need Achi?

5 S *hə hə*
Uh-huh

6 AT *mə-ʳgo?*
NEG-need
Don't need?

7 AT *na atɕʰi ani-sa tʰur-ra-toŋ-a*
then achi ani-NMLZ towards-LOC-IMP-EMP
Achi, follow me, then

8 S *hə hə*
Uh-huh

9 AL *o: na?*
EXCL then
Oh well?

10 AT *atɕʰi ani-kə ⁿdʑo-kə-dʑak̚-kə-taŋ-ŋa*
achi ani-ERG go-CVB-CAUS-CVB-AUX\PST-EGO
Ani made Achi leave

((Y follows AT, moving near the apartment door.))

11 AL *o.ta kʰe-a atɕʰi me-la*
EXCL 3-OBL achi COP\NEG-EPIS
Well then, it seems he has no Achi

12 AT *atɕʰi baɪ-baɪ atɕʰi baɪ-baɪ ze ⁿdʑo-kə-dʑak̚-kə-toŋ*
achi bye-bye achi bye-bye say go-CVB-CAUS-CVB-IMP
Say "Bye-bye, Achi! Bye-bye Achi!" to make her leave

13 S *hə hə*
Uh-huh

14 AT *atɕʰi mə-ʳgo*
achi NEG-need
(You) don't need Achi

15 S *mm*
Mm hmm

16 AT *ja ja ŋi atɕʰi Yeshi ⁿdʑo-kə-dʑak̚-kə-taŋ-ŋa*
ok ok 1\ERG achi Yeshi go-CVB-CAUS-CVB-PST-EGO
Okay, then, I made Achi Yeshi leave

17 AT *ani ra atɕʰi ɣɲikə ⁿdʑo-kə-dʑak̚-kə-taŋ-ŋa*
ani and achi both go-CVB-CAUS-CVB-PST-EGO
Both Ani and Achi left

18 S *hə hə*
Uh-huh

19 AT *na ani e-ʳgo*
then ani Q-need
Then, do you need Ani?

20 S *go-a!*
need-EMP
(I) need!

21 AT *go-a?*
need-EMP
(You) need?

22 S *ⁿdi mə-ʳgo*
DEM NEG-need
(I) don't need her ((pointing to Yeshi))

23 AT *ja na atɕʰi go-ne-soŋ*
ok then achi door-ABL-go\IMP
Okay, then, Achi, go outside

24 AT *atɕʰi xok̚ awu-kə tɕʰu mə-ʳgo ze-kə*
achi come\IMP awu-ERG 2\OBL NEG-need say-DE
Achi, come. Awu says he doesn't need you

25 AL *e-go-a? ze-kə-ja rema go-a ze*
Q-need-EMP say-DE-EMP quickly need-EMP say\IMP
She's saying "Do you need me?" Okay, quickly say, "I need you!"

26 AT *atɕʰi ⁿdʑo-soŋ*
achi go-PST
Achi left

27 S ***shenme! shenme ! shenme !***
what what what
What! What! What!

28 AT *awu baɪ-baɪ ze-toŋ-ja atɕʰi*
awu bye-bye say-IMP-EMP achi
Brother, say "bye-bye" to Achi

29 S ***shenme?***
what
What?

30 AL *ma-ⁿdʑo ze-toŋ-ja rema*
NEG-go\IMP say-IMP-EMP quickly
Quickly, say "Don't go!"

31 S *shenme*
what
What

32 AL *daŋ tɕ^{h}e:: ze-toŋ-ja rema*
love big say-IMP-EMP quickly
Quickly, say "I love you!"

33 S *shenme*
what
What

34 AL *shenme ze-zək̚*
what say\PST-IE
(You) said "**what**"

35 S *shenme*
what
What

((Ten seconds omitted. S turns in circles and points his hands towards the ceiling.))

36 S *awu-kə atɕ^{h}i Yeshi ^{h}ta-kə-^{n}dʑo*
awu-ERG achi Yeshi see-CVB-go
Awu's going to see Achi Yeshi

37 AL *[ai:::]*
Aww

38 AT *[a::] atɕ^{h}i raŋ-ki naŋ-ŋa xok̚*
aw achi self-INS inside-LOC come\IMP
Aw, Achi, bring yourself inside!

39 AT *jaŋ awu-kə go-ze*
again awu-ERG need-QUOT
Again, Awu's saying he needs you

Excerpt 3.3: "How Much Do You Love Me?"

Context: Yeshi has returned to the apartment following excerpt 3.2. She goes into her bedroom, while I stay in the living room with Sonam [S], Ani Tsering Kyi [AT], and Ayi Lhamo [AL]. Ani Tsering Kyi elicits statements of love from Sonam.

1 AT *ja na tɕʰo ani daŋ-e-tɕʰe*
EMP then 2 ani love-Q-big
So, then, do you love Ani a lot?

2 S *tɕʰe*
big
A lot

3 AT *daŋ tɕʰe tɕi.mo.zək̚ daŋ tɕʰe*
love big how_much love big
A lot. How much do you love (me)?

4 S *apʰa daŋ tɕʰe*
apha love big
(I) love Apha a lot

5 AT *apʰa daŋ tɕʰe?*
apha love big
(You) love Apha a lot?

6 S *ama daŋ tɕʰe*
ama love big
(I) love Ama a lot

7 AT *ama ra daŋ tɕʰe? ani daŋ tɕʰe-a?*
ama and love big ani love big-EMP
(You) also love Ama a lot? Do (you) love Ani a lot?

8 S *apʰa daŋ tɕʰe ama daŋ tɕʰe aji daŋ tɕʰe*
apha love big ama love big ayi love big
(I) love Apha a lot, (I) love Ama a lot, (I) love Ayi a lot

9 AT *aji daŋ mə-tɕʰe apʰa daŋ mə-tɕʰe ama daŋ mə-tɕʰe*
ayi love NEG-big apha love NEG-big ama love NEG-big
(You) don’t love Ayi a lot, (you) don’t love Apha a lot,
(you) don’t love Ama a lot

10 AT *ani tɕɨk̚.ko daŋ tɕʰe-a*
ani refuse love big-EMP
(You) refuse to love Ani

11 AT *na rema ani uba-ɕe*
then quickly ani hug-VZR
Then, quickly hug Ani.

12 AT *ʰkepa zək̚ xtɕik̚ doŋ-ŋa-toŋ uba-ɕe*
neck DA one give-CVB-IMP hug-VZR
Give one hug around the neck

13 AT *lokwa ɣɲi-kə uba-ɕe-taŋ*
hands both-INS hug-VZR-IMP
Hug with both your hands

((S turns and hugs AT.))

14 AT *ama ama tɕʰo da xtɕik̚ ɲen-kə-a-ze*
EXCL EXCL 2 EMP EMP good-DE-EMP-EPIS
Wow, wow! You are certainly such a good boy

15 AT *tɕʰo da raŋ-ŋa xtɕik̚ ma-re jin-na*
2 EMP self-PRT EMP NEG-COP COP-COND
(Before) you weren't yourself, right?

16 AT *Sonam ⁿdi.ⁿdʐa xtɕik̚ ɲen-go*
Sonam like_this EMP good-PRT
Sonam is good like this

Excerpt 4.1: "You Have a Goat's Mouth!"

Context: Lhamo [L] (age 3 years, 11 months) and Dolma [D] (5 years, 7 months), and their cousins Dawa [DW] (5 years, 7 months) and Dolkar [DK] (3 years) are folding paper into different shapes in Lhamo and Dolma's home. Lhamo and Dolma's mother, Ama [A], is playing with them. Mandarin words are bolded.

1 DW *L ⁿdi.gə ɕatok̚ li-dʑi-re-ja jin-na?*
L like_this hat make-FUT-FUT-EMP COP-COND
Lhamo, we'll make a hat like this. Right?

2 L *ɕatok̚li-dʑi-ma-re-ja* ***feiji feiji***
hat make-FUT-NEG-FUT-EMP **airplane airplane**
We won't make a hat. **An airplane, an airplane**

3 DW *ŋi mtsʰodzu li-dʑi*
1\ERG boat make-FUT
I'll make a boat

4 A *ɣnamdzu ze-nə-re*
plane say-FCT-FCT
One says "airplane"

5 D *ŋa-tsʰo* ***feiji*** *li-dʑi* ***feiji*** *da =*
1-PL **airplane** make-FUT **airplane** EMP
We'll make **an airplane**. **An airplane**, then

6 DW *= ŋa-ts^{h}o-gə mts^{h}odʑu li-dʑi*
1-PL-ERG boat make-FUT
We'll make a boat

7 DW *ŋa-ɣɲi-gə mts^{h}odʑu li-dʑi jin-na*
1-DU-ERG boat make-FUT COP-COND
We two ((pointing to D)) will make a boat, right?

8 DK *ŋa-ts^{h}o ɣnamdʑu li-dʑi ak^{h}ə-ɣɲi-gi mts^{h}odʑu li-a*
1-PL airplane make-FUT 2-DU-ERG boat make-EMP
((pointing to D)) We'll make an airplane. ((pointing to DW and L)) You two make boats

9 DW *ŋa mts^{h}odʑu li-mə-xi-a =*
1 boat make-NEG-know-EMP
I don't know how to make a boat

10 D *= tɕ^{h}e-tɕ^{h}u da* ***feiji*** *li-mə-xi-a*
2-PL EMP **airplane** make-NEG-know-EMP
You all don't know how to make **an airplane** then

11 D *ŋi mts^{h}odʑu li-a =*
1\ERG boat make-EMP
I'll make a boat

12 A *=ama ra-ma-lik̚ ɣnamdʑu ze-nə-re =*
EXCL goat-NEG-sheep airplane say-FCT-FCT
My goodness! Neither goat nor sheep! One says "airplane"

13 L ***=feiji*** *da* ***feiji*** *li-go-a*
airplane EMP **airplane** make-want-EMP
(I) want to make **an airplane**, then, **an airplane**!

14 A *ŋo-ts^{h}a rama k^{h}a tɕ^{h}o*
face-hot goat mouth 2
((to L)) Shame. Like a goat's mouth!

15 D *L da ŋo-mə-ts^{h}a rama k^{h}a*
Lhamo EMP face-NEG-hot goat mouth
Lhamo's not ashamed, then. Goat's mouth!

((L wails and runs outside to the porch, where she is comforted by cousin Tashi.))

Excerpt 4.2: "I Won't Go to the Homeland!"

Context: Aphu Lhundhup [AL] is discussing Sonam's language use with me. Ayi Lhamo sits on the couch with baby cousin Sherab on her lap. Sonam [S] (age 3 years, 8 months) interjects in Aphu Lhundhup's talk. Mandarin words are bolded.

1 AL *kʰə-a gen-na ^{n}dʑo-go* ***you'eryuan*** *-na ^{n}dʑo-go*
3-DAT over_there-LOC go-need **preschool**-LOC go-need
He has to go over there, to the **preschool**

2 AL *kʰə-a ʳdʑaʰke zək̚ ma-lʰəb-na*
3-DAT Chinese DA NEG-learn-COND
If he doesn't learn any Chinese,

3 AL *ɕipa-kə ^{n}di.^{n}dʐa mə-ko-ki-a*
children-ERG like_this NEG-understand-EVID-EMP
the other children won't understand him

4 AL *ɕoŋ.la.ta ə-tɕʰu ^{n}de-ni kʰor-kʰor ɕe*
so 3-PL DEM-ABL around-RED do
So, when they go around,

5 AL *^{n}de-na kʰorjul ^{n}də.^{n}dʐa mə-xa-kə*
DEM-COND environment like_that NEG-good-DE
then the environment isn't good like that

6 AL *kʰə-a go-a ʰtsʰe-ne ɕipa-ki ʰtsʰe-ki-soŋ-ŋa*
2-DAT outside-LOC play-ABL children-ERG play-CVB-go-CVB
When he plays outside, when the children go to play,

7 AL *kʰə-ʳkə ʰtsʰe tsʰaŋma ʳdʑa tak̚-tak̚ re*
3-GEN play all Chinese exactly-RED COP
their play is all exactly Chinese

8 AL *kʰə-a ʳdʑajik̚ ma-tʰon-na ^{n}dʑo-sa me-la*
3-DAT Chinese NEG-know-COND go-NMLZ COP-EPIS
If he doesn't know written Chinese, he will have nowhere to go

9 AL *kʰə kʰəmo re-a*
3 alone COP-EMP
He's alone, then

10 S *apʰu::* ***ni bie dasheng yidian***
aphu **2 NEG/IMP big_voice a_little**
Aphu, **don't talk so loudly**

11 AL *ja (.) ze.na.ta ŋa-tsʰo jul-va ^{n}dʑo pʰajul-va ^{n}dʑo*
ok so 1-PL land-LOC go homeland-LOC go
Okay. Then, if we go to our land, to our homeland,

12 AL *kʰə-a kʰorjul-ki laka xa-kə*
3-DAT environment-GEN all_those good-DE
everything in the environment is good for him

13 AL *tsʰaŋma woʳke ɸɕe-no ^{n}di ɸɕe-na*
all Tibetan speak-NMLZ DEM speak-COND
Because everyone speaks Tibetan,

14 AL *kʰə jaŋ woʳke ɸɕe*
2 also Tibetan speak
he will also speak Tibetan

15 S ***ni bie dasheng yidian ni bie dasheng yidian***
2 NEG/IMP big_voice a_little 2 NEG/IMP big_voice a_little
Don't talk so loudly, don't talk so loudly

16 AL *o.ta pʰajul-va ^{n}dʑo-dʑi?*
EXCL homeland-LOC go-FUT
Oh, then, will (you) go to the homeland?

17 S *pʰajul mə-^{n}dʑo*
homeland NEG-go
(I) won't go to the homeland

18 AL *Tsachen ^{n}dʑo-la akʰə-tɕʰo ʰtsʰerok˺ jo*
Tsachen go-LOC 1-PL playmate COP
If (you) go to Tsachen, all our playmates are there

19 S ***bu yao wo yao wo gege***
NEG want 1 want 1\GEN older_brother
(I) don't want (them). I want my older brother

20 AL *do-a do-a akʰə-tɕʰo tɕʰimtsʰaŋ tsʰaŋma jo-no*
wait-EMP wait-EMP 1-PL family all COP-NMLZ
Wait, wait, all our family is there

21 S ***bu yao wo yao wo gege***
NEG want 1 want 1\GEN older_brother
(I) don't want (them). I want my older brother!

22 AL *aləi*
EXCL
Oh

23 S ***chao si le(.) wo yao wo gege***
noise die EMP 1 want 1\GEN older_brother
It's so loud! I want my older brother!

24 AL *^{n}dʑo-la Tsachen ^{n}dʑo-na ak^{h}ə-tɕ^{h}o awu Dawa atɕ^{h}i Dolma*
go-LOC Tsachen go-COND 1-PL awu Dawa achi Dolma
If you go to Tsachen, there's our Awu Dawa and Achi Dolma

25 S *ap^{h}u* ***chao si le chao si le !***
aphu **noise die EMP noise die EMP**
Aphu, it's so loud, it's so loud!

26 AL *k^{h}a rok˺ do (.) ^{n}də.gə ji ɲen-nə-ma-re*
mouth quiet stay\IMP like_this do good-FCT-NEG-FCT
Be quiet. Doing like this isn't good

27 S *na ŋi k^{h}a rok˺* ***shuo*** *! o! tɕ^{h}i tɕ^{h}its^{h}ək* ***shuo*** *? ap^{h}u!*
EXCL 1\ERG mouth quiet **say** EXCL 2 what **say** aphu
Then, I **said** be quiet! Oh! What are you **saying**? Aphu!

28 AL *ap^{h}u ɸɕe-ko-no mə-t^{h}un-nə-re?*
grandpa say-PROG-NMLZ NEG-agree-FCT-FCT
Don't (you) agree with what Aphu is saying?

29 S ***chao si le***
noise die EMP
It's so loud

30 AL ***chao si le?*** *ap^{h}u ɸɕe-ko-no e-ko-kə?*
noise die EMP aphu say-PROG-NMLZ Q-understand-DE
It's so loud? Do (you) understand what Aphu is saying?

31 S *mə-ko-kə*
NEG-understand-DE
(I) don't understand

Excerpt 5.1: "What Is 'Turtle'?"

Context: Volunteer teacher Rinchen [R] is leading a class session of "I Read." Amdo Tibetan children Zangmo [Z] (age 7), Ribu [RI] (6), Gracie [G] (5), and Migmar (6), and Han Chinese children Joshua (6) and Janet (5) sit around a table with Rinchen. I [S] observe with two parents from seats against the side wall. Rinchen and the children use Mandarin and English to identify animals from a picture book, *Spring Is Here*. Mandarin words are bolded.

1 R ***ranhou na ge*** *tur↓tles turtle* ***shi shenme ya***
then that PRT turtles turtle **is what EMP**
Then, those "turtles," **what is** "turtle"?

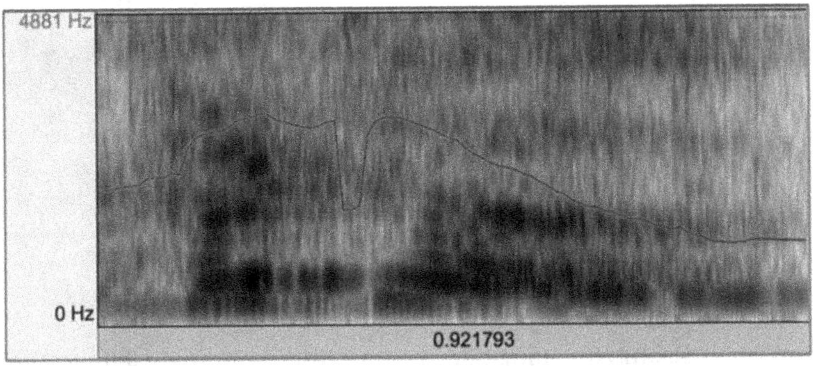

Figure 10. Pitch contour of "turtles" (excerpt 5.1, line 1)

2 Z *tu↓zi*
rabbit
Rabbit

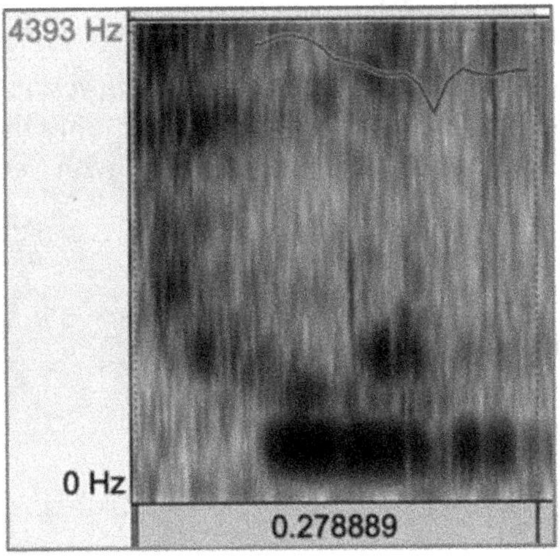

Figure 11. Pitch contour of "***tuzi***" (excerpt 5.1, line 2)

3 R *hu::h*
Huh?

4 G ***tuzi***
rabbit
Rabbit

5 R *tu::rtle=*
Turtle

6 Z ***=xiao tuzi***
small rabbit
Bunny

7 R *no::↓**tuzi** **shi shenme ya**(.) ra?*
no **rabbit is what EMP** ra
No. **What is "rabbit"**? Ra?

8 G *[rabbit]*
Rabbit! ((making bunny ears with fingers at her temples))

9 S *[oh rabbit]*
Oh, rabbit

10 R *[yeah]*
Yeah

11 R ***na*** *turtle* ***shi shenme ya***
then turtle **is what EMP**
Then, what is "turtle"?

12 R *turtle* ***shi na zhong hen man shangmian you [na ge qiao]***
turtle **is that kind very slow above has that PRT shell**
Turtle **is the kind that moves slowly with a shell on top**

13 Z ***[a::: woniu]=***
ah snail
Ah, **snail!**

14 RI ***=wo zhidao wo zhidao=***
1 know 1 know
I know, I know!

15 Z ***=woniu=***
snail
Snail

16 RI ***=woniu=***
snail
Snail

17 G ***=woniu***
snail
Snail

((R looks down at image of a turtle in the picture book.))

18 RI *bu [shi a wugui]=*
NEG is EMP turtle
Ah, no it's turtle.

19 R *[a::]*
Ah

20 Z *=wugui wugui=*
turtle turtle
Turtle, turtle

21 R *=very good=*
Very good!

22 Z *=wugui=*
turtle
Turtle

23 R *=ya::y ye::s=* ((reaching to high-five RI))
Yay! Yes!
((The participants laugh as R gives RI a high-five.))

Excerpt 5.2: "'Bow' Means 'Sunshine'"

Context: Volunteer teacher Rinchen [R] is leading a class session of "I Read." Amdo Tibetan children Zangmo [Z] (age 7), Ribu [RI] (6), Gracie [G] (5), and Migmar (6), and Han Chinese children Joshua [J] (6) and Janet (5) sit around a table with Rinchen. I [S], along with two mothers, observe from seats against the side wall. Rinchen and the children had finished singing a song called "I Can Sing a Rainbow." Rinchen began reading a book that featured an image of a rainbow. Mandarin words are bolded.

1 R *rain[bo::w↓]*
Rainbow

((Eleven turns omitted, while the children repeat "rainbow" in turn and in unison.))

2 Z *[rainbow rainbow **wo jian guo** rainbow]*
rainbow rainbow **1 see PST** rainbow
Rainbow, rainbow **I've seen** a rainbow

3 R *[rainbow (.) rainbow (.) rain]=*
Rainbow, rainbow, rain

4 J *=wo ye jian guo rainbow (.) wo [jian guo]*
1 also see PST rainbow **1 see PST**
I've also seen a rainbow. I've seen

5 Z *[bow bow]*
bow bow
Bow, bow

6 Z ***shi taiyang de yise***
is sunshine GEN meaning
means "sunshine"

7 R *da tɕʰo jar laŋ ⁿde-ni jar laŋ ɸdʑok̚ ⁿde-ni*
EMP 2 up rise there-ABL up rise stand there-ABL
((to Z)) Okay, you get up there. Get up and stand there

8 R *tɕʰo ⁿde ɸɕe ɸɕe-jaŋ* ***taiyang shi shenme*** *(.) sun*
2 DEM say say-NMLZ **sunshine is what** sun
You said this, this way, **"sunshine" is what**? Sun

9 Z *[sun]*
Sun

10 J *[sunny!]*
Sunny!

11 RI *[sunny?]=*
Sunny?

12 R *=sunny? sunny* ***jiu shi qingtian de yise*** *=*
sunny? sunny **just is sunny GEN meaning**
Sunny? Sunny **means "sunny"**

13 Z ***qingtian***
sunny
Sunny

14 R *ok tɕʰi mə-ɲen*
ok 2 NEG-good
Okay, you're not good

15 Z *a*
Ah

16 R *aləi kʰa rok̚ ɲen-a-do*
EXCL mouth shut good-CVB-stay
Okay, sit and listen quietly

17 Z *a*
Ah

18 R *yinwei we are going to: you are going to: be: a Grade 1 student hu:h?*
Because we are going to, you are going to be, a Grade 1 student, huh?

19 S *hu:h?*
Huh?

20 R *you have to lea::rn to li::sten to teacher (.) ok=*
You have to learn to listen to teacher, okay?

21 Z *=ok=*
Okay

22 R *=and follow teacher (.) ok?*
And follow teacher, okay?

23 Z *ok=*
Okay

24 R *=this is the ru::le of our class (.)*
This is the rule of our class

25 R ***zhe shi women yi ge zunhsou de yi ge** (.) rule **shi zhe li** ok?*
this is our one PRT follow GEN one PRT rule **is this here** ok
This is our one thing to follow. This rule **here**, okay?

((Z begins to cough.))

26 R *ok? very goo::d very good (.) ok ok ok rainbow=*
Okay? Very good, very good. Okay, okay, okay. Rainbow

27 J *=rainbow*
Rainbow

Excerpt 5.3: "A Thousand Years of History"

Context: Volunteer teacher Rinchen [R] is leading a session of "I Read." Amdo Tibetan children Zangmo [Z] (age 7), Tenzin [T] (6), Ribu [RI] (6), Gracie [G] (5), and Han Chinese children Joshua [J] (6) and Janet [JA] (5) sit around a table. I [S] am sitting against the back wall with Joshua, Gracie, and Janet's mothers. Rinchen and the children are naming food items in a picture book. Mandarin words are bolded.

1 R ***na zhe shi shenme***
then this is what
Then, what is this? ((pointing to image of yogurt in picture book))

2 G *suannai=*
yogurt
Yogurt

3 R *=suannai dui bu dui*
yogurt right NEG right
Yogurt, right?

4 G *u::h u:h*
Uh-huh

5 R *yogurt=*
Yogurt

6 S *=yogurt*
Yogurt

7 R *ɕo ɕo*
yogurt yogurt
Yogurt, yogurt

8 R *yogurt e:: zangyu na ge suannai*
yogurt EXCL **Tibetan that PRT yogurt**
Eh, **in Tibetan that "suannai"**

9 R *ye shi ɕo jiu shi [yogurt]*
also is yogurt **just is** yogurt
is "ɕo," **which means** "yogurt"

10 RI *[ɕo]=*
yogurt
Yogurt

11 S *[ɕo]=*
yogurt
Yogurt

12 G *=apple=*
Apple

13 R *=youdian jia na ge*
somewhat resemble that PRT
Looks a little bit like that

14 G *apple=*
Apple

15 R *=qian nian de lishi dui bu dui*
thousand year GEN history right NEG right
A thousand years of history, right?

16 R *suannai de lishi*
yogurt GEN history
The history of yogurt

17 R *ok apple apple*
Okay, apple! Apple

Glossary

Kinship Terms

Achi: older sister

Akha: uncle
Ama: mother
Ani: aunt
Apha: father
Aphu: grandfather
Awu: older brother
Ayi: grandmother

Place Names

Amdo (*a mdo*): northeastern Tibet; one of three imperial Tibetan provinces

Chentsa (Tib. *gcan tsha,* Ch. *Jianzha xian*): Chentsa Tibetan Autonomous County in Amdo

Golog (Tib. *mgo log bod rigs rang skyong khul,* Ch. *Guoluo zangzu zizhizhou*): Golog Tibetan Autonomous Prefecture, located in southeastern Amdo

Hualong (Tib. *dpa' lung rdzong,* Ch. *Hualong huizu zizhixian*): Hualong Hui Autonomous County, located in northeastern Qinghai

Kham (*khams*): southeastern Tibet; one of three imperial Tibetan provinces

Kumbum (*sku 'bum byams pa gling*): Kumbum monastery, located on the outskirts of Xining

Labrang (*bla brang bkra shis 'khyil*): an eminent monastery in Amdo

Lhasa (*lha sa*): the capital of imperial Tibet and the historical home of the Dalai Lama lineage

Lungma: pseudonym; a county in Tsholho Tibetan Autonomous Prefecture

Rebgong (Tib. *reb gong*, Ch. *tongren shi*): a monastery city in eastern Amdo

Rongwo (*rong bo'i dgon chen*): Rongwo monastery in Rebgong

Tsachen: pseudonym; a village in Tsholho Tibetan Autonomous Prefecture

Tsholho (Tib. *mtsho lho bod rigs rang skyong khul*, Ch. *Hainan zangzu zizhizhou*): Tsholho Tibetan Autonomous Prefecture, located south of Tsho Ngonpo

Tsho Ngonpo (*mtsho sngon po*): Tibet's great salt lake, located in Amdo

U-tsang (*dbus gtsang*): central Tibet; one of three imperial Tibetan provinces

Xining (Ch. *xining shi*): the capital city of Qinghai Province

Xunhua (Ch. *Xunhua salazu zizhixian*): Xunhua Salar Autonomous County, located in northeastern Qinghai

Ziling (Ch. *Xining*): the Tibetan name for Qinghai's provincial capital city

Written Tibetan

***'bri*:** female yak

***'brog skad*:** Nomad Talk, the mother tongue of Amdo Tibetan nomads

***'dang*:** to love, a formulaic expression of love and affection

***'jig rten*:** the material world

***'thab 'dzing*:** "struggle sessions," a form of re-education practised during the Cultural Revolution

***'then thug*:** pulled noodles

***am ja*:** Amdo salted milk tea

***a mdo brnyan 'phrin khang*:** Amdo provincial television station

***a mdo skad*:** the Amdo Tibetan language, encompassing both Nomad Talk and Farmer Talk

***ba mo*:** cow

***bla ma*:** Tibetan Buddhist teacher

***bod kyi skad yig*:** the Tibetan language, both spoken and written

***bod skad*:** spoken Tibetan

bod ja: Tibetan butter tea

bod yig: written Tibetan

byang chub kyi sems: altruism

chu pa: traditional Tibetan dress

chol kha gsum: the "three provinces" of imperial Tibet, U-tsang, Kham, and Amdo

chos skad: a register of literary Tibetan specific to Buddhist texts

dag yig: a traditional Tibetan treatise on orthography and spelling

dge bshes: a title awarded to scholars who have passed the curriculum in Gelukpa Buddhist philosophy

dge lugs pa: Gelukpa, the school of Tibetan Buddhism that, supported by the patronage of the Mongol leader Altan Khan, established the Dalai Lama lineage and gained dominance in the seventeenth century

dgos: to need, a formulaic expression of interdependence

dpal be'u: image of the eternal knot that represents karma

gangs ljongs: the land of snows; a name for cultural Tibet

go re: Amdo Tibetan bread

g.yag: male yak

ja khang: teahouse

khang: a sleeping platform, connected to an iron stove providing heat, that is located in the central living room of many Amdo Tibetan houses

khyim tshang: household

lang: to rise, a verbalizer used to describe experiences of emotion

lam rim chen mo: "Great Treatise on the Stages of the Path" by Je Tsongkhapa

las: karma, the cycle of rebirths resulting from accumulated actions

lo gsar: the new year

ma la: rosary

ma ni khang: temple

mi brje: person-exchange, a form of intermarriage

mog mog: Tibetan dumplings

mtsho sngon bod skad rgyang sgrog khang: Tsho Ngonpo Tibetan radio station

pha skad gtsang ma: pure father tongue; a term used to describe an imagined standard Tibetan language

pha yul: homeland

phan tshun che ba: strong relationship, characterized by mutual exchange

phyag 'tshal: prostration

rgod po: wild; a characterization of young children's natural proclivities

rgya skad: spoken Chinese

rgya yig: written Chinese

rig gnas gsar brje: the Cultural Revolution

rlung rta: prayer flags, stamped with the auspicious image of a "wind horse"

rong ma 'brog: neither farmer nor nomad; a subsistence practice involving settled pastoralism

rong skad: Farmer Talk, a label that encompasses multiple mother tongues of settled Amdo Tibetan communities

rtsam pa: barley flour, a staple of Tibetan diets

***sdug bsngal bshad pa* (Ch. *suku*)**: speaking bitterness; the practice of narrating pre-Communist oppression, associated with the "Anti-Feudalism Campaign" during the 1958 Democratic Reforms

sems: heart-mind, the centre of a person's consciousness

sems byung: mental factors, or malleable states of mind

sems can: sentient beings

sems chung: small heart, an adjective for a person prone to intense emotional states

sems kyis shes: knowing from the heart and mind, a concept that guides Tibetan theories of learning

skad: speech, spoken language

skor ba: circumambulation

sman pa: Tibetan medical doctor

snying rje: compassion; a term used in formulaic displays of emotion

spyi skad: common language; a lingua franca based on Lhasa's dialect of central Tibetan that is used in diasporic communities

spyi tshogs gsar pa: new society; the period after the founding of the People's Republic of China in 1949

spyi tshogs rnying pa: old society; the period before the founding of the People's Republic of China in 1949

srung ma: the lineage deity, whose patronage is passed down within a family

sum cu pa: a treatise on traditional Tibetan grammar

thos bsam bsgom gsum: hearing, thinking, and meditating; three stages of knowledge acquisition in Buddhist education

tshe ring lo brgya: long life, one hundred years; an Amdo farewell

tsho ba: an extended kin unit that shares patronage of a Buddhist teacher and practises intermarriage

yig skad: literary Tibetan

yul lha: deities who inhabit land formations

yul skad: land speech; local spoken language varieties that are the mother tongues of young Tibetan children

zho: yogurt made from yak milk

Mandarin

baozi: steamed, stuffed buns

dusheng zinü zhengce: one-child policy; a family planning policy that ran from 1979 to 2015

fangyan: topolects; place-based languages varieties

gaige kaifang: Reform and Opening; economic liberalization reforms led by Deng Xiaoping

gaokao: university entrance exam

gege: older brother

gongchandang: Communist Party

gongchandang de zhengce: the policies of the Communist Party

guanxi: mutually beneficial relationships

hanhua: sinification, the process of becoming Chinese; a national project expressed in writings from China's Republican era

hebing zhengce: School Consolidation Policy, which centralized rural primary and secondary schools into larger administrative units

heping jiefang: peaceful liberation; the Communist understanding of the political incorporation of Tibet into China

Hongjun: the Red Army (Communist China's army from 1928 to 1937)

hongzao: red dates

huacha: tea scented with dried flowers

hukou: household registration

jiejichengfen: class status

jiu shehui: old society; the period prior to the founding of the People's Republic of China in 1949

minkaomin: minority nationality university entrance exams, written in the recognized language of the nationality rather than Chinese

minzu: nationality

minzhu gaige: Democratic Reforms; a program initiated by the Chinese Communist Party in 1958

minzu tuanjie: national unity; a goal for harmonious multiculturalism, especially as articulated in writings from China's Republican era

neidiban: boarding schools for children from minoritized nationalities, which are located in central China

Qinghai hua: Qinghai's dialect of Mandarin

qinghai lan qingke: literally "blue barley," the highland barley grown in Tibet

Qinghai minzu daxue: Qinghai Nationalities University, in Xining

renlei shajie: killing and destruction of humanity; a homonym for the Tibetan term meaning "Cultural Revolution"

renmin jiefangjun: the People's Liberation Army

salazu: the Salar nationality

shaoshu minzu: minoritized nationality whose boundaries are defined by the Chinese state; any state-recognized nationality other than Han Chinese

shehui zhuyi jiaoyu: socialist education; a process of political re-education practised during the Cultural Revolution

suku (Tib. *sdug bsngal bshad pa*): speaking bitterness; the practice of narrating pre-Communist oppression, associated with the Anti-Feudalism Campaign during the 1958 Democratic Reforms

suzhi: quality; a term referring to conceptions of human capital articulated in Chinese state discourse

tongyi zhanxian: the United Front, a Chinese Communist Party political strategy associated with the 1958 Democratic Reforms

tuzu: the Tu nationality

xiangmu: local development project

xibu da kaifa: Open Up the West; an economic development campaign beginning in 1999

xin shehui: new society; the period after the founding of the People's Republic of China in 1949

you'eryuan: preschool

zangzu: the Tibetan nationality

zhongguo meng: Chinese dream; a term for national modernization associated with leader Xi Jinping

zhongyang minzu daxue: Minzu University of China in Beijing

zhongyang renmin guangbo diantai: China National Radio

Notes

Introduction

1 A rich literature outlining the urgency of language endangerment charts its foundations in colonization. For example, Hale (1992) defined the centrality of language endangerment to the field of linguistics. Grenoble and Whaley (1998) provide an overview of the complex sociological, economic, and political factors that are exacerbating the loss of native speakers across the globe. King et al. (2008) present opportunities to support language vitality.

2 A recent UNESCO report (Ball 2011) notes the negative social and psychological consequences that follow from a lack of access to early childhood mother tongue education. Demonstrating these negative consequences in the context of India, Mohanty (2010) argues that the marginalization of Indigenous languages has sparked social and political conflict. Skutnabb-Kangas (2000) asserts that, despite good intentions, formal education in Indigenous languages cannot replace traditional forms of cultural and linguistic transmission across generations.

3 "127935 Tibetans Living Outside Tibet: Tibetan Survey," *Hindustan Times*, 28 September 2011, https://web.archive.org/web/20110927215516/http://www.hindustantimes.com/127935-Tibetans-living-outside-Tibet-Tibetan-survey/Article1-634405.aspx.

4 The CCP's use of the term *minzu* derives from the Soviet Union's nationality policy, and is thus generally translated into English as "nationality." While other translations are possible, I retain the standard translation to differentiate *minzu* from the multiple forms of identification that occur within and across these state-designated categories. I translate *shaoshu* as "minoritized" rather than "minority" to emphasize that minority status is an emergent, constructed category. Although *minzu* policy is associated primarily with the Republican and Communist

Chinese states, historians, in fact, locate its origins in China's last dynasty, the Qing (1644–1912). The term *minzu* was first formulated in the late 1800s, and entered into Chinese political writings in the first decades of the twentieth century (Leibold 2007, 8). Despite state claims to the fundamental unity of China's diverse citizens, the *minzu* concept is a relatively recent political construct.

5 In order to protect the confidentiality of participants, I have given pseudonyms to most rural places, including Tsachen Village and Lungma County.

6 Hainan State Government (*hainan zhou zhengfu*), "Inside Hainan," (*zoujin hainan*), http://www.hainanzhou.gov.cn/zjhn/, accessed 24 August 2021.

7 Tibetan linguists Dondrup Tsering (2011) and Padma Lhundrup (2009) provide documentation of Amdo's diverse *yul skad*, and further describe the distinction between Nomad Talk and Farmer Talk.

8 Literature in linguistic anthropology has revealed cultural bias in common Western psychological measures of children's linguistic development, which frame non-white, non–middle class children's language use through deficit discourses (see, for example, Avineri et al. 2015; Blum 2017; Heath 1982). As this monograph demonstrates, routines prescribed by Western psychologists do not necessarily support language vitality or validate multilingual children's communicative competence.

9 While the relationship of language to thought has been examined from a variety of standpoints, Slobin (1996) presents the most cogent approach to this question as it relates to language acquisition. Slobin's (1985) edited volume provides more specific evidence, from a variety of languages across the globe, that linguistic structures affect children's performance on psychological and elicitation-based tests. Tomasello (2003b) presents interdisciplinary, cognitive approaches to the study of language and thought. Levinson (2003) outlines the most commonly accepted examples of linguistic structures that are believed to influence thought.

10 Previous ethnographies about endangered language communities have supported the viewpoint that the social identities and expectations placed upon children may contribute to language loss. For example, Barbra Meek (2012) found that a Kaska community's framing of their mother tongue as the specialized knowledge of elders inhibited children from speaking it. Kaska children did not, however, passively abandon this language, but instead conceptualized Kaska linguistic competence as a progression through social statuses. In a study in Gapun, Papua New Guinea, Don Kulick (1992) found that adults blamed children for the loss of Taiap, their mother tongue, when people of all ages in Gapun were shifting away from Taiap in favour of the dominant language, Tok Pisin.

11 The relationship of Amdo to imperial Tibet prior to the thirteenth century is not well documented. The absence of a linear history connecting imperial Tibet to the contemporary region of greater cultural Tibet complicates attempts to assert a unified Tibetan past. Amdo's history was shaped by the relations not only between imperial centres and peripheries, but also between settled and nomadic communities. David Sneath's (2007) assertion that the Indigenous societies of Inner Asia are best understood as "headless states" – or polities that retain flexible forms of authority, arbitration, and distinctions between governing and governed persons that are not emblematic of either kinship or empire – remains useful for locating Amdo between Tibet and China.

12 Gray Tuttle, "An Overview of Amdo (Northeastern Tibet) Historical Politics," *Essays of Places*, n.d., http://places.kmaps.virginia.edu/descriptions/1228.xml.

13 In Amdo, monastic polities comprised interlocking social units. The full meanings of and distinctions between social units, including Tib. *shog pa* and *tsho ba* and Ch. *buluo* are not fully understood. Paul Nietupski's (1999) study of Labrang (Tib. *bla brang*) monastery provides an in-depth exploration of Amdo social groups in this polity in the period 1921–49 (54–61).

14 Max Oidtmann (2018) provides a detailed examination of the relationships between Qing courts and monastic polities, especially by documenting how Buddhist leaders translated Manchu law for Tibetan civil society.

15 Tibetans' territory was of particular political concern to the Guomindang, because both Great Britain and the Soviet Union viewed Tibet as a buffer zone between China and their own expanding empires. Great Britain's involvement in diplomacy between Lhasa, the capital of imperial Tibet, and Republican China is particularly notable (Shakya 2000, 278–286).

16 Leibold (2007) describes the racism inherent to twentieth-century Chinese nationalism. Both Republican and Communist discourses positioned *minzu* on a linear scale of evolution, with the majority Han Chinese located at a higher level of development than the minoritized *shaoshu minzu*. According to this racial logic, the advancement of the nation-state depended on the cultural evolution of non-Han persons. Kuper (1988) theorizes the development of racialized evolutionary logics in a variety of political contexts, including Communist states (239–40).

17 Tibetans sometimes employ the synonymous calque, "old world" (Tib. *'jig rten rnying pa*) (see, for example, Makley 2005, 59).

18 International Campaign for Tibet, "Protests by Students against Downgrading of Tibetan Language Spread to Beijing," 22 October 2010, https://savetibet.org/protests-by-students-against-downgrading-of-tibetan-language-spread-to-beijing/.

19 These forms of territorial control over diverse persons have led scholars to compare China's current ethnic policy through economic development campaigns to settler colonization (see Bulag 2002; Hansen 2006).

1 Local Histories and Language Variation in Amdo

1 Features that characterize Tsachen and Hualong's *yul skad* include a uvular fricative before some affricate consonants, unique personal pronouns, and a set of sentence final discourse markers shared with Salar. Salar is a Turkic language spoken by a minoritized nationality native to Hualong. Based on fieldwork, linguists have documented extensive structural convergence resulting from language contact in Amdo. Dwyer (2022) noted morphosyntactic convergence among Sinitic, Tibetic, and Turko-Mongolic languages in Amdo. Simon (2016) demonstrated a largely unidirectional morphosyntactic shift from Amdo Tibetan to Salar, particularly in the perspective marking system. More generally, Tsering Samdrup and Hiroyuki Suzuki (2017) point towards the significance of *tsho ba* allegiances and associated migration histories in establishing the boundaries of Amdo Tibetan varieties.

2 Ethnographers Andrew Grant (2018a) and Charlene Makley (2003) note similar examples of how Amdo Tibetans adapt Buddhist circumambulation practices to urban and semi-urban environments in China.

3 Goffman (1972) defines "line" as a trajectory of conversational activity marked by participants' display of a consistent attitude towards themselves, one another, and their shared talk (6).

4 As ethnographer Minhua Ling's (2019) study of migrant youth demonstrates, even when rural-to-urban migrants manage to shift their registration status to their current place of habitation, they face continued discrimination in the areas of employment and education due to their rural origins.

5 Zhan (2017) argues that the revenue-generating potential of rural land transfers serves as an underlying motivation for *hukou* reforms.

6 These attitudes among Tsachen's families stand in contrast to many nomads' experiences of coerced settlement (Tashi Nyima 2014).

7 Additional radio and television programming in Tibetan languages is operated from Beijing, through China National Radio (Ch. *zhongyang renmin guangbo diantai*), as well as in the Tibet Autonomous Region, Gansu, and Sichuan. These networks are available throughout Qinghai.

8 While little is known about Old Tibetan, existing scholarship supports the notion that Nomad Talk has experienced less divergence from a source language than Farmer Talk's *yul skad*. For example, Zoe Tribur (2017b) compared phonological and grammatical innovation across dialects of

Amdo Tibetan, noting a tendency for endoteric nomad communities to exhibit complexification while exoteric farming communities exhibited more extensive structural divergence.

9 Due to the extent of contemporary structural convergence among unrelated languages, linguists refer to Amdo as a *sprachbund*, or a geographic region characterized by linguistic hybridity. Janhunen (2012) provides a typology of convergent features, noting a tendency towards regularity in the distribution of shared features among Turko-Mongolic, Sinitic, and Tibetan spheres (179).

10 While trade relationships between Hui merchants and Tibetan pastoralists prior to the rise of the PRC are particularly well-documented (Lipman 1984, 291–2), Kazakhs, Mongols, and Salar and Tu people also engaged in exchange with Amdo Tibetans.

11 For example, the Chinese-Tibetan-Mongolian language Wutun may have developed from intermarriage between Chinese soldiers and Tibetan and Mongolian women during the Ming and Qing dynasties (Cabras 2019, 30).

12 Some relationships have been amended to maintain confidentiality.

13 Sørensen and Hazod describe Amdo traditions of *mi brje* (2007, 412). Levine (2015) also documents Amdo Tibetan household organization, in the context of changing economic practices. While Tuttle (n.d.) notes that *tsho ba* are inherently exogamous, this description does not align with the use of the term by my interlocutors, who described endogamy within their *tsho ba*. It is possible that, as the family's *tsho ba* migrated, existing rules for exogamy shifted.

14 Qi (2013) describes the role of *srung ma* in facilitating cultural continuity across generations (129–30).

15 Efforts to standardize education in Qinghai extended to mosques, temples, and monasteries. Among the Hui, Islamic education often supported literacy in Chinese and tended to follow a syncretic doctrine influenced by Confucianism (Lipman 1984, 296–7). The functions of religious education in literacy instruction may have supported the outgrowth of secular schools from religious institutions.

16 While some historians have studied the development of secular education in Amdo in the twentieth century, this topic is better documented in the Tibet Autonomous Region. Since 1927, Mao Zedong had supported both community- and state-funded schools in central Tibet (Bass 1998, 26–7). As the PRC took power, they developed an education policy for minoritized nationalities explicitly focused on political education in the mother tongue. Schools in the Tibet Autonomous Region employed Tibetan monks as well as lay Tibetan and Chinese teachers, but, with the Cultural Revolution, mother tongue education was largely abandoned (ibid., 29–34).

17 Aphu Lhundhup's oral history interview stated that Lungma's middle school was established in 1976, at the end of the Cultural Revolution. Analysis of primary source documents suggests that a middle school may have existed in Lungma County prior to Cultural Revolution, but may have been reorganized by Qinghai's provincial education department at a later date (Haas 2013, 165).

18 In this particular statement, Ayi Khangmo was referring to a time in the late 1960s. Scholars have generally located the evaluation of Tibetans' class status, especially based on land holdings, in the 1958 Democratic Reforms (see, for example, Hayes 2014, 134; Makley 2005, 46).

19 More specifically, Goffman's concept of "footing" examined speakers' positioning with respect to their talk and to other interactive participants, in order to challenge the notion of interaction as a dyadic exchange between speaker and hearer. With the concept of "footing," Goffman differentiated speakers and hearers into multiple participation roles that can be inhabited by one or more participants (1981, 144–5).

20 Reynolds's (2012) sociolinguistic study of one *yul skad* of Amdo Farmer Talk suggests that language ideologies, especially concerns over the encroachment of Chinese among educated speakers, may contribute to the reinterpretation of converged features as related to Chinese. More generally, these attitudes can drive resistance to phonological innovation.

2 The Grammar of Belonging: Spatial Deixis in Situated Family Interaction

1 Jacka (2009) examines the historical development of *suzhi* discourse. Murphy (2004) describes the role of this discourse in shaping the behaviour and ideologies of rural parents, teachers, and children in Jiangxi province. Scholars of Tibetan communities in the PRC have noted that policies for modernization concentrate essential human services, including education, in cities as part of broader efforts for assimilation and territorial control (Yeh and Makley 2019; Roche, Leibold, and Hillman 2020).

2 Linguistic anthropologists offer several perspectives about the relationship between cultural practices, social identity, and language change. Literature in the tradition of language ideologies argues that social differentiation drives linguistic change, through rationalizations that link linguistic features to social categories (Agha 2005; Irvine and Gal 2000; Silverstein 2003). Language socialization scholars draw on the framework of language ideologies to examine how perduring typifications of groups and individuals emerge in situated language practices and routine activities (Kulick and Schieffelin 2004; Ochs 1992; C. Goodwin 2007; M.H. Goodwin 2011). However, the traditions of language socialization and language

ideologies differ in where each locates the origin of language change. The literature on language ideologies used the writings of Charles Sanders Peirce (1955) to posit that semiotic processes drive language change (see also Mertz 2007). Language socialization scholars built on practice theory to argue that everyday communicative routines motivate language change (Garrett and Baquedano-López 2002, 344–5).

3 Scholars examining conversation through different methodologies engage in lively debate about which specific mechanisms of turn-taking are universal. Ethnographic studies suggest that language ideologies influence how participants experience and describe conversational turn-taking (Reisman 1974, 112–14). At the same time, quantitative studies have suggested an ethological foundation to turn-taking. For example, Stivers et al. (2009) measured the time intervals between conversational turns in ten different languages. They found that speakers across languages minimize silence between turns, while also avoiding overlap and differentiating types of speech acts.

4 Psycholinguistic researchers use infants' head-turning and rates of sucking to measure their selective attention (Kuhl et al. 1992; Vouloumanos and Werker 2007; Werker and Hensch 2015)

5 Developmental psychologists posit a complex relationship between referential gesture and language production. For example, Iverson and Goldin-Meadow's (2005) study of communicative behaviour in infants aged ten to twenty-four months demonstrated that gesture not only predates, but also facilitates, infants' language production (see also Goldin-Meadow 2007; Tomasello, Carpenter, and Liszkowski 2007).

6 For example, English demonstratives (this, that, these, those) refer to different places or things, depending on the speaker's location and position.

7 As Hanks (2005) compellingly demonstrates, deictic markers index interactive contexts that are not only physical and spatial, but also phenomenological. Specifically, deictic markers establish relationships between agents and objects that co-constitute embedded dimensions of an interaction, such as participants' physical positioning, stances or states of knowledge, and social typifications.

8 Charles Goodwin (2000) defines "cognition" as shared knowledge built from the social and material environment in an interactive context.

9 The spatial deictic system is shared across varieties of Amdo Tibetan and written Tibetan. Speakers adapt the deictic markers to the sound system of their *yul skad*.

10 Brown and Levinson (1993) describe a similar system of spatial deixis in Tzeltal Mayan.

11 Spatial deictics are bolded in quoted speech. A full transcript of quoted speech, including morpheme glossing, is included in the appendix.

12 Spatial deictics are bolded in quoted speech. A full transcript of quoted speech, including morpheme glossing, is included in the appendix.
13 Spatial deictics are bolded, and Mandarin loan words are bolded and underlined in quoted speech. A full transcript of quoted speech, including morpheme glossing, is included in the appendix.
14 The kin terms *Awu* and *Achi* translate literally to "older brother" and "older sister." They are used in a caregiving register to refer to all children, regardless of relative age. When used by peers, the kin terms denote relative age. Amdo Tibetan toddlers often use these kin terms to refer to themselves in the third person.
15 Scholars of conversation analysis argue that certain universal preferences influence the content of sequential turns-at-talk (C. Goodwin and Heritage 1990, 296–8; Schegloff 2007, 58–63). Unexpected answers, contradictions, and interruptions, known as "dispreferred seconds," subtly indicate an anti-social stance because they display a lack of alignment between the speaker and recipient. While particular language structures and cultural norms may influence how speakers display alignment or disalignment, conversation follows an "essential generic organization of practice" across human societies (Sidnell 2007, 240).
16 Language socialization scholars have argued that caregivers use prompting routines to explicate for children culturally particular norms surrounding language use (Demuth 1986, 55–6; Schieffelin 1990, 75–7). As Berman and Smith (2021) note, prompting routines also "recruit addressees into immature subject positions" by enforcing an asymmetry in who can shape the trajectory of an unfolding activity (595).
17 Although spatial deixis is one of the earliest grammatical systems that children produce, children do not demonstrate adult-like knowledge of deictic contrasts in comprehension experiments until several years later (Clark and Sengul 1978, 457). Given that comprehension of this system tends to develop more slowly than its production, we can assume that Sonam may not have acquired understanding of Amdo's deictic contrasts before shifting to Mandarin.
18 Berman and Smith (2021) argue that children and other novices are not only socialized into knowledge. They are also socialized into a *lack* of particular knowledges, which creates their subject position as novices.

3 Socializing Compassion: Buddhist Theories of Emotion and Relationality in the Production of Social Difference

1 A full discussion of canonical writings on compassion and motherhood, including important distinctions in the treatment of these topics across Buddhist schools of philosophy, goes beyond the scope of this chapter.

Nonetheless, Tsongkhapa's meditations on motherhood remain relevant to understanding verbal displays of compassion in Tsachen and Xining, given that these practices invoke images of the mother and of other foundational kin relationships.

2 More specifically, a particular type of metalanguage, known as metapragmatic discourse, articulates the social functions of language forms. Metapragmatic discourse rationalizes and justifies local communicative practices, leading to the dynamic potential for continuity or change in language use (Silverstein 1979, 233). With metapragmatic discourse, speakers define the moral connotations of affective displays and associate these moral values with enduring social characteristics.

3 The notion of *guanxi* is central to local models of relationality in multiple Chinese communities (Kipnis 1997; Yan 2011; Yang 2002). In this analysis, I report commentary provided by my Amdo interlocutors but do not engage in a full analysis of the varied cultural meanings and social functions of *guanxi*. For example, Xu (2017) noted that Han Chinese parents articulated concerns about preschool similar to those of Amdo Tibetan parents. Chinese parents, however, discussed *guanxi* as a means of resolving the breakdown of morality in the early twenty-first century.

4 Naftali (2016) provides a comprehensive account of how changing birth policies in the twentieth century have shaped childhood in China.

5 Emotional states are generally configured as stative clauses and are marked with an imperfective direct evidential *-kə* (Tribur 2017a, 396–8).

6 Mandarin loan words are bolded in quoted speech. A full transcript of quoted speech, including morpheme glossing, is presented in the appendix.

7 M. Goodwin, Cekaite, and C. Goodwin (2012) note that vowel lengthening and exaggerated pitch contour similarly function to indicate heightened emotion in American adolescents' conversations. The extent to which this function of prosody is used cross-linguistically has not been established.

8 As anthropologist Penelope Brown (2002) demonstrated in a study of Mayan caregivers' talk to young children, hypothetical threats are often organized according to culturally specific themes. In Amdo families, the threat of bugs or mice entering children's stomachs was frequently offered as a means of controlling unwanted behaviour.

9 For a more complete discussion of cross-cultural research on attachment theory, see van Ijzendoorn and Sagi-Schwartz (2008), LeVine (2014), Quinn and Mageo (2013), and Weisner (2005).

10 Mandarin loan words are bolded in quoted speech. A full transcript of quoted speech, including morpheme glossing, is presented in the appendix.

11 Marjorie Goodwin (2017) found that families in California similarly used hugging as reconciliation following displays of aggression or agonism, and that it was particularly common for children to hug adults to repair their relationship following an identified transgression.
12 A full transcript of quoted speech, including morpheme glossing is presented in the appendix.
13 This translation was completed alongside a native speaker present during the interaction, with *tɕik̚.ko* understood as "refuse." However, this word could also correspond to the written Tibetan *gcig po* (only), in which case a more accurate translation would be "you only love Ani."

4 Learning Standard Language Ideologies: Education Policy and Colonial Alienation between the Homeland and the City

1 Language ideologies, more generally, influence how people use language and, in so doing, shape language structures, including the boundaries between different languages and the vitality of entire codes. In linguistic anthropology, the paradigm of language ideologies has been central to understanding language maintenance and change. For example, Silverstein (1993, 2001) argued that ethnometapragmatics, or rationalizations of language use explicitly articulated in discourse, (re) formulate the indexical associations that structure language forms and their contexts of use. Silverstein's integration of the concept of ideology, through ethnometapragmatic discourse, into the study of language contributed to foundational debates about the location and circulation of power and authority (see, for example, Briggs 1998; Kroskrity 1998).
2 For example, Bauman and Briggs (2003) traced the belief that a single country should share one language to eighteenth-century German philosophy, which codified shared cultures through vernacular literatures. Lesley Milroy (2001) explained that the political and economic history of labour and migration in twentieth-century Britain and the United States led to contrasting definitions of standard English. Whereas standard British English is a marked prestige variety acquired through schooling, standard American English is an unmarked norm devoid of nonstandard features. In the twentieth century, Chinese state language planning built on these European notions of linguistic nationality for the purposes of modernization, but also responded to the unification of diverse spoken languages through a shared literary tradition – a linguistic ecology specific to this region of East Asia.
3 For example, McGranahan (2019) extensively charts competing imperial histories in Tibet, which have engendered contemporary settler colonial formations under Communist China. Hansen (2006) argues that the

Chinese state's targeted movement of Han persons into Tibet, often accompanying resource extraction, represents a structure of settler colonization. Scholars who apply the framework of settler colonization to China's relationship with other minoritized nationalities include Bulag (2002), who documents the Mongol experience under Chinese colonialism, and Mullaney (2010), who discusses the foundations of the PRC's census – which defined *minzu* categories – in British and Qing colonial logics.

4 While the official language, Mandarin (Ch. *Putonghua*), is now the mother tongue of an estimated 900 million speakers, it was constructed through explicit planning in the nineteenth and twentieth centuries. Recent estimates note between twelve and twenty mutually unintelligible varieties of Chinese (Handel 2015, 35), which are further differentiated into *fangyan*. The term *fangyan* is used loosely by speakers of Chinese to describe place-based linguistic diversity in China, but does not map onto linguists' definitions of the boundaries of languages and dialects.

5 Tam (2020) describes in more detail how language reformers in both the Republican and Communist eras grappled with tensions between a desire for standardization and a vision of China's diverse *fangyan* as carriers of the culture of the masses.

6 Tam demonstrates that these evolutionary logics borrowed from Soviet nationality policy to assert a natural process of unification through linguistic assimilation (2020, 163–7). Similarly, Ji (2003) documents how language reforms beyond the standardization of Mandarin, including the engineering of a new political vocabulary, sought to ideologically transform the Communist nation. While the PRC applied the same logics of evolution, and similar practices of developing official political vocabularies, in language planning for *shaoshu minzu*, these language policies were ideologically motivated by the Chinese state's interest in language standardization for Han persons (Tam 2020, 163).

7 Rohsenow (2004) closely documents the processes and debates surrounding script reform, which involved both creating a Romanized transliteration system (Ch. *pinyin*) and simplifying the Chinese script.

8 Thirty-eight minoritized nationalities were recognized in the first census, an additional fifteen were recognized in the 1964 census, and an additional two were recognized between 1965 and 1979 (Zhou 2003, 12–13).

9 Over the past seven decades, the constitutional provision for minoritized language rights has been complicated by three factors. First, language rights apply only to those groups officially recognized by the state as *shaoshu minzu* or minoritized nationalities. Many ethnolinguistic groups – such as the Baima, who are currently incorporated into the Tibetan ethnicity (Ch. *zangzu*) – remain unrecognized by the Chinese state and have resisted their state classification partly to gain language rights

(Upton 2000). Second, provisions for language rights narrowly focus on writing systems rather than spoken languages. Third, state education policies have come in waves of supporting constrained multilingualism or favouring total assimilation to Mandarin (Beckett and Postiglione 2011, 4). Since the middle of the first decade of this century, there has been a shift away from pluralism and towards assimilation in the realm of education policy for minoritized nationalities.

10 Tibetan linguistic diversity extends beyond mutually intelligible *yul skad*, to include languages that are not historically tied to literary Tibetan. Gerald Roche provides the most extensive documentation of these "unrecognized" Tibetan languages, which are doubly marginalized by the Chinese state as well as by speakers of more standard Tibetan varieties (Roche 2019; Roche and Suzuki 2018; Roche and Tsomu 2018).

11 Dwyer (1998) notes five tiers in the PRC's language hierarchy: 1) *Putonghua*; 2) recognized standards of large multilingual communities (such as Tibetan); 3) "primary minority languages" such as Korean, Manchu, and non-standard varieties of Chinese that the state has historically recognized; 4) "secondary minority" languages that are unwritten; and 5) unrecognized and unclassified languages.

12 Nietupski (1999) provides a detailed case study of the historical role of Tibetan monasteries in education and governance. Kapstein (2002) charts the forms of exchange that accompanied the spread of monastic Buddhism in Tibet. Schaeffer, Kapstein, and Tuttle (2013) provide a comprehensive textual analysis of 180 works of Tibetan and Buddhist scholarship, which evidence the role of monasteries as cosmopolitan centres.

13 In the year 2000, the central government expanded the *neidiban* system to include students from the Xinjiang Uyghur Autonomous Region. From 2000 to 2019, more than 100,000 Uyghur students have attended *neidiban* (Leibold 2019, 6).

14 While written Tibetan (Tib. *bod yig*) refers to both secular and religious literary traditions, canonical Buddhist writings (Tib. *chos skad*) present grammatical and lexical differences from modern written Tibetan. Written Tibetan is not fully standardized across Tibetan regions. Nonetheless, Tibetan writing more generally remains associated with Buddhism.

15 Thurston (2018b) locates discourses of purity in Buddhist traditions. "Purity" refers to spiritual, bodily, or behavioural cleanliness that supports good fortune (204).

16 The following conversation took place in English and was rendered based on fieldnotes from the author.

17 The phrase *lu-taŋ* (Tib. *glu dang*) may be code-mixed between central Tibetan and Amdo Tibetan. The word for "song," *glu* is typical of Amdo, as opposed to the word *gzhas* common in central Tibetan. However, the

imperative verbalizer *dang* is common in central Tibetan, while *longs* is more commonly employed across Amdo.

18 Ward (2022a) provides a more detailed ethnographic examination of this rhetorical question in the context of children's language socialization.

19 Mandarin loan words are bolded in quoted speech. A full transcription of excerpts, including morpheme glossing, is presented in the appendix.

20 A similar dynamic between standard language ideologies and aged identities has been noted in other ethnographic settings. For example, linguistic anthropologist Jennifer Reynolds (2009) found that pan-Mayan language ideologies hold youth responsible for ensuring cultural and linguistic continuity by rejecting outside influences and learning their heritage languages, even when adults may not (see also Kulick 1992, and Meek 2007).

21 Mandarin loan words are bolded in quoted speech. A full transcription of excerpts, including morpheme glossing, is presented in the appendix.

22 As linguist Lily Wong Fillmore (1991) argued in a study of immigrant children's language practices in the United States, there are both external and internal factors that lead young children to give up their native languages after learning English. While external factors include the dominance of English and peers' expectations, internal factors include children's own identification with the English language (342–6).

5 Reading in the City: Literacy as Belonging in Urban China

1 Features of prosody are distinct from a language's phonemes, or meaningful units of sound. Research in sociolinguistics has shown that, across languages, speakers use prosody to organize the boundaries of turns at talk (Szczepek Reed 2009, 1243), and to display attention to others' previous utterances (Couper-Kuhlen 2014, 222). These two functions of prosody influence how participants sequentially build shared understanding.

2 In an ethnographic study of reading and writing in Samoan-American families, Duranti and Ochs (1997) developed the concept of "syncretic literacy" to describe a similar "intermingling or merging of culturally diverse traditions [that] informs and organizes literacy activities" (172).

3 Scholars have generally mapped this specific route, known as "Tea Horse Road" (Ch. *chamadao*) from contemporary Sichuan to India. Wei (2023) argues for more comprehensive attention to a "Plateau Silk Road" that moved through contemporary Amdo/Qinghai and was characterized by extensive inter-ethnic exchange. Further demonstrating the historical links between Tibet and China, a common narrative holds that tea was first introduced to Tibet following King Songtsen Gampo's marriage to Chinese

princess Wencheng. The marriage of Songsten Gampo and Wencheng is used in performance and narrative to exemplify the primordial unity of Tibet and China. However, as Warner (2011) argues through his engagement with texts from eastern Tibet, the story of Songtsen Gampo and Wencheng is best read as a demonstration of the early political autonomy of Tibet, coupled with cultural hybridity.

4 During fieldwork in 2016–18, my research participants referenced an English language requirement in Xining's public schools, but I did not examine Xining's curricular policies for verification. Ma and Renzeng (2015) noted that policy documents in Qinghai province lay out a curriculum that includes English from Grades 3 or 5 onwards (103); however, it is possible that this requirement has changed since 2015.

5 One example of an evangelical Christian organization that supports missionization in Amdo/Qinghai is the Joshua Project (Joshua Project, "Rongmahbrogpa Amdo in China," https://joshuaproject.net/people_groups/18394/CH, accessed 26 September 2023).

6 Ethnographers have identified preschool as a site for heightened concerns about moral development. For example, anthropologist Jing Xu (2017) found that, in Shanghai, early childhood education has become a lens through which urban Chinese adults grapple with the tension between collectivism and individual achievement at the forefront of contemporary debates about morality (7–11). In their cross-cultural comparison of preschools in Japan, China, and the United States, Joseph Tobin, David Wu, and Dana Davidson (1991) similarly suggested that preschools institutionalize models of relationality that reflect broader moral concerns.

7 Amdo Tibetan words are italicized. Mandarin words are bolded and italicized. The appendix includes a morpheme-by-morpheme glossing of the excerpts, as well as spectrogram images of selected pitch contours.

8 Amdo Tibetan words are italicized. Mandarin words are bolded and italicized. The appendix includes a morpheme-by-morpheme glossing of the excerpts.

9 Amdo Tibetan words are italicized. Mandarin words are bolded and italicized. The appendix includes a morpheme-by-morpheme glossing of the excerpts.

References

A M and Darren Byler. 2022. "Alienation and Educational 'Third Space': English Learning and Uyghur Subject Formation in Xinjiang, China." *Anthropology & Education Quarterly* 53(4): 396–415. https://doi.org/10.1111/aeq.12434.

Adams, Vincanne. 2001. "The Sacred in the Scientific: Ambiguous Practices of Science in Tibetan Medicine." *Cultural Anthropology* 16(4): 542–75. https://doi.org/10.1525/can.2001.16.4.542.

Agha, Asif. 2005. "Voice, Footing, Enregisterment." *Journal of Linguistic Anthropology* 15(1): 38–59. https://doi.org/10.1525/jlin.2005.15.1.38.

Ainsworth, Mary D. Salter, Mary C. Blehar, Everett Waters, and Sally N. Wall. 2015. *Patterns of Attachment: A Psychological Study of the Strange Situation*. New York: Psychology Press.

Ainsworth, Mary D. Salter, and John Bowlby. 1991. "An Ethological Approach to Personality Development." *American Psychologist* 46: 333–41. https://doi.org/10.1037/0003-066X.46.4.333.

Allen, Joseph P. 2008. "The Attachment System in Adolescence." In *Handbook of Attachment: Theory, Research, and Clinical Applications*, edited by Jude Cassidy and Philip R. Shaver, 419–35. New York: Guilford Press.

Andersen, Elaine. 2014. *Speaking with Style: The Sociolinguistics Skills of Children*. London: Routledge.

Avineri, Netta, Eric Johnson, Shirley Brice-Heath, Teresa McCarty, Elinor Ochs, Tamar Kremer-Sadlik, Susan Blum, et al. 2015. "Invited Forum: Bridging the 'Language Gap.'" *Journal of Linguistic Anthropology* 25(1): 66–86. https://doi.org/10.1111/jola.12071.

Bakhtin, Mikhail. 1981. *The Dialogic Imagination: Four Essays*. Edited by Michael Holquist. Translated by Caryl Emerson and Michael Holquist. Austin: University of Texas Press.

Ball, Jessica. 2011. "Enhancing Learning of Children from Diverse Backgrounds: Mother-Tongue Based Bilingual or Multilingual Education in the Early Years." Paris: UNESCO.

Baquedano-López, Patricia. 2000. "Narrating Community in Doctrina Classes." *Narrative Inquiry* 10(2): 1–24. https://doi.org/10.1075/ni.10.2.07baq.

Barnett, Robert. 2009. "The Tibet Protests of Spring 2008." *China Perspectives* 2009(3): 6–23. https://doi.org/10.4000/chinaperspectives.4836.

– 2012. "Political Self-Immolation in Tibet: Causes and Influences." *Revue d'Études Tibétaines* 25: 41–64.

Bass, Catriona. 1998. *Education in Tibet: Policy and Practice since 1950*. London: Tibet Information Network.

Bateson, Mary Catherine. 1975. "Mother-Infant Exchanges: The Epigenesis of Conversational Interaction." *Annals of the New York Academy of Sciences* 263(1): 101–13. https://doi.org/10.1111/j.1749-6632.1975.tb41575.x.

Bauman, Richard, and Charles Briggs. 2003. *Voices of Modernity: Language Ideologies and the Politics of Inequality*. New York: Cambridge University Press.

Beckett, Gulbahar H., and Gerard A. Postiglione, eds. 2011. *China's Assimilationist Language Policy: The Impact on Indigenous/Minority Literacy and Social Harmony*. London: Routledge.

Berman, Elise, and Benjamin Smith. 2021. "De-Naturalizing the Novice: A Critique of the Theory of Language Socialization." *American Anthropologist* 123(3): 590–602. https://doi.org/10.1111/aman.13624.

Bhum, Pema, and Lauran Hartley. 2001. "Mao's Cuckoo." *Index on Censorship* 30(1): 176–81. https://doi.org/ 10.1080/03064220108536886.

Björk-Willén, Polly. 2007. "Participation in Multilingual Preschool Play: Shadowing and Crossing as Interactional Resources." *Journal of Pragmatics* 39(12): 2133–58. https://doi.org/10.1016/j.pragma.2007.05.010.

Blum, Susan D. 2017. "Unseen WEIRD Assumptions: The So-Called Language Gap Discourse and Ideologies of Language, Childhood, and Learning." *International Multilingual Research Journal* 11(1): 23–38. https://doi.org/10.1080/19313152.2016.1258187.

Bourdieu, Pierre. 1991. *Language and Symbolic Power*. Edited by John B. Thompson. Translated by Gino Raymond and Matthew Adamson. Cambridge, MA: Polity Press.

Bowlby, John. 1983. *Attachment and Loss*, vol. 1. New York: Basic Books.

Bradley, David. 2005. "Introduction: Language Policy and Language Endangerment in China." *International Journal of the Sociology of Language* 173: 1–21. https://doi.org/10.1515/ijsl.2005.2005.173.1.

Briggs, Charles. 1998. "'You're a Liar – You're Just Like a Woman!' Constructing Dominant Ideologies of Language in Warao Men's Gossip." In *Language Ideologies: Practice and Theory*, edited by Bambi B. Schieffelin, Kathryn A. Woolard, and Paul V. Kroskrity, 229–55. New York: Oxford University Press.

Briggs, Charles, and Richard Bauman. 1992. "Genre, Intertextuality, and Social Power." *Journal of Linguistic Anthropology* 2(2): 131–72. https://doi.org/10.1525/jlin.1992.2.2.131.

Brown, Penelope. 2002. "Everyone Has to Lie in Tzeltal." In *Talking to Adults: The Contribution of Multiparty Discourse to Language Acquisition*, edited by Shoshana Blum-Kulka and Catherine E. Snow, 241–75. Mahwah, NJ: Erlbaum.

Brown, Penelope, and Stephen C. Levinson. 1993. "'Uphill' and 'Downhill' in Tzeltal." *Journal of Linguistic Anthropology* 3(1): 46–74. https://doi.org/10.1525/jlin.1993.3.1.46.

Buckley, Chris. 2021. "Tibetan Who Spoke Out for Language Rights Is Freed from Chinese Prison." *New York Times*, 29 January. https://www.nytimes.com/2021/01/29/world/asia/tibet-china-tashi-wangchuk.html.

Bulag, Uradyn E. 2002. *The Mongols at China's Edge: History and the Politics of National Unity*. Lanham, MD: Rowman & Littlefield.

Burdelski, Matthew. 2010. "Socializing Politeness Routines: Action, Other-Orientation, and Embodiment in a Japanese Preschool." *Journal of Pragmatics* 42(6): 1606–21. https://doi.org/10.1016/j.pragma.2009.11.007.

Burdelski, Matthew, and Ann-Carita Evaldsson. 2019. "Young Children's Multimodal and Collaborative Tellings in Family and Preschool Interaction." *Research on Children and Social Interaction* 3(1–2): 1–5. https://doi.org/10.1558/rcsi.38982.

Cabras, Giulia. 2019. "Language, thang ka and Buddhism: Ethnogenesis and Identity Construction in the Seng ge gshong (Wutun) Community in Amdo Tibet." In *Wind Horses: Tibetan, Himalayan and Mongolian Studies*, edited by Giacomella Orofino, 29–48. Naples: Università degli studi di Napoli "L'Orientale."

Casillas, Marisa. 2014. "Turn-Taking." In *Pragmatic Development in First Language Acquisition*, edited by Danielle Matthews, 53–70. Amsterdam: John Benjamins.

Cekaite, Asta, and Polly Björk-Willén. 2013. "Peer Group Interactions in Multilingual Educational Settings: Co-Constructing Social Order and Norms for Language Use." *International Journal of Bilingualism* 17(2): 174–88. https://doi.org/10.1177/1367006912441417.

Cekaite, Asta, and Ann-Carita Evaldsson. 2019. "Stance and Footing in Multilingual Play: Rescaling Practices and Heritage Language Use in a Swedish Preschool." *Journal of Pragmatics* 144 (April): 127–40. https://doi.org/10.1016/j.pragma.2017.11.011.

Cencetti, Elisa. 2014. "New Settlements on the Tibetan Plateau of Amdo-Qinghai: Spatialized Power Devices." In *On the Fringes of Harmonious Society: Tibetans and Uyghurs in Socialist China*, edited by Trine Brox and Ildikó Bellér-Hann, 159–82. Copenhagen: Nordic Institute of Asian Studies Press.

Chapin, Bambi L. 2014. *Childhood in a Sri Lankan Village: Shaping Hierarchy and Desire*. New Brunswick, NJ: Rutgers University Press.

Clancy, Patricia. 1986. "The Acquisition of Japanese Communicative Style." In *Language Acquisition and Socialization across Cultures*, edited by Elinor Ochs and Bambi B. Schieffelin, 213–50. New York: Cambridge University Press.

Clark, Eve V. 1978. "From Gesture to Word: On the Natural History of Deixis in Language Acquisition." In *Human Growth and Development: Wolfson College Lectures 1976*, edited by Jerome Bruner and Alison Garton, 85–120. Oxford: Oxford University Press.

Clark, Eve V., and C.J. Sengul. 1978. "Strategies in the Acquisition of Deixis." *Journal of Child Language* 5: 457–75. https://doi.org/10.1017/S0305000900002099.

Clifford, James. 1986. "On Ethnographic Allegory." In *Writing Culture: The Poetics and Politics of Ethnography*, 98–121. Berkeley: University of California Press.

Committee on Economic, Social and Cultural Rights. 2023. *Concluding Observations on the Third Periodic Report of China, Including Hong Kong, China, and Macao, China*. UNESCO, 73rd session, 30th meeting (3 March). UN Doc E/C.12/CHN/CO/3.

Cook, Haruko Minegishi. 2014. "Language Socialization and Stance-Taking Practices." In *The Handbook of Language Socialization*, edited by Alessandro Duranti, Elinor Ochs, and Bambi B. Schieffelin, 296–321. Malden, MA: Wiley-Blackwell.

Corsaro, William A. 1992. "Interpretive Reproduction in Children's Peer Cultures." *Social Psychology Quarterly* 55(2): 160–77. https://doi.org/10.2307/2786944.

Couper-Kuhlen, Elizabeth 2014. "Prosody as Dialogic Interaction." In *Prosodie und Phonetik in der Interaktion / Prosody and Phonetics in Interaction*, edited by Dagmar Barth-Weingarten and Beatrice Szczepek Reed, 221–51. Verlag fuer Gespraechsforschung.

Dawa Norbu. 2001. *China's Tibet Policy*. Surrey, UK: Curzon.

Dechun, Li, and Gerald Roche. 2017. *Long Narrative Songs from the Mongghul of Northeast Tibet: Texts in Mongghul, Chinese, and English*. Cambridge: Open Book Publishers.

Demick, Barbara. 2020. *Eat the Buddha: Life and Death in a Tibetan Town*. New York: Random House.

Demuth, Katherine. 1986. "Prompting Routines in the Language Socialization of Basotho Children." In *Language Socialization across Cultures*, edited by Bambi B. Schieffelin and Elinor Ochs, 51–79. Cambridge: Cambridge University Press.

Diessel, Holger, and Kenny R. Coventry. 2020. "Demonstratives in Spatial Language and Social Interaction: An Interdisciplinary Review." *Frontiers in Psychology* 11. https://doi.org/10.3389/fpsyg.2020.555265.

Dondrup Tsering. 2011. *Bod Kyi Yul Skad Rnam Bshad* [Commentary on Tibet's Dialects]. Beijing: krong go'i bod rig pa dpe skrun khang [China Tibetan Publishing House].

Dreyfus, George. 2002. "Is Compassion an Emotion? A Cross-Cultural Exploration of Mental Typologies." In *Visions of Compassion: Western Scientists and Tibetan Buddhists Examine Human Nature*, edited by Richard J. Davidson and Anne Harrington, 31–45. Oxford: Oxford University Press.

Dui Hua Foundation. 2020. "Court Statistics on Splittism and Inciting Splittism, Part II: Uyghurs & Tibetans." *Dui Hua Human Rights Journal*, 16 July. http://www.duihuahrjournal.org/2020/07/court-statistics-on-splittism-inciting.html.

Duranti, Alessandro, and Elinor Ochs. 1997. "Syncretic Literacy in a Samoan American Family." In *Discourse, Tools, and Reasoning: Essays on Situated Cognition*, edited by Lauren Resnick, Roger Säljö, Clotilde Pontecorvo, and Barbara Burge, 169–202. New York: Springer.

Dwyer, Arienne M. 1998. "The Texture of Tongues: Languages and Power in China." In *Nationalism and Ethnoregional Identities in China*, edited by William Safran, 68–85. London: Routledge.

– 2022. "Typological Patterning of Contact-Induced Morphosyntactic Shift in Amdo Tibet." In *Endangered Languages of Northeast Asia*, edited by Elisabetta Ragagnin and Bayarma Khabtagaeva, 81–99. Leiden: Brill.

Eberhard, David, Gary Simons, and Charles Fennig, eds. 2023. *Ethnologue: Languages of the World*. 26th ed. SIL International. www.ethnologue.com

Ekvall, Robert Brainerd. 1968. *Fields on the Hoof: Nexus of Tibetan Nomadic Pastoralism*. Long Grove, IL: Waveland Press.

Fader, Ayala. 2006. "Learning Faith: Language Socialization in a Hasidic Community." *Language in Society* 35(2): 205–28. https://doi.org/10.1017/S004740450606009X.

Ferguson, Jenanne K. 2016. "Code-Mixing among Sakha-Russian Bilinguals in Yakutsk: A Spectrum of Features and Shifting Indexical Fields." *Journal of Linguistic Anthropology* 26(2): 141–61. https://doi.org/10.1111/jola.12123.

Fillmore, Lily Wong. 1991. "When Learning a Second Language Means Losing the First." *Early Childhood Research Quarterly* 6(3): 323–46. https://doi.org/10.1016/S0885-2006(05)80059-6.

Fischer, Andrew Martin. 2013. *The Disempowered Development of Tibet in China: A Study in the Economics of Marginalization*. Lanham, MD: Lexington Books.

Fung, Heidi, and Mai Thị Thu. 2019. "Cultivating Affection-Laden Hierarchy: Embodied Moral Socialization of Vòng Tay (Khoanh Tay) with Children in Southern Vietnam." *Ethos* 47(3): 281–306. https://doi.org/10.1111/etho.12247.

García-Sánchez, Inmaculada M. 2014. *Language and Muslim Immigrant Childhoods: The Politics of Belonging*. Malden, MA: Wiley-Blackwell.

Garrett, Paul B., and Patricia Baquedano-López. 2002. "Language Socialization: Reproduction and Continuity, Transformation and Change." *Annual Review of Anthropology* 31: 339–61. https://doi.org/10.1146/annurev.anthro.31.040402.085352.

Goffman, Erving. 1972. "On Face-Work: An Analysis of Ritual Elements in Social Interaction." In *Communication in Face to Face Interaction: Selected Readings*, edited by John Laver and Sandy Hutcheson, 319–47. Harmondsworth: Penguin.

– 1976. "Replies and Responses." *Language in Society* 5(3): 257–313.

– 1981. *Forms of Talk*. Philadelphia: University of Pennsylvania Press.

Goldin-Meadow, Susan. 2007. "Pointing Sets the Stage for Learning Language – and Creating Language." *Child Development* 78(3): 741–45. https://doi.org/10.1111/j.1467-8624.2007.01029.x. Medline:17517001.

Goldstein, Melvyn C. 1999. *The Snow Lion and the Dragon: China, Tibet, and the Dalai Lama*. Berkeley: University of California Press.

Goodman, David S.G. 2004a. "The Campaign to 'Open Up the West': National, Provincial-Level and Local Perspectives." *China Quarterly* 178 (June): 317–34. https://doi.org/10.1017/S0305741004000190.

– 2004b. "Qinghai and the Emergence of the West: Nationalities, Communal Interaction and National Integration." *China Quarterly* 178 (June): 379–99. https://doi.org/10.1017/S0305741004000220.

Goodwin, Charles. 2000. "Action and Embodiment within Situated Human Interaction." *Journal of Pragmatics* 32(10): 1489–1522. https://doi.org/10.1016/S0378-2166(99)00096-X.

– 2006. "Retrospective and Prospective Orientation in the Construction of Argumentative Moves." *Text & Talk* 26(4–5): 443–61. https://doi.org/10.1515/TEXT.2006.018.

– 2007. "Interactive Footing." In *Reporting Talk: Reported Speech in Interaction*, edited by Elizabeth Holt and Rebecca Clift, 16–46. Cambridge: Cambridge University Press.

– 2018. *Co-operative Action*. Cambridge: Cambridge University Press.

Goodwin, Charles, and John Heritage. 1990. "Conversation Analysis." *Annual Review of Anthropology* 19: 283–307. https://doi.org/10.1146/annurev.an.19.100190.001435.

Goodwin, Marjorie Harness. 1991. *He-Said–She-Said: Talk as Social Organization among Black Children*. Bloomington: Indiana University Press.

– 2011. "Engendering Children's Play: Person Reference in Children's Conflictual Interaction." In *Conversation and Gender*, edited by Susan A. Speer and Elizabeth Stokoe, 250–71. Cambridge: Cambridge University Press.

– 2017. "Haptic Sociality: The Embodied Interactive Constitution of Intimacy through Touch." In *Intercorporeality: Emerging Socialities in Interaction*, edited by Christian Meyer, Jürgen Streeck, and J. Scott Jordan, 73–102. Oxford: Oxford University Press.

Goodwin, Marjorie Harness, Asta Cekaite, and Charles Goodwin. 2012. "Emotion as Stance." In *Emotion in Interaction*, edited by Anssi Peräkylä and Marja-Leena Sorjonen, 16–40. Oxford: Oxford University Press.

Grant, Andrew. 2016. "Belonging and Ethnicity in China's West: Urbanizing Minorities in Xining City on the Eastern Tibetan Plateau." PhD diss., University of California, Los Angeles.

– 2018a. "Channeling Xining: Tibetan Place-Making in Western China during the Era of Commodity Housing." *Annals of the American Association of Geographers* 108(5): 1457–71. https://doi.org/10.1080/24694452.2018.1446821.

– 2018b. "Hyperbuilding the Civilized City: Ethnicity and Marginalization in Eastern Tibet." *Critical Asian Studies* 50(4): 537–55. https://doi.org/10.1080/14672715.2018.1514270.

Gratier, Maya. 2020. "Insights from Infancy: The Felt Basis of Language in Interpersonal Engagement." In *The Routledge Handbook of Language and Emotion*, edited by Sonya E. Pritzker, Janina Fenigsen, and James M. Wilce, 13–27. New York: Routledge Taylor & Francis Group.

Green, R. Jeffrey. 2012. "Amdo Tibetan Media Intelligibility." SIL Electronic Survey Report 2012–019. SIL International.

Grenoble, Lenore A., and Lindsay J. Whaley, eds. 1998. *Endangered Languages: Language Loss and Community Response*. Cambridge: Cambridge University Press.

Gumperz, John J. 1982. "Conversational Code Switching." In *Discourse Strategies*, 59–99. Cambridge: Cambridge University Press.

Gumperz, John, and Jenny Cook-Gumperz. 2008. "Discourse, Cultural Diversity and Communication: A Linguistic Anthropological Perspective." In *Handbook of Intercultural Communication*, edited by Helga Kotthoff and Helen Spencer-Oatey, 13–29. Berlin: Walter de Gruyter.

Gyal, Huatse. 2019. "'I Am Concerned with the Future of My Children': The Project Economy and Shifting Views of Education in a Tibetan Pastoral Community." *Critical Asian Studies* 51(1): 12–30. https://doi.org/10.1080/14672715.2018.1544500.

Haas, William Brent. 2013. "Qinghai across Frontiers: State- and Nation-Building under the Ma Family, 1911–1949." PhD diss., University of California, San Diego.

Hale, Ken. 1992. "Endangered Languages." *Language* 68(1): 1–42. https://doi.org/10.1353/lan.1992.0052.

Handel, Zev. 2015. "The Classification of Chinese: Sinitic (The Chinese Language Family)." In *The Oxford Handbook of Chinese Linguistics*, edited by William S-Y. Wang and Chaofen Sun, 35–44. Oxford: Oxford University Press.

Hanks, William. 1992. "The Indexical Ground of Deictic Reference." In *Rethinking Context: Language as Interactive Phenomenon*, edited by Alessandro Duranti and Charles Goodwin, 43–76. Cambridge: Cambridge University Press.
– 2005. "Explorations in the Deictic Field." *Current Anthropology* 46(2): 191–220. https://doi.org/10.1086/427120.
– 2009. "Fieldwork on Deixis." *Journal of Pragmatics* 41(1): 10–24. https://doi.org/10.1016/j.pragma.2008.09.003.
Hansen, Mette Halskov. 2006. *Frontier People: Han Settlers in Minority Areas of China*. Vancouver: UBC Press.
Hartley, Lauran R. 1996. "The Role of Regional Factors in the Standardization of Spoken Tibetan." *Tibet Journal* 21(4): 30–57.
Hayes, Jack Patrick. 2014. *A Change in Worlds on the Sino-Tibetan Borderlands: Politics, Economies, and Environments in Northern Sichuan*. New York: Lexington Books.
Heath, Shirley Brice. 1982. "What No Bedtime Story Means: Narrative Skills at Home and School." *Language in Society* 11(1): 49–76. https://doi.org/10.1017/S0047404500009039.
Hoffman, Eva. 1990. *Lost in Translation: A Life in a New Language*. Reprint. New York: Penguin Books.
Hostetler, Laura. 2001. *Qing Colonial Enterprise: Ethnography and Cartography in Early Modern China*. Chicago: University of Chicago Press.
Hua Kan, ed. 2002. *Zangyu Anduo Fangyan Cihui* [Comparative Dictionary of Amdo Tibetan]. Lanzhou: Gansu Nationalities Publishing House.
Ijzendoorn, Marinus H. van, and Abraham Sagi-Schwartz. 2008. "Cross-Cultural Patterns of Attachment: Universal and Contextual Dimensions." In *Handbook of Attachment: Theory, Research, and Clinical Applications*, edited by Jude Cassidy and Phillip R. Shaver, 880–905. New York: Guilford Press.
Irvine, Judith, and Susan Gal. 2000. "Language Ideology and Linguistic Differentiation." In *Regimes of Language: Ideologies, Polities, and Identities*, edited by Paul Kroskrity, 35–84. Santa Fe, NM: School of American Research Press.
Iverson, Jana M., and Susan Goldin-Meadow. 2005. "Gesture Paves the Way for Language Development." *Psychological Science* 16(5): 367–71. https://doi.org/10.1111/j.0956-7976.2005.01542.x. Medline:15869695.
Jacka, Tamara. 2009. "Cultivating Citizens: *Suzhi* (Quality) Discourse in the PRC." *positions: asia critique* 17(3): 523–35. https://doi.org/10.1215/10679847-2009-013.
Jaffe, Alexandra. 2009. "Introduction: The Sociolinguistics of Stance." In *Stance: Sociolinguistic Perspectives*, edited by Alexandra Jaffe, 1–28. Oxford: Oxford University Press.

Jakobson, Roman. 1980. "Metalanguage as a Linguistic Problem." In *The Framework of Language*, 81–92. Ann Arbor: Michigan Studies in the Humanities.

Janhunen, Juha A. 2012. "On the Hierarchy of Structural Convergence in the Amdo Sprachbund." In *Argument Structure and Grammatical Relations: A Crosslinguistic Typology*, edited by Pirkko Suihkonen, Bernard Comrie, and Valery Solovyev, 177–90. Amsterdam: John Benjamins.

Jefferson, Gail. 2004. "Glossary of Transcript Symbols with an Introduction." In *Conversation Analysis: Studies from the First Generation*, edited by Gene H. Lerner, 13–31. Amsterdam: John Benjamins.

Ji, Fengyuan. 2003. *Linguistic Engineering: Language and Politics in Mao's China*. Honolulu: University of Hawaii Press.

Johnson, Sarah Jean, and Hasmik Avetisian Cochran. 2021. "Collaborative Research into the 'Hidden Worlds' of Children's Peer Reading." *Journal of Early Childhood Research* 19(3): 381–95. https://doi.org/10.1177/1476718X20983846.

Kapstein, Matthew T. 2002. *The Tibetan Assimilation of Buddhism: Conversion, Contestation, and Memory*. Oxford: Oxford University Press.

King, Kendall A., Natalie Schilling-Estes, Lyn Fogle, Jia Jackie Lou, and Barbara Soukup, eds. 2008. *Sustaining Linguistic Diversity: Endangered and Minority Languages and Language Varieties*. Washington, DC: Georgetown University Press.

Kipnis, Andrew. 1997. *Producing Guanxi: Sentiment, Self, and Subculture in a North China Village*. Durham, NC: Duke University Press.

Kolås, Åshild, and Monika P. Thowsen. 2005. *On the Margins of Tibet: Cultural Survival on the Sino-Tibetan Frontier*. Seattle: University of Washington Press.

Koven, Michèle. 2007. *Selves in Two Languages: Bilinguals' Verbal Enactments of Identity in French and Portuguese*. Philadelphia: John Benjamins Publishing.

Kroskrity, Paul. 1998. "Arizona Tewa Kiva Speech as a Manifestation of a Dominant Language Ideology." In *Language Ideologies: Practice and Theory*, edited by Bambi B. Schieffelin, Kathryn A. Woolard, and Paul V. Kroskrity, 103–22. New York: Oxford University Press.

Kuan, Teresa. 2015. *Love's Uncertainty: The Politics and Ethics of Child Rearing in Contemporary China*. Berkeley and Los Angeles: University of California Press.

Kuhl, Patricia, Karen Williams, Francisco Lacerda, Kenneth Stevens, and Björn Lindblom. 1992. "Linguistic Experience Alters Phonetic Perception in Infants by 6 Months of Age." *Science* 255(5044): 606–8. https://doi.org/10.1126/science.1736364.

Kulick, Don. 1992. *Language Shift and Cultural Reproduction: Socialization, Self and Syncretism in a Papua New Guinean Village*. Cambridge: Cambridge University Press.

Kulick, Don, and Bambi B. Schieffelin. 2004. "Language Socialization." In *A Companion to Linguistic Anthropology*, edited by Alessandro Duranti, 347–68. Malden, MA: Blackwell Publishing.

Kuper, Adam. 1988. *The Invention of Primitive Society: Transformations of an Illusion*. New York: Routledge.

Kyratzis, Amy. 2017. "Peer Ecologies for Learning How to Read: Exhibiting Reading, Orchestrating Participation, and Learning over Time in Bilingual Mexican-American Preschoolers' Play Enactments of Reading to a Peer." *Linguistics and Education* 41: 7–19. https://doi.org/10.1016/j.linged.2017.07.005.

Kyratzis, Amy, and Sarah Jean Johnson. 2017. "Multimodal and Multilingual Resources in Children's Framing of Situated Learning Activites: An Introduction." *Linguistics and Education* 41: 1–6. https://doi.org/10.1016/j.linged.2017.07.002.

Leibold, James. 2007. *Reconfiguring Chinese Nationalism: How the Qing Frontier and Its Indigenes Became Chinese*. New York: Palgrave Macmillan US.

– 2019. "Interior Ethnic Minority Boarding Schools: China's Bold and Unpredictable Educational Experiment." *Asian Studies Review* 43(1): 3–15. https://doi.org/10.1080/10357823.2018.1548572.

Lempert, Michael. 2012. *Discipline and Debate: The Language of Violence in a Tibetan Buddhist Monastery*. Berkeley and Los Angeles: University of California Press.

León, Lourdes de. 2014. "Language Socialization and Multiparty Participation Frameworks." In *The Handbook of Language Socialization*, edited by Alessandro Duranti, Elinor Ochs, and Bambi B. Schieffelin, 81–111. Malden, MA: Wiley-Blackwell.

Levine, Nancy E. 2015. "Transforming Inequality: Eastern Tibetan Pastoralists from 1955 to the Present." *Nomadic Peoples* 19(2): 164–88. https://doi.org/10.3197/np.2015.190202.

LeVine, Robert A. 2014. "Attachment Theory as Cultural Ideology." In *Different Faces of Attachment: Cultural Variations on a Universal Human Need*, edited by Hiltrud Otto and Heidi Keller, 50–65. New York: Cambridge University Press.

LeVine, Robert A., and Karin Norman. 2001. "The Infant's Acquisition of Culture: Early Attachment Re-examined in Anthropological Perspective." In *The Psychology of Cultural Experience*, edited by Carmella C. Moore and Holly F. Mathews, 83–104. Cambridge: Cambridge University Press.

Levinson, Stephen. 2003. "Language and Mind: Let's Get the Issues Straight!" In *Language in Mind: Advances in the Study of Language and Thought*, edited by Dedre Gentner and Susan Goldin-Meadow, 25–46. Cambridge, MA: MIT Press.

Lewis, Sara E. 2013. "Trauma and the Making of Flexible Minds in the Tibetan Exile Community." *Ethos* 41(3): 313–36. https://doi.org/10.1111/etho.12024.

Lhagyal, Dak. 2021. "'Linguistic Authority' in State-Society Interaction: Cultural Politics of Tibetan Education in China." *Discourse: Studies in the Cultural Politics of Education* 42(3): 353–67. https://doi.org/10.1080/01596306.2019.1648239.

Lhamo Pemba. 2007. *Tibetan Proverbs*. Dharamsala, India: Library of Tibetan Works and Archives.

Ling, Minhua. 2019. *The Inconvenient Generation: Migrant Youth Coming of Age on Shanghai's Edge*. Stanford, CA: Stanford University Press.

Lipman, Jonathan N. 1984. "Ethnicity and Politics in Republican China: The Ma Family Warlords of Gansu." *Modern China* 10(3): 285–316. https://doi.org/10.1177/009770048401000302.

Lo, Adrienne, and Heidi Fung. 2014. "Language Socialization and Shaming." In *The Handbook of Language Socialization*, edited by Alessandro Duranti, Elinor Ochs, and Bambi B. Schieffelin, 169–89. Malden, MA: Wiley-Blackwell.

Lucy, John A. 1993. "Metapragmatic Presentationals: Reporting Speech with Quotatives in Yucatec Maya." In *Reflexive Language: Reported Speech and Metapragmatics*, edited by John A. Lucy, 91–126. New York: Cambridge University Press.

Ma, Fu and Renzeng. 2015. "Ethnolinguistic Vitality, Language Attitudes and Language Education in Tibetan Schools in Qinghai." In *Trilingualism in Education in China: Models and Challenges*, edited by Anwei Feng and Bob Adamson, 103–15. Dordrecht: Springer Netherlands.

Maconi, Lara. 2008. "One Nation, Two Discourses: Tibetan New Era Literature and the Language Debate." In *Modern Tibetan Literature and Social Change*, edited by Lauran R. Hartley and Patricia Schiaffini-Vedani, 173–201. Durham, NC: Duke University Press.

Makley, Charlene. 2003. "Gendered Boundaries in Motion: Space and Identity on the Sino-Tibetan Frontier." *American Ethnologist* 30(4): 597–619. https://doi.org/10.1525/ae.2003.30.4.597.

– 2005. "'Speaking Bitterness': Autobiography, History, and Mnemonic Politics on the Sino-Tibetan Frontier." *Comparative Studies in Society and History* 47(1): 40–78. https://doi.org/10.1017/S0010417505000034.

Max Planck Institute for Evolutionary Anthropology. 2015. "Leipzig Glossing Rules." https://www.eva.mpg.de/lingua/resources/glossing-rules.php.

McGranahan, Carole. 2019. "Chinese Settler Colonialism: Empire and Life in the Tibetan Borderlands." In *Frontier Tibet: Patterns of Change in the Sino-Tibetan Borderlands*, edited by Stéphane Gros, 517–40. Amsterdam: Amsterdam University Press.

Meek, Barbra A. 2007. "Respecting the Language of the Elders: Ideological Shift and Linguistic Discontinuity in a Northern Athapascan Community." *Journal of Linguistic Anthropology* 17(1): 23–43. https://doi.org/10.1525/jlin.2007.17.1.23.

– 2012. *We Are Our Language: An Ethnography of Language Revitalization in a Northern Athabaskan Community*. Tucson: University of Arizona Press.
– 2019. "Language Endangerment in Childhood." *Annual Review of Anthropology* 48(1): 95–115. https://doi.org/10.1146/annurev-anthro-102317-050041.
Merleau-Ponty, Maurice. 2010 [1945]. *Phenomenology of Perception*. Translated by Donald Landes. London: Routledge.
Mertz, Elizabeth. 2007. "Semiotic Anthropology." *Annual Review of Anthropology* 36: 337–53. https//doi.org/10.1146/annurev.anthro.36.081406.094417.
Michael, Lev. 2015. "The Cultural Bases of Linguistic Form: The Development of Nanti Quotative Evidentials." In *Language Structure and Environment: Social, Cultural, and Natural Factors*, edited by Rik De Busser and Randy J. LaPolla, 99–130. Amsterdam: John Benjamins.
Milroy, James. 2001. "Language Ideologies and the Consequences of Standardization." *Journal of Sociolinguistics* 5(4): 530–55. https://doi.org/10.1111/1467-9481.00163.
Milroy, Lesley. 2001. "Britain and the United States: Two Nations Divided by the Same Language (and Different Language Ideologies)." *Journal of Linguistic Anthropology* 10(1): 56–89. https://doi.org/10.1525/jlin.2000.10.1.56.
Mohanty, Ajit K. 2010. "Languages, Inequality and Marginalization: Implications of the Double Divide in Indian Multilingualism." *International Journal of the Sociology of Language* 205: 131–54. https://doi.org/10.1515/ijsl.2010.042.
Moore, Leslie C. 2006. "Learning by Heart in Qur'anic and Public Schools in Northern Cameroon." *Social Analysis* 50(3): 109–26. https://doi.org/10.3167/015597706780459421.
Morcom, Anna. 2018. "The Political Potency of Tibetan Identity in Pop Music and Dunglen." *Himalaya, the Journal of the Association for Nepal and Himalayan Studies* 38(1): 127–44.
Morelli, Gilda. 2015. "The Evolution of Attachment Theory and Cultures of Human Attachment in Infancy and Early Childhood." In *The Oxford Handbook of Human Development and Culture: An Interdisciplinary Perspective*, edited by Lene Arnett Jensen, 149–64. Oxford: Oxford University Press.
Mullaney, Thomas. 2010. *Coming to Terms with the Nation: Ethnic Classification in Modern China*. Berkeley: University of California Press.
Murphy, Rachel. 2004. "Turning Peasants into Modern Chinese Citizens: 'Population Quality' Discourse, Demographic Transition and Primary Education." *China Quarterly* 177 (May): 1–20. https://doi.org/10.1017/S0305741004000025.
Naftali, Orna. 2016. *Children in China*. Malden, MA: John Wiley & Sons.
Nelson, Katherine. 2009. *Young Minds in Social Worlds: Experience, Meaning, and Memory*. Cambridge, MA: Harvard University Press.

Nietupski, Paul Kocot. 1999. *Labrang: A Tibetan Buddhist Monastery at the Crossroads of Four Civilizations (Photos from the Griebenow Archives, 1921–1949).* Ithaca, NY: Snow Lion Publications.

Ochs, Elinor. 1979. "Transcription as Theory." In *Developmental Pragmatics*, edited by Elinor Ochs and Bambi Schieffelin, 43–72. New York: Academic Press.

– 1985. "Variation and Error: A Sociolinguistic Approach to Language Acquisition in Samoa." In *The Crosslinguistic Study of Language Acquisition*, vol. 1, edited by Dan Slobin, 783–838. Hillside, NJ: Lawrence Erlbaum Associates.

– 1988. *Culture and Language Development: Language Acquisition and Language Socialization in a Samoan Village*. Cambridge: Cambridge University Press.

– 1992. "Indexing Gender." In *Rethinking Context: Language as an Interactive Phenomenon*, edited by Alessandro Duranti and Charles Goodwin, 335–358. Cambridge: Cambridge University Press.

– 1996. "Linguistic Resources for Socializing Humanity." In *Rethinking Linguistic Relativity*, edited by John J. Gumperz and Stephen C. Levinson, 407–37. Cambridge: Cambridge University Press.

Ochs, Elinor, and Lisa Capps. 2001. *Living Narrative: Creating Lives in Everyday Storytelling*. Cambridge, MA: Harvard University Press.

Ochs, Elinor, and Bambi B. Schieffelin. 1984. "Language Acquisition and Socialization: Three Developmental Stories and Their Implications." In *Culture Theory: Essays on Mind, Self and Emotion*, edited by Richard A. Shweder and Robert A. Levine, 276–320. Levine, NY: Cambridge University Press.

– 1995. "The Impact of Language Socialization on Grammatical Development." In *The Handbook of Child Language*, edited by Paul Fletcher and Brian MacWhinney, 73–94. Oxford: Blackwell.

Oidtmann, Max. 2018. *Forging the Golden Urn: The Qing Empire and the Politics of Reincarnation in Tibet*. New York: Columbia University Press.

Ozawa-de Silva, Chikako, and Brendan R. Ozawa-de Silva. 2011. "Mind/Body Theory and Practice in Tibetan Medicine and Buddhism." *Body & Society* 17(1): 95–119. https://doi.org/10.1177/1357034X10383883.

Padma Lhundrup. 2009. *A Mdo'i Yul Skad Kyi Sgra Gdangs La Dpyad Pa* [A Phonological Analysis of Amdo Tibetan Dialects]. Xining: Mtsho sngon mi rigs deb skrun khang [Mtsho ngon Nationalities Press].

Park, Eunjin. 2006. "Grandparents, Grandchildren, and Heritage Language Use in Korean." In *Heritage Language Development: Focus on East Asian Immigrants*, edited by Kimi Kondo-Brown, 57–86. Amsterdam: John Benjamins.

Paugh, Amy L. 2005. "Multilingual Play: Children's Code-Switching, Role Play, and Agency in Dominica, West Indies." *Language in Society* 34(1): 63–86. https://doi.org/10.1017/S0047404505050037.

Peirce, Charles Sanders. 1955. "Logic as Semiotic: The Theory of Signs." In *Philosophical Writings of Peirce*, edited by Justus Buchler, 98–115. New York: Dover.

Postiglione, Gerard A. 2008. "Making Tibetans in China: Educational Challenges for Harmonious Multiculturalism." *Educational Review* 60(1): 1–20. https://doi.org/10.1080/00131910701794481.

– 2009. "Dislocated Education: The Case of Tibet." *Comparative Education Review* 53(4): 483–512. https://doi.org/10.1086/603616.

Powers, John, and Deane Curtin. 1994. "Mothering: Moral Cultivation in Buddhist and Feminist Ethics." *Philosophy East and West* 44(1): 1–19. https://doi.org/10.2307/1399802.

Prins, Marielle. 2002. "Toward a Tibetan Common Language: A Mdo Perspectives on Attempts at Language Standardization." In *Amdo Tibetans in Transition: Society and Culture in the Post-Mao Era*, edited by Toni Huber, 27–51. Leiden: Brill.

Ptáčková, Jarmila. 2020. *Exile from the Grasslands: Tibetan Herders and Chinese Development Projects*. Seattle: University of Washington Press.

Qi, Wu. 2013. "Tradition and Modernity: Cultural Continuum and Transition among Tibetans in Amdo." PhD diss., University of Helsinki.

Quinn, Naomi, and Jeannette Marie Mageo, eds. 2013. *Attachment Reconsidered: Cultural Perspectives on a Western Theory*. New York: Palgrave Macmillan /Springer Nature.

Reisman, Karl. 1974. "Contrapuntal Conversations in an Antiguan Village." In *Explorations in the Ethnography of Speaking*, edited by Richard Bauman and Joel Sherzer, 110–24. Cambridge: Cambridge University Press.

Reynolds, Jennifer. 2009. "Shaming the Shift Generation: Intersecting Ideologies of Family and Linguistic Revitalization in Guatemala." In *Native American Language Ideologies: Beliefs, Practices, and Struggles in Indian Country*, edited by Paul V. Kroskrity and Margaret C. Field, 213–37. Tucson: University Arizona Press.

Reynolds, Jermay. 2012. "Language Variation and Change in an Amdo Tibetan Village: Gender, Education and Resistance." PhD diss., Georgetown University.

Robin, Françoise. 2016. "Discussing Rights and Human Rights in Tibet." In *Ethnic Conflict and Protest in Tibet and Xinjiang: Unrest in China's West*, edited by Ben Hillman and Gray Tuttle, 60–9. New York: Columbia University Press.

Roche, Gerald. 2019. "Articulating Language Oppression: Colonialism, Coloniality and the Erasure of Tibet's Minority Languages." *Patterns of Prejudice* 53(5): 487–514. https://doi.org/10.1080/0031322X.2019.1662074.

– 2021a. "Lexical Necropolitics: The Raciolinguistics of Language Oppression on the Tibetan Margins of Chineseness." *Language & Communication* 76 (January): 111–20. https://doi.org/10.1016/j.langcom.2020.10.002.

– 2021b. "Tibetan Language Rights and Civil Society in the People's Republic of China: Challenges of and for Rights." *Asian Studies Review* 45(1): 67–82. https://doi.org/10.31235/osf.io/a3ktz.

Roche, Gerald, Madoka Hammine, Jesus Federico C. Hernandez, and Jess Kruk. 2023. "The Politics of Fear and the Suppression of Indigenous Language Activism in Asia: Prospects for the United Nations' Decade of Indigenous Languages." *State Crime Journal* 12(1): 29–50. https://doi.org/10.13169/statecrime.12.1.0029.

Roche, Gerald, James Leibold, and Ben Hillman. 2020. "Urbanizing Tibet: Differential Inclusion and Colonial Governance in the People's Republic of China." *Territory, Politics, Governance* 11(2): 394–414. https://doi.org/10.1080/21622671.2020.1840427.

Roche, Gerald, and Hiroyuki Suzuki. 2018. "Tibet's Minority Languages: Diversity and Endangerment." *Modern Asian Studies* 52(4): 1227–78. https://doi.org/10.1017/S0026749X1600072X.

Roche, Gerald, and Yudru Tsomu. 2018. "Tibet's Invisible Languages and China's Language Endangerment Crisis: Lessons from the Gochang Language of Western Sichuan." *China Quarterly* 233: 186–210. https://doi.org/10.1017/S0305741018000012.

Rohlf, Gregory. 2016. *Building New China, Colonizing Kokonor: Resettlement to Qinghai in the 1950s*. Lanham, MD: Lexington Books.

Rohsenow, John S. 2004. "Fifty Years of Script and Written Language Reform in the P.R.C." In *Language Policy in the People's Republic of China: Theory and Practice Since 1949*, edited by Minglang Zhou and Hongkai Sun, 21–43. New York: Kluwer Academic Publishers.

Saillard, Claire. 2004. "On the Promotion of *Putonghua* in China: How a Standard Language Becomes a Vernacular." In *Language Policy in the People's Republic of China: Theory and Practice since 1949*, edited by Minglang Zhou and Hongkai Sun, 163–76. New York: Kluwer Academic Publishers.

Samdrup, Tsering, and Hiroyuki Suzuki. 2017. "Migration History and *Tsowa* Divisions as a Supplemental Approach to Dialectology in Amdo Tibetan: A Case Study on Mangra County." In *Studies in Asian Geolinguistics*, vol. 7: *Tone and Accent*, edited by Mitsuaki Endo, 57–65. Tokyo: Research Institute for Languages and Cultures of Asia and Africa.

Schaeffer, Kurtis R., Matthew T. Kapstein, and Gray Tuttle, eds. 2013. *Sources of Tibetan Tradition*. New York: Columbia University Press.

Schegloff, Emanuel A. 2007. "The Organization of Preference/Dispreference." In *Sequence Organization in Interaction: A Primer in Conversation Analysis*, 58–96. Cambridge: Cambridge University Press.

Schieffelin, Bambi B. 1983. "Talking like Birds: Sound Play in a Cultural Perspective." In *Acquiring Conversational Competence*, edited by Elinor Ochs and Bambi B. Schieffelin, 177–84. Boston: Routledge & Kegan Paul.

– 1990. *The Give and Take of Everyday Life: Language Socialization of Kaluli Children*. Cambridge: Cambridge University Press.
– 2007. "Found in Translating: Reflexive Language across Time and Texts in Bosavi, Papua New Guinea." In *Consequences of Contact: Language Ideologies and Sociocultural Transformations in Pacific Societies*, edited by Miki Makihara and Bambi B. Schieffelin, 140–65. Oxford: Oxford University Press.
Schieffelin, Bambi B., and Elinor Ochs, eds. 1986. *Language Socialization across Cultures*. Cambridge: Cambridge University Press.
Shakabpa, Tsepon Wangchuk Deden. 2010. *One Hundred Thousand Moons: An Advanced Political History of Tibet*. Translated by Derek F. Maher. Leiden: Brill.
Shakya, Tsering. 2000. *The Dragon in the Land of Snows: A History of Modern Tibet since 1947*. New York: Penguin Books.
Shneiderman, Sara. 2006. "Barbarians at the Border and Civilising Projects: Analysing Ethnic and National Identities in the Tibetan Context." In *Tibetan Borderlands*, edited by P. Christiaan Klieger, 9–34. Leiden: Brill.
Sidnell, Jack. 2007. "Comparative Studies in Conversation Analysis." *Annual Review of Anthropology* 36: 229–44. https://doi.org/10.1146/annurev.anthro.36.081406.094313.
Silverstein, Michael. 1979. "Language Structure and Linguistic Ideology." In *The Elements: A Parasession on Linguistic Units and Levels*, edited by Paul R. Clyne, William F. Hanks, and Carol L. Hofbauer, 193–247. Chicago: Chicago Linguistic Society.
– 1993. "Metapragmatic Discourse and Metapragmatic Function." In *Reflexive Language: Reported Speech and Metapragmatics*, edited by John A. Lucy, 33–58. New York: Cambridge University Press.
– 2001. "The Limits of Awareness." In *Linguistic Anthropology: A Reader*, edited by Alessandro Duranti, 382–407. Malden, MA: Blackwell Publishing.
– 2003. "Indexical Order and the Dialectics of Sociolinguistic Life." *Language & Communication* 23(3–4): 193–229. https://doi.org/10.1016/S0271-5309(03)00013-2.
Simon, Camille. 2016. "Morphosyntaxe et sémantique grammaticale du Salar et du Tibétain de l'amdo." PhD diss., Université Sorbonne Nouvelle-Paris 3.
Skutnabb-Kangas, Tove. 2000. *Linguistic Genocide in Education – or Worldwide Diversity and Human Rights?* London: Routledge.
Slobin, Dan I., ed. 1985. *The Crosslinguistic Study of Language Acquisition*, vol. 1: *The Data*. Hillsdale, NJ: Lawrence Erlbaum Associates.
– 1996. "From 'Thought and Language' to 'Thinking for Speaking.'" In *Rethinking Linguistic Relativity*, edited by John J. Gumperz and Stephen C. Levinson, 70–96. Cambridge: Cambridge University Press.

Sneath, David. 2007. *The Headless State: Aristocratic Orders, Kinship Society, and Misrepresentations of Nomadic Inner Asia*. New York: Columbia University Press.

Song, Juyong. 2009. "Bilingual Creativity and Self-Negotiation: Korean American Children's Language Socialization into Korean Address Terms." In *Beyond Yellow English: Toward a Linguistic Anthropology of Asian Pacific America*, edited by Angela Reyes and Adrienne Lo, 213–32. Oxford: Oxford University Press.

Sørensen, Per K., and Guntram Hazod. 2007. *Rulers on the Celestial Plain: Ecclesiastic and Secular Hegemony in Medieval Tibet: A Study of Tshal Gung-thang*. Vienna: Verlag der Österreichischen Akademie der Wissenschaften.

Stern, Daniel. 1985. *The Interpersonal World of the Infant: A View from Psychoanalysis and Developmental Psychology*. New York: Basic Books.

Stivers, Tanya, N.J. Enfield, Penelope Brown, Christina Englert, Makoto Hayashi, Trine Heinemann, Gertie Hoymann, et al. 2009. "Universals and Cultural Variation in Turn-Taking in Conversation." *Proceedings of the National Academy of Sciences of the United States of America* 106(26): 10587–92. https://doi.org/10.1073/pnas.0903616106.

Szczepek Reed, Beatrice. 2009. "Prosodic Orientation: A Practice for Sequence Organization in Broadcast Telephone Openings." *Journal of Pragmatics* 41(6): 1223–47. https://doi.org/10.1016/j.pragma.2008.08.009.

Takada, Akira. 2013. "Generating Morality in Directive Sequences: Distinctive Strategies for Developing Communicative Competence in Japanese Caregiver–Child Interactions." *Language & Communication* 33(4, Part A): 420–38. https://doi.org/10.1016/j.langcom.2013.03.012.

– 2014. "Preverbal Infant-Caregiver Interaction." In *The Handbook of Language Socialization*, edited by Alessandro Duranti, Elinor Ochs, and Bambi B. Schieffelin, 56–80. Malden, MA: Wiley-Blackwell.

Tam, Gina Anne. 2020. *Dialect and Nationalism in China, 1860–1960*. Cambridge: Cambridge University Press.

Tashi Nyima. 2014. "In the Name of Conservation and Harmonious Development: The Separation of Pastoralists from Pastures in Tibet." In *On the Fringes of the Harmonious Society: Tibetans and Uyghurs in Socialist China*, edited by Trine Brox and Ildikó Bellér-Hann, 127–58. Copenhagen: Nordic Institute of Asian Studies.

Taylor, Talbot J. 2000. "Language Constructing Language: The Implications of Reflexivity for Linguistic Theory." *Language Sciences* 22: 483–99. https://doi.org/10.1016/S0388-0001(00)00016-4.

Thiong'o, Ngũgĩ wa. 1986. "The Language of African Literature." In *Decolonising the Mind: The Politics of Language in African Literature*, 4–33. Nairobi: East African Educational Publisher.

Thurston, Timothy. 2018a. "On Artistic and Cultural Generations in Northeastern Tibet." *Asian Ethnicity* 19(2): 143–62. https://doi.org/10.1080/14631369.2017.1386542.

– 2018b. "The Purist Campaign as Metadiscursive Regime in China's Tibet." *Inner Asia* 20: 199–218. https://doi.org/10.1163/22105018-12340107.

Tobin, Joseph J., David Y.H. Wu, and Dana H. Davidson. 1991. *Preschool in Three Cultures: Japan, China and the United States*. New Haven, CT: Yale University Press.

Tomasello, Michael. 2003a. *Constructing a Language: A Usage-Based Theory of Language Acquisition*. Cambridge, MA: Harvard University Press.

– 2003b. "The Key Is Social Cognition." In *Language in Mind: Advances in the Study of Language and Thought*, edited by Dedre Gentner and Susan Goldin-Meadow, and 47–58. Cambridge, MA: MIT Press.

Tomasello, Michael, Malinda Carpenter, and Ulf Liszkowski. 2007. "A New Look at Infant Pointing." *Child Development* 78(3): 705–22. https://doi.org/10.1111/j.1467-8624.2007.01025.x.

Tomasello, Michael, Gina Conti-Ramsden, and Barbara Ewert. 1990. "Young Children's Conversations with Their Mothers and Fathers: Differences in Breakdown and Repair." *Journal of Child Language* 17(1): 115–30. https://doi.org/10.1017/s0305000900013131. Medline:2312636.

Tournadre, Nicolas, and Sangda Dorje. 2003. *Manual of Standard Tibetan: Language and Civilization*. Ithaca, NY: Snow Lion Publications.

Tribur, Zoe. 2017a. "Observations on Factors Affecting the Distributional Properties of Evidential Markers in Amdo Tibetan." In *Evidential Systems of Tibetan Languages*, edited by Lauren Gawne and Nathan W. Hill, 367–422. Boston: De Gruyter.

– 2017b. "Social Network Structure and Language Change in Amdo Tibetan." *International Journal of the Sociology of Language* 245: 169–206. https://doi.org/10.1515/ijsl-2017-0007.

Tsering Woeser. 2020. *Forbidden Memory: Tibet during the Cultural Revolution*. Lincoln: University of Nebraska Press.

Tunzhi (Sonam Lhundrop), Hiroyuki Suzuki, and Gerald Roche. 2019. "Language Contact and the Politics of Recognition amongst Tibetans in the People's Republic of China: The rTa'u-Speaking 'Horpa' of Khams." In *The Politics of Language Contact in the Himalaya*, edited by Selma K. Sonntag and Mark Turin, 17–48. Cambridge: Open Book Publishers.

Tuttle, Gray. n.d. "An Overview of Amdo (Northeastern Tibet)." *Mandala Collections*. https://texts.mandala.library.virginia.edu/text/overview-amdo-northeastern-tibet-historical-polities.

Upton, Janet L. 2000. "Notes towards a Native Tibetan Ethnology: An Introduction to and Annotated Translation of dMu dge bSam gtan's Essays on Dwags po (Baima Zangzu)." *Tibet Journal* 25(1): 3–26.

Vouloumanos, Athena, and Janet F. Werker. 2007. "Listening to Language at Birth: Evidence for a Bias for Speech in Neonates." *Developmental Science* 10 (2): 159–64. https://doi.org/10.1111/j.1467-7687.2007.00549.x.

Vygotsky, Lev S. 1978. *Mind in Society: The Development of Higher Psychological Processes*. Edited by Michael Cole, Vera Jolm-Steiner, Sylvia Scribner, and Ellen Souberman. Cambridge, MA: Harvard University Press.

Wang, C. 2013. "An Examination of the Effects and Issues of Tibetan Nomadic Boarding Schools: A Case Study in Xinghai County, Qinghai." *Journal of Beifang University of Nationalities* 111: 104–10.

Ward, Shannon. 2022a. "Playing with Language Boundaries: Heteroglot Standard Language Ideology and Linguistic Belonging among Amdo Children." In *Bordering Tibetan Languages: Making and Marking Languages in Transnational High Asia*, edited by Gerald Roche and Gwendolyn Hyslop, 31–52. Amsterdam: Amsterdam University Press.

– 2022b. "Spatializing Kinship: The Grammar of Belonging in Amdo, Tibet." *Pragmatics* 32(3): 452–87. https://doi.org/10.1075/prag.20039.war.

Ward, Shannon, and Gerald Roche. 2020. "Language." In *Historical Dictionary of Tibet*, edited by John Powers and David Templeman, 2nd ed., 371–7. Lanham, MD: Scarecrow Press.

Warner, Cameron David. 2011. "A Miscarriage of History: Wencheng Gongzhu and Sino-Tibetan Historiography." *Inner Asia* 13: 239–64. https://doi.org/10.1163/000000011799297663.

Washul, Eveline. 2018. "Tibetan Translocalities: Navigating Urban Opportunities and New Ways of Belonging in Tibetan Pastoral Communities in China." *Critical Asian Studies* 50(4): 493–517. https://doi.org/10.1080/14672715.2018.1520606.

Wei, Huo. 2023. "On the 'Plateau Silk Road' Jointly Created by Ancient People of Various Ethnic Groups on the Qinghai-Tibet Plateau." *China and Asia* 5(1): 50–78. https://doi.org/10.1163/2589465X-05010003.

Weiner, Benno. 2020a. "The Aporia of Re-remembering: Amdo's 'Early-Liberation Period' in the Qinghai *Wenshi Ziliao*." In *Conflicting Memories: Tibetan History under Mao Retold*, edited by Robert Barnett, Benno Weiner, and Françoise Robin, 41–77. Leiden: Brill.

– 2020b. *The Chinese Revolution on the Tibetan Frontier*. Ithaca, NY: Cornell University Press.

Weisner, Thomas S. 2005. "Attachment as a Cultural and Ecological Problem with Pluralistic Solutions." *Human Development* 48: 89–94. https://doi.org/10.1159/000083219.

Weng, Jeffrey. 2018. "What Is Mandarin? The Social Project of Language Standardization in Early Republican China." *Journal of Asian Studies* 77(3): 611–33. https:// doi.org/10.1017/S0021911818000487.

Werker, Janet F., and Takao K. Hensch. 2015. "Critical Periods in Speech Perception: New Directions." *Annual Review of Psychology* 66: 173–96. https://doi.org/10.1146/annurev-psych-010814-015104.

Werker, Janet F., and Richard C. Tees. 1999. "Influences on Infant Speech Processing: Towards a New Synthesis." *Annual Review of Psychology* 50: 509–35. https://doi.org/10.1146/annurev.psych.50.1.509.

Woolard, Kathryn A. 1998. "Simultaneity and Bivalency as Strategies in Bilingualism." *Journal of Linguistic Anthropology* 8(1): 3–29. https://doi.org/10.1525/jlin.1998.8.1.3.

– 2011. "Is There Linguistic Life after High School? Longitudinal Changes in the Bilingual Repertoire in Metropolitan Barcelona." *Language in Society* 40(5): 617–48. https://doi.org/10.1017/S0047404511000704.

Wright, Stuart. 2019. "Governing Social Change in Amdo: Tibetans in the Era of Compulsory Education and School Consolidation." PhD diss., University of Sheffield.

Wylie, Turrell V. 1959. "A Standard System of Tibetan Transcription." *Harvard Journal of Asiatic Studies* 22: 261–7. https://doi.org/10.2307/2718544.

Xu, Jing. 2017. *The Good Child: Moral Development in a Chinese Preschool.* Stanford, CA: Stanford University Press.

Yan, Yunxiang. 2011. "The Changing Moral Landscape." In *Deep China: The Moral Life of the Person*, by Arthur Kleinman, Yunxiang Yan, Jun Jing, Sing Lee, Everett Zhang, Pan Tianshu, Wu Fei, and Guo Jinhua, 36–77. Berkeley and Los Angeles: University of California Press.

Yang, Mayfair Mei-hui. 2002. "The Resilience of *Guanxi* and Its New Deployments: A Critique of Some New *Guanxi* Scholarship." *China Quarterly* 170: 459–76. https://doi.org/10.1017/S000944390200027X.

Yao, Shujie. 2000. "Economic Development and Poverty Reduction in China over 20 Years of Reforms." *Economic Development and Cultural Change* 48(3): 447–74. https://doi.org/10.1086/452606.

Yeh, Emily T. 2003. "Tibetan Range Wars: Spatial Politics and Authority on the Grasslands of Amdo." *Development and Change* 34(3): 499–523. https://doi.org/10.1111/1467-7660.00316.

– 2013. *Taming Tibet: Landscape Transformation and the Gift of Chinese Development*. Ithaca, NY: Cornell University Press.

Yeh, Emily, and Charlene Makley. 2019. "Urbanization, Education, and the Politics of Space on the Tibetan Plateau." *Critical Asian Studies* 51(1): 1–11. https://doi.org/10.1080/14672715.2018.1555484.

Ying, Yumjyi Ji. 2023. "'To Be Included among People': Families' Perceptions of Schooling and Contingent Negotiations in a Rural Tibetan Community in China." *Compare: A Journal of Comparative and International Education* 53(5): 855–72. https://doi.org/10.1080/03057925.2021.1976617.

Zeng, Yukun. 2022. "How to Read the Analects Eight Hours a Day: The Variety of Dujing (Reading Classics) Experiences amid the Confucian Revival." *China Perspectives* 2 (June): 17–28. https://doi.org/10.4000/chinaperspectives.13890.

Zenz, Adrian. 2010. "Beyond Assimilation: The Tibetanisation of Tibetan Education in Qinghai." *Inner Asia* 12(2): 293–315. https://doi.org/10.1163/000000010794983478.

– 2014. *"Tibetanness" under Threat? Neo-Integrationism, Minority Education and Career Strategies in Qinghai, P.R. China*. Leiden: Global Oriental.

Zhan, Shaohua. 2017. "Hukou Reform and Land Politics in China: Rise of a Tripartite Alliance." *China Journal* 78 (July): 25–49. https://doi.org/10.1086/690622.

Zhang, Lubei, and Linda T.H. Tsung. 2019. "Tibetan Bilingual Education in Qinghai: Government Policy vs Family Language Practice." *International Journal of Bilingual Education and Bilingualism* 22(3): 290–302. https://doi.org/10.1080/13670050.2018.1503226.

Zhang, Qing. 2013. "Language Policy and Ideology: Greater China." In *The Oxford Handbook of Sociolinguistics*, edited by Robert Bayley, Richard Cameron, and Ceil Lucas, 563–86. Oxford: Oxford University Press.

Zhou, Minglang. 2003. *Multilingualism in China: The Politics of Writing Reforms for Minority Languages 1949–2002*. New York: Mouton de Gruyter.

– 2017. "Language Policy and Education in Greater China." In *Encyclopedia of Language and Education*, vol. 1: *Language Policy and Political Issues in Education*, edited by Stephen May and Teresa L. McCarty, 463–77. New York: Springer International Publishing.

Zhou, Minglang, and Heidi A. Ross. 2004. "The Context of the Theory and Practice of China's Language Policy." *In Language Policy in the People's Republic of China: Theory and Practice since 1949*, edited by Minglang Zhou and Hongkai Sun, 1–18. New York: Kluwer Academic Publishers.

Index

ANTHROPOLOGICAL HORIZONS

Editor: Michael Lambek, University of Toronto

Published to date:

The Varieties of Sensory Experience: A Sourcebook in the Anthropology of the Senses / Edited by David Howes (1991)
Arctic Homeland: Kinship, Community, and Development in Northwest Greenland / Mark Nuttall (1992)
Knowledge and Practice in Mayotte: Local Discourses of Islam, Sorcery, and Spirit Possession / Michael Lambek (1993)
Deathly Waters and Hungry Mountains: Agrarian Ritual and Class Formation in an Andean Town / Peter Gose (1994)
Paradise: Class, Commuters, and Ethnicity in Rural Ontario / Stanley R. Barrett (1994)
The Cultural World in Beowulf / John M. Hill (1995)
Making It Their Own: Severn Ojibwe Communicative Practices / Lisa Philips Valentine (1995)
Merchants and Shopkeepers: A Historical Anthropology of an Irish Market Town, 1200–1991 / P.H. Gulliver and Marilyn Silverman (1995)
Tournaments of Value: Sociability and Hierarchy in a Yemeni Town / Ann Meneley (1996)
Mal'uocchiu: Ambiguity, Evil Eye, and the Language of Distress / Sam Migliore (1997)
Between History and Histories: The Making of Silences and Commemorations / Edited by Gerald Sider and Gavin Smith (1997)
Eh, Paesan! Being Italian in Toronto / Nicholas DeMaria Harney (1998)
Theorizing the Americanist Tradition / Edited by Lisa Philips Valentine and Regna Darnell (1999)
Colonial "Reformation" in the Highlands of Central Sulawesi, Indonesia, 1892–1995 / Albert Schrauwers (2000)
The Rock Where We Stand: An Ethnography of Women's Activism in Newfoundland / Glynis George (2000)
"Being Alive Well": Health and the Politics of Cree Well-Being / Naomi Adelson (2000)
Irish Travellers: Racism and the Politics of Culture / Jane Helleiner (2001)
Of Property and Propriety: The Role of Gender and Class in Imperialism and Nationalism / Edited by Himani Bannerji, Shahrzad Mojab, and Judith Whitehead (2001)
An Irish Working Class: Explorations in Political Economy and Hegemony, 1800–1950 / Marilyn Silverman (2001)

The Double Twist: From Ethnography to Morphodynamics / Edited by Pierre Maranda (2001)

The House of Difference: Cultural Politics and National Identity in Canada / Eva Mackey (2002)

Writing and Colonialism in Northern Ghana: The Encounter between the LoDagaa and "the World on Paper," 1892–1991 / Sean Hawkins (2002)

Guardians of the Transcendent: An Ethnography of a Jain Ascetic Community / Anne Vallely (2002)

The Hot and the Cold: Ills of Humans and Maize in Native Mexico / Jacques M. Chevalier and Andrés Sánchez Bain (2003)

Figured Worlds: Ontological Obstacles in Intercultural Relations / Edited by John Clammer, Sylvie Poirier, and Eric Schwimmer (2004)

Revenge of the Windigo: The Construction of the Mind and Mental Health of North American Aboriginal Peoples / James B. Waldram (2004)

The Cultural Politics of Markets: Economic Liberalization and Social Change in Nepal / Katharine Neilson Rankin (2004)

A World of Relationships: Itineraries, Dreams, and Events in the Australian Western Desert / Sylvie Poirier (2005)

The Politics of the Past in an Argentine Working-Class Neighbourhood / Lindsay DuBois (2005)

Youth and Identity Politics in South Africa, 1990–1994 / Sibusisiwe Nombuso Dlamini (2005)

Maps of Experience: The Anchoring of Land to Story in Secwepemc Discourse / Andie Diane Palmer (2005)

We Are Now a Nation: Croats between "Home" and "Homeland" / Daphne N. Winland (2007)

Beyond Bodies: Rain-Making and Sense-Making in Tanzania / Todd Sanders (2008)

Kaleidoscopic Odessa: History and Place in Contemporary Ukraine / Tanya Richardson (2008)

Invaders as Ancestors: On the Intercultural Making and Unmaking of Spanish Colonialism in the Andes / Peter Gose (2008)

From Equality to Inequality: Social Change among Newly Sedentary Lanoh Hunter-Gatherer Traders of Peninsular Malaysia / Csilla Dallos (2011)

Rural Nostalgias and Transnational Dreams: Identity and Modernity among Jat Sikhs / Nicola Mooney (2011)

Dimensions of Development: History, Community, and Change in Allpachico, Peru / Susan Vincent (2012)

People of Substance: An Ethnography of Morality in the Colombian Amazon / Carlos David Londoño Sulkin (2012)

"We Are Still Didene": Stories of Hunting and History from Northern British Columbia / Thomas McIlwraith (2012)

Being Māori in the City: Indigenous Everyday Life in Auckland / Natacha Gagné (2013)
The Hakkas of Sarawak: Sacrificial Gifts in Cold War Era Malaysia / Kee Howe Yong (2013)
Remembering Nayeche and the Gray Bull Engiro: African Storytellers of the Karamoja Plateau and the Plains of Turkana / Mustafa Kemal Mirzeler (2014)
In Light of Africa: Globalizing Blackness in Northeast Brazil / Allan Charles Dawson (2014)
The Land of Weddings and Rain: Nation and Modernity in Post-Socialist Lithuania / Gediminas Lankauskas (2015)
Milanese Encounters: Public Space and Vision in Contemporary Urban Italy / Cristina Moretti (2015)
Legacies of Violence: History, Society, and the State in Sardinia / Antonio Sorge (2015)
Looking Back, Moving Forward: Transformation and Ethical Practice in the Ghanaian Church of Pentecost / Girish Daswani (2015)
Why the Porcupine Is Not a Bird: Explorations in the Folk Zoology of an Eastern Indonesian People / Gregory Forth (2016)
The Heart of Helambu: Ethnography and Entanglement in Nepal / Tom O'Neill (2016)
Tournaments of Value: Sociability and Hierarchy in a Yemeni Town, 20th Anniversary Edition / Ann Meneley (2016)
Europe Un-Imagined: Nation and Culture at a French-German Television Channel / Damien Stankiewicz (2017)
Transforming Indigeneity: Urbanization and Language Revitalization in the Brazilian Amazon / Sarah Shulist (2018)
Wrapping Authority: Women Islamic Leaders in a Sufi Movement in Dakar, Senegal / Joseph Hill (2018)
Island in the Stream: An Ethnographic History of Mayotte / Michael Lambek (2018)
Materializing Difference: Consumer Culture, Politics, and Ethnicity among Romanian Roma / Péter Berta (2019)
Virtual Activism: Sexuality, the Internet, and a Social Movement in Singapore / Robert Phillips (2020)
Shadow Play: Information Politics in Urban Indonesia / Sheri Lynn Gibbins (2021)
Suspect Others: Spirit Mediums, Self-Knowledge, and Race in Multiethnic Suriname / Stuart Earle Strange (2021)
Exemplary Life: Modeling Sainthood in Christian Syria / Andreas Bandak (2022)
Without the State: Self-Organization and Political Activism in Ukraine / Emily Channell-Justice (2022)

Truly Human: Indigeneity and Indigenous Resurgence on Formosa / Scott Simon (2023)
Moral Figures: Making Reproduction Public in Vanuatu / Alexandra Widmer (2023)
Moving Words: Literature, Memory, and Migration in Berlin / Andrew Brandel (2023)
Untold Stories: Legacies of Authoritarianism among Spanish Labour Migrants in Later Life / David Divita (2024)